Samantha Rastles
the Woman Question

D1111838

MARIETTA HOLLEY

Samantha Rastles the Woman Question

Edited with an Introduction by
JANE CURRY

UNIVERSITY OF ILLINOIS PRESS

Urbana and Chicago

This book is printed on acid-free paper.

Library of Congress Cataloging in Publication Data

Holley, Marietta, 1836–1926.
  Samantha rastles the woman question.

  Excerpts from the author's writings published
between 1873 and 1914.
  Bibliography: p.
  Includes index.
  1. Women's rights—Anecdotes, facetiae, satire, etc.
2. Sex role—Anecdotes, facetiae, satire, etc.
I. Curry, Jane, 1945–   . II. Title.
PS1949.H5A6   1983   814'.4   82-13482
ISBN 0-252-01020-5 (cloth)
ISBN 0-252-01306-9 (paper)

For Jim and Norma Werden Curry,
who encouraged both laughter and independence

Acknowledgments

When I first discovered Marietta Holley's Samantha more than a decade ago, several mentors and friends shared my enthusiasm over the find. The late Joe Lee Davis and Marvin Felheim encouraged me to pursue and develop my inquiries; Elizabeth Douvan laughed with me and gave counsel; Adam Simms first suggested compiling an anthology of the women humorists I was reading; Lee Chambers-Schiller, Doug Davies, and Janette Weisberg Simms took time from their own studies to listen to the latest "episoddin' " according to Samantha.

I want to thank my editor, Carole Appel, for making suggestions for revisions, and Mary Anne Ferguson, who read the entire manuscript and offered excellent criticism for improving the book's usefulness to students.

'Course, I'm 'sponsible fer th' final form, so dontcha go faultin' nobody elst if'n there's mistakes. Though anon or oftener I wundered who'd read th' book win it was rote, my pardner wuzn't as dubersome and tejus as Josiah. See, he thinks wimmen ort to hav their rights too. His name is David Lund, and I'm bound to him by a cast-iron affection.

Contents

Preface

Marietta Holley is unique among nineteenth-century American humorists in her treatment of women. As she labored over her prefaces, Holley's character, Samantha Allen, invariably received supportive remarks from her "pardner" Josiah, who cried from the wings: "But who will read the Book, Samantha, when it is rote?" Josiah was a pessimist. Holley's books, published regularly from 1873–1914 (many under the name of Josiah Allen's Wife), were a popular success, and her stance regarding women's rights paralleled considerable activity in the society at large dealing with the question of suffrage and assignation of sex roles. Unfortunately, many who study women's history and the suffrage movement are unacquainted with Holley's work and many who study American humor have failed to appreciate her special contribution.[1] This collection is meant to correct that neglect and give students of the nineteenth century other artifacts by women from popular culture to supplement sentimental novels and ladies magazines on the one hand and suffrage tracts on the other.

In the humorous writings of the nineteenth century, women occupy a remarkably undeviating sphere. The conventional stereotypes that take up American residence are transformed by regional peculiarities (i.e. Yankee marms, superstitious swamp dames, settlement snoops, etc.) but the outline remains unmistakable. Again and again, American humorists endow their female characters with thoroughly undesirable qualities. Woman is nearly always one or more of the following: vain, scolding, capricious, coquettish, unpredictable, curious, impractical, loquacious, gullible, muddle-headed, gossippy, gushy, backbiting, jealous, or vindictive. Woman's wagging tongue seldom rests, and petticoat government via the "curtain-lecture" rarely abates. Domestic martyrs dot the landscape as carping wife and long-suffering husband do the daily battle of marital bliss. Women "gushers" hold almost exclusive copyright to the bad "poitry" of effusive self-indulgence and sentimentality inspired by some misguided muse in inordinate quantities.

Whether tamer of the human gamecocks or reformer of domesticated males, women retain their role as guardian of the home, the family, the cultural mores in general. Occasionally, women (usually widows like Benjamin Shillaber's Mrs. Partington or Ben Franklin's Silence Dogood) are allowed a place among the crackerbox philosophers, but they are as foolish as they are wise. The widow who has satisfied society's expectations can be both independent and wise, though of course Mrs. Partington is noticeably muddle-headed and malapropistic. Both male and female humorists portray most single or widowed women as inveterate man-chasers, as people devoid of any personal status unless affiliated with that of a man.

The masculine southwest tradition reinforces the same images and patterns — women tame the alligators, are superstitious, coquettish, curious, etc. However, in the area of sexual candor, the southwest humorists stand apart from fellow funny men of the nineteenth century in their reflection of women. Implicit in some descriptions of sexual play (particularly as rhapsodized by Sut Lovingood) is the acknowledgment of a positive sexuality for women. Like men, women enjoy, desire, and even need sexual activity.[2] Only in Mark Twain's long unpublished *Letters From the Earth* does another humorist explicitly describe women's enjoyment of sexual intercourse: " . . . she wants that candle — yearns for it, longs for it, hankers after it, as commanded by the law of God in her heart."

When it comes to explicit reference to "the woman question," suffrage, or women's rights, there is a near unanimity among writers. With the exception of Marietta Holley, nineteenth-century humorists are against changes, modifications, or reversals of the traditionally defined roles assigned men and women in our culture. Josh Billings (Shaw), Seba Smith, Frances Whitcher, Artemus Ward (Browne), Mr. Dooley (Dunne), and John Kendrick Bangs all denounce to some degree admitted proponents of women's rights. (Neither Twain nor the southwest humorists make specific references to the "woman question," but the relationship between their male and female characters would make a favorable inclination highly unlikely). A favorite technique of many humorists was to undercut prosuffrage or pro–women's rights ideas by putting them in the mouth of a Mrs. Partington, a Betsey Jane Ward, a Xanthippe, or some other "feroshus female" or "slab-sided, coarse lookin' critter." Only Holley wrote consistently from a pro–women's rights point of view and exposed as foolish the various arguments against the development of full human potential for women.[3]

One's first glance through critical accounts seems to suggest that women apparently composed no deliberate humor, though they wrote sentimental novels by the carriage load. However, Holley was not alone in the nineteenth century. Frances Whitcher's Widow Bedott sketches had appeared in magazines of the 1840s and '50s. Whitcher's emphasis was decidedly on women – and the women were generally undesirable people. They dominate both the action and the maliciousness of her sketches. While male characters display the usual human foibles, their shortcomings are more irritating than maligning. More than the men, it seems, her women are spurred by motivations of jealousy and blatant self-interest. And the Widow Bedott violates all the virtues of womanhood: she is most of the things a woman ought not be. Like her male counterparts, the Widow makes fun of "manly" women, of women who dare to lecture in public, of the Professor who advocates adjustment of the artificially determined sex roles. But to determine Whitcher's view on such matters is more difficult; we have to consider the source – Widow Bedott. On one level, by making the widow so conglomerately unappealing, Whitcher indirectly reinforces values presumably shared by her audience. On another, since she criticizes the very characteristics she herself exemplifies, the widow becomes a vehicle for Whitcher to satirize popular forms such as sentimental writing and unappealing qualities such as gossiping, vanity, and foolish pride.[4]

Marietta Holley, on the other hand, uses the same characters – the wise sage, the foolish foil, the love-hungry spinster – but she reverses the sympathies. The sage advocates a moderate position in favor of women's rights. The foolish foil clumsily presents what can only be seen as the laughable logic of an inept man trying to preserve the power he undeservedly inherited by being born male. The love-hungry spinster accepts prevailing sex role values and is consequently the ridiculous creature we see. Holley uses horse sense to undermine what were the generally shared values of the culture regarding the spheres of men and women.

While popular art in general has usually been devoted to perpetuating accepted ways of seeing things, to confirming the experience of the majority, humor has often been an avenue of social criticism. The reasons for the enormous popularity of Holley's books may lie in the composition of the audience, the travel format of many of the books, and the mother-wit style of presentation.

We can often locate sales figures or other indicators of popularity;[5] it is much more difficult to ascertain who actually bought and read the books in question. One purchased book may be passed among many family members, neighbors, and friends.[6] Literature that becomes popular usually doesn't have to persuade or innovate; it addresses readers who are ready for it. Holley's writings on the woman question (and other social issues as well) may not have brought about precipitous changes in the ideas or behavior of her readers, but they may have hastened or clarified a change already in progress for segments of the population.[7]

Holley's frequently used travel format, like Twain's *Innocents Abroad* or Artemus Ward's travels, was a well-established, popular way to observe and comment on places, people, and values through the eyes of a "wise innocent." And, of course, though dialect humor was waning, horse sense still won out over book sense for many Americans. In the preface to *Horse Sense in American Humor*, Walter Blair traces the propensity of the American public to revere horse sense (also read: "common sense, homespun philosophy, pawkiness, crackerbox philosophy, gumption, or mother-wit.")[8] Horse sense refers both to a way of thinking and the kind of ideas a person gets by thinking that way. According to Blair, from Ben Franklin to the present,[9] "our racy humor and horse sense have been blended to persuade or enlighten the people of this country and . . . had appealed to our love for home-grown laughter and our almost religious faith in mother-wit."[10] Ben Franklin, Davy Crockett, Simon Suggs, Jack Downing, Josh Billings, Mark Twain, Mrs. Partington, and Samantha Allen are among those Blair considers in the horse sense tradition. As regards women, then, most common sense pronouncements favor women "in their place" and make ugly, grotesque, or ridiculous those women who fail to conform.

Samantha Allen stands out as the lone mother-wit who appeals in a moderate way for gumption of a different order, who appeals for the sensible scenario of men and women sitting side by side as they tackle what life has to offer them. Her spinster, like those of many other writers, is also a voracious man-hunter, is ugly, sentimental, and pathetically ridiculous. But unlike other humorists who simply ascribe such traits to their women, Marietta Holley uproots the clinging vine/stately tree expectations and exposes the reasons which lie behind the development of such an unfortunate character.

So, women as subjects of nineteenth-century American humor seem to suffer from sex-linked frailities not shared by their male counterparts. Male characters are shown to have their shortcomings and are variously vain, foolish, shortsighted, pompous, etc., but these foibles do not seem genetically tied to their maleness. They suffer human inadequacies. The double x chromosomes, however, seem to predestine females to all manner of special weaknesses. Women as writers of humor on the one hand conspire to uphold stereotypes by presenting a Widow Bedott; on the other hand, they subvert the established order by putting potentially unpopular notions in the mouth of sensible Samantha. It is in this context that I introduce Marietta Holley and offer selected readings from Josiah Allen's Wife.

NOTES

1. In the critical accounts of American humor, Holley is given extensive treatment only in Walter Blair's *Horse Sense in American Humor* (Chicago, 1942). There is no reference to her in Constance Rourke's classic *American Humor* (New York, 1931); she rates a footnote in Jesse Bier's *Rise and Fall of American Humor* (New York, 1968); and in Jennette Tandy's *Crackerbox Philosophers* (New York, 1925) she surfaces only as a name among other names. Recently more attention has been paid to Holley's work, as reflected in the bibliography for this anthology.

2. I make the case for this perception of the treatment of women in southwest humor in "The Ring-Tailed Roarers Rarely Sang Soprano," *Frontiers*, II:3 (Fall, 1977), 129–40.

3. To check the documentation and interpretation that leads me to these conclusions see Curry, "Women as Subjects and Writers of Nineteenth-Century American Humor," (Ph.D. dissertation, University of Michigan, 1975).

4. For an examination of Whitcher's humor, see Curry's article entitled "Yes, Virginia, There Were Female Humorists" in *University of Michigan Papers in Women's Studies*, I:1 (1974) 74–90. Also see Nancy Walker's article in *American Studies* XXII: 2 (Fall, 1981) "Wit, Sentimentality, and the Image of Women in the Nineteenth Century."

Whitcher's Widow Bedott sketches began appearing in 1846 in Joseph Neal's *Saturday Gazette and Lady's Literary Museum* and then in *Godey's Lady's Book*. In 1856 her sketches were collected in one volume, *The Widow Bedott Papers*, the first edition of which sold over

100,000 copies. A reprint was published in 1969 by Gregg Press, Upper Saddle River, N.J.

5. See introduction, p. 3n5.

6. My personal hunch is that the primary audience was women, who passed it along to daughters and other women with considerable delight. This hunch is based on a thoroughly unscientific survey: of the eight Holley books I've been able to acquire, four are signed. Three belonged to women and one (the 1891 edition of Betsey Bobbet) is inscribed "Dorothy from Mother Aug 19–98." While doing performances as Samantha, I have met one older woman who remembers her mother reading to her (with laughter and spirit) from Holley's books, and another who read Samantha books as a child.

Elinore Pruitt Stewart, whose *Letters of a Woman Homesteader* were the basis for the recent movie *Heartland*, was apparently a Holley fan as well. In her letters, dated from April, 1900, to November, 1913, she twice refers to Holley's characters. Speaking of a trip to the county seat with a neighbor, she remarks: "I had more fun to the square inch than Mark Twain or Samantha Allen *ever* provoked." In an October, 1911, letter, she says: "As soon as I could, I made myself scarce about the granary and very busy about the house, and like Josiah Allen, I was in a very 'happified' state of mind." Elinore Pruitt Stewart described herself as a southerner but wrote these letters to a Denver friend from her homestead in Wyoming.

7. For a discussion of popular arts and their basic differentiation from elite art, see Russell Nye, *The Unembarrassed Muse* (New York, 1970), introduction.

8. The "present" Blair refers to is 1942.

9. Walter Blair, *Horse Sense in American Humor* (Chicago, 1942), p. vi. In his most recent book, coauthored with Hamlin Hill and entitled *America's Humor: From Poor Richard to Doonesbury* (New York, 1978), Blair gave Holley but a paragraph: "In the era of the Phunny Phellows, Marietta Holley edged closer to today's women comic writers when she created and quoted a Phunny Phemale, 'Josiah Allen's Wife,' Samantha. Ms. Holley, a feminist, satirized religious hypocrisy, political skulduggery, and male chauvinism. But she was an unschooled rustic with sound mare sense, a Christian, a loving wife and a model housekeeper, and therefore could never have become as popular today as she did during her lifetime" (p. 496). One wonders which of the characteristics would disqualify her. As one who performs as Samantha before "popular audiences," I could "soar into eloquence" debating the point.

10. Blair, *Horse Sense*, pp. x–xi.

Marietta Holley

Introduction

A writer for *The Critic* of January, 1905, said of Marietta Holley: "As 'Josiah Allen's Wife,' she has entertained as large an audience, I should say, as has been entertained by the humor of Mark Twain." That puts Holley and her folksy, common-sense character Samantha Allen in illustrious company. Marietta Holley made a special contribution to nineteenth-century American humor — not because of innovative comic style or technique, for even in her own time the mother-wit, dialect style was anachronistic; nor because she was our only woman humorist, for the nineteenth century claimed Frances Whitcher, "Fanny Fern," and others; but rather because she was the only humorist whose main character was a woman who spoke specifically about women's rights.

Much of Holley's humor strikes a resonant note of familiarity with modern readers — in terms of language and images as well as in terms of some conservative ideas that have stubbornly persisted into late-twentieth-century culture — and establishes her kinship with latter-day feminists, some of whom sound the same arguments but withhold the same good humor. When one reads the Samantha books, she begins to view the nineteenth century not as "then" so much as it was the beginning of "now." One may be struck by the same confusion Ann Douglas notes in *The Feminization of American Culture* when she describes the process of researching and writing her book on nineteenth-century America: "I expected to find my fathers and my mothers; instead I discovered my fathers and my sisters. The best of the men had access to solutions, and occasionally inspiring ones, which I appropriate only with the anxiety and effort that attend genuine aspiration. The problems of the women correspond to mine with a frightening accuracy that seems to set us outside the process of history; the answers of even the finest of them were often mine, and sometimes largely unacceptable to me. . . . "[1]

Of course, in certain ways, Holley's humor is definitely dated. Her comic style, like that of other mainstream nineteenth-century American humorists such as Seba Smith, Josh Billings, and Artemus Ward (Browne), utilized a dialect dependent on misspellings to conjure sounds of the spoken word and hence reflect (or affect) the rustic flavor so popular among the horse-sense-loving public. Thus, "says" becomes "sez," "was" becomes "wuz," and "medium" becomes "megum." Since twentieth-century humor eschews reliance on "spelling dialect" to convey regional or class linguistic peculiarities, modern readers may at first need to read a few sentences aloud to catch on to the dialect aspect of Holley's work.

Likewise, some of her issues, such as suffrage and temperance, belong particularly to movements and events of the late nineteenth and early twentieth centuries. Indeed, her humor can be seen as a reflection of and argument against late-nineteenth-century social and political reality. But Holley's verbal wit transcends both the situational provenience and the stereotypical characters thereby providing a freshness that reminds us that the "woman question" goes beyond social mores and politics to the most basic assumptions of our culture.

Marietta Holley, born on the family farm in Jefferson County, New York, in 1836, very early began writing verses generally of pious and sentimental poetry. Her brothers teased her endlessly about these verses, and she later blamed that unmerciful teasing for her life-long case of extreme shyness that even in the height of her popularity inhibited her from making public appearances. Her formal education at the district school ended when she was fourteen because of family financial difficulties, but she developed a passion for music and was assisted by an uncle who paid for piano lessons. Teaching seemed an appropriate way for a young lady to make a living, and she did so with her family's approval. Holley apparently admired a local young schoolteacher who did not follow the approved route and instead quit teaching in order to become a book agent. She was, of course, considered by the community to be "forward." A woman's place was by the "fireside where sheltered by a man's personality she could labor from dawn to dark safe from the vulgar gaze of the public."[2] This woman likewise claimed other-world spiritual communication which also impressed the young Marietta. A religious woman, like Samantha, Holley thoroughly believed both in direct divine guidance via the Bible and in spiritualism. "Every morning she picked up her Bible, held it in her left hand,

and opened it with her right. The verse upon which her right thumb rested was the law for the day."[3]

When her first book, *My Opinions and Betsey Bobbet's*, appeared in 1873, it was sold by subscription and found its greatest appeal in rural sections of the country. It was published and circulated by the American Publishing Company, the same publisher that sold 150,000 copies of Twain's *Innocents Abroad* and 80,000 copies of *Roughing It*. The Samantha books, which eventually numbered twenty-one and came out regularly until the last in 1914, were a popular success as evidenced by her large sales, frequent public readings, the success of a Neil Burgess dramatization,[4] and the eagerness of publishers to bring out her new work. Holley was offered a $14,000 advance by Funk & Wagnalls for her 1893 book called *Samantha at the World's Fair*.[5] The propaganda value of her feminist view early caught the attention of Frances Willard and Susan B. Anthony. Willard invited her to be a delegate at the 1877 WCTU (Woman's Christian Temperance Union) convention and Anthony urged her to attend the 1878 National Woman Suffrage Association, but Holley never attended a convention and was terrified at the idea of being on a public stage. Even Anthony's suggestion that she come "incog" couldn't persuade her to attend.[6]

She became famous and financially comfortable, but she still refused to attend conventions or appear publicly and in fact refused the offers of various publishers to send her to Europe or St. Louis or Chicago in order to write her books on travel and expositions. With the exception of her trips to Saratoga and to Coney Island, she never visited any of the places before she wrote about them. Instead, she assiduously studied maps, guidebooks, descriptions, etc., and then wrote her narratives without the encumbrance of directly observed reality.

Though her success and fame were attached to her humorous work, Holley continued to write poetry throughout her life and considered poetry the far more valid literary form. She allowed Samantha to speak her ideas and thus endow her principles with personality, but she resembled Samantha in neither appearance, culture, nor status. "Miss Holley is more like a Grand Duchess than the homely character she has immortalized. Her spectacles are a pair of gold lorgnettes, her gowns are made by a French modiste, and she has no need of a cap."[7] Though she chose to remain in the country, her society was not the local society of country folk but rather people of prominence. And though Samantha praised the "cast-iron affection" that bound her to Josiah and glorified the virtues of home and family, Marietta Holley never married. Aside from the good humor and solid common sense they shared, Samantha seems to have exhibited precisely those traits not attributable to Holley. Samantha is aggressive, loquacious, well traveled, and plain.

By the time she died in 1926 at the age of ninety, Holley's books were scarcely read. The ideas and issues so relevant to late-nineteenth-century America had become by then commonplace and lacked the urgency and appeal that had preceded the war and the Nineteenth Amendment. Her later books had become endlessly repetitious and her rustic philosopher, an anachronistic comic convention even in 1900, was yet more incongruous in the increasingly urban 1920s.

My Opinions and Betsey Bobbet's (1873) introduces us to the rustic philosopher of sound country stock whose ideas on various issues are grounded in an affection for common sense and faith in its applicability to problems. Jonesville's Samantha Smith Allen is hefty in both principles and weight. By her own admission, she is a wise, religious, compassionate, loyal, faithful, and loving 204-pound wife. She is possessed of endless good judgment, is adept at moral "eppisodin'," and is a first-rate housekeeper and cook. Though she protests both categories, she is also immodest and ceaselessly talkative. She proclaims immediately that "sentiment ain't my style, and I abhor all kinds of shams and deceitfulness."[8] She is a good Christian Methodist who reserves judgment on people until all the facts are known and refuses to participate in malicious gossip feeding upon unfounded rumors. On the other hand, she recognizes the genuinely foolish or destructive qualities of her "sect" such as the use of corsets, bustles, and pantaloons in order to be stylish, and the tendency to gossip. She extols the virtues and recognizes the duties of wives and mothers, and prides herself on being a loyal wife to Josiah and a good mother to his children. At the same time, she sees no conflict between devotion to one's "pardner" and family and a belief in women's rights. She does, however, see a conflict between devotion to family and the licensing of liquor by the government. Thus, Samantha is both prosuffrage and protemperance.

One of the foolish foils whose opinions are set against Samantha's is her husband, Josiah Allen. A widower with two children when she married him, he is a lightweight both as "measured by the steelyards" and as measured by intelligence. He and Samantha have been married fourteen years or so in *Opinions* and forty years by the time the last book is published. This 100-pound, bald weakling displays a tendency toward sentimental foolishness and impractical, adventuresome schemes that Samantha is of course obliged to break off. He is naturally vain, proud, and egotistical and can be easily swayed even from moral good sense by his yearnings to be fashionable. Samantha complains that he is "clost" with his money, and he is continually inventing schemes to acquire more. He is a good pardner, but he's incapable of exercising good judgment. Since he also fails to heed Samantha's reliable advice, his plans are generally utter catastrophes.

Josiah presents the egotistical masculine argument that would keep women strictly in the home because that's what it says in the Bible, because women have weak minds, and because they are constitutionally fragile and must be protected by their stronger menfolk. He is, on the one hand, portrayed as the reversal of the standard male stereotype: he is smaller, dumber, prouder, and more irrational than his female counterpart. On the other hand, he fits the comic stereotype of the small, weak husband henpecked by his larger wife. Whenever they have a discussion in which Samantha has logically boxed him into a corner, he nearly always remembers that he has to milk the cow, or plow the field, or devour his dinner. This is a clear reversal of the usual stereotype of the female who, when losing an argument on rational grounds, will dissolve in torrents of tears guaranteed to soften the heart of her beloved.

Betsey Bobbet is weak sentimentality set against Samantha's absolute practicality. In a glaring understatement, Samantha described her: "Betsey haint handsome." Samantha goes on to depict the stereotypical skinny, ugly old maid whose complexion isn't good, whose eyes are little and deep set, whose large nose has remained steadfastly in place though both teeth and hair have long since fallen away. She mouths the views of the genteel female whose "gushings of a tendah soul" display affectation of speech and agreement with the view that "women's speah" is to cling, to coo, to smile, and to soothe. She agrees with the masculine argument that "it is wimmen's duty to marry, and not to vote." She has a sentimental and impractical picture of marriage and, like Frances Whitcher's Widow Bedott, writes "dretful" poetry and is reduced to vulgar coquetries in her desperate pursuit of the dignity that the state of marriage would bring her. Unfortunately for Betsey, though she is more than willing to be a clinging vine, there seem no men willing to become her stately tree.

To make one's ultimate goal in life the snaring of a husband, Holley suggests, is to transform women into ridiculous buzzards swooping voraciously on their prey; into lonely, bitter people who feel totally defeated because of unhappy love matches contracted for the wrong reasons; into showpieces who have been socialized to value the status of a title—Mrs.—over the quality and dignity of honest loving relationships. Girls must have self-respect and be industrious. "Marryin' ain't the only theme to lay holt of. . . . No woman can feel honorable and reverential toward themselves, when they are foldin' their useless hands over their empty souls, waitin' for some man, no matter who, to marry 'em and support 'em."[9]

No husband can make up for the loss of self-respect. But Betsey does not heed Samantha's advice. She considers it her "duty" to marry, and so she relentlessly pursues eligible men and finally snares Simon Slimpsey, dooming herself to a hard life caring for his several children and coping with his laziness, poverty, and drunkenness. But, pitifully, she still would never part with the "dignity" she has achieved simply by becoming a married woman.

Samantha's constant stance is that of "megumness" ["mediumness"]. She avoids the extremes of any idea and circles all the way around to see all sides. For example, she includes both corsets and pantaloons in her category of female foolishness. Both the genteel ladies of fashion who obstruct normal breathing patterns and the more immodest, boyish women who wear trousers in public are slapped on the hand for failing to be "megum" and sensible. She admits that men are "curious, vain and tejus" but also admits that "so be women." Both "sects" are about equally foolish and disagreeable, good and noble.

Representatives of various viewpoints take their turns confronting and arguing with Samantha, with Samantha's opinions nearly always seeming eminently sane and correct. Samantha's persona as sensible, reasonable sage provides a distance from her various foils. Additionally, the distance between Holley and Samantha as a literary as well as a personal fact allows the reader to perceive Samantha's shortcomings, malapropisms, and loyalties that may seem inimical to her self-perceived stature. For example, the reader sees that though Samantha outdid herself in eloquence while chastizing Victoria Woodhull regarding free love and divorce (Selection 12), Victoria remains unconvinced and unconverted. Samantha may think she has won the debate, but the reader knows better. In Selection 1, Holley has her rustic character use an abstract literary device — allegory — to make her point to a decidedly dull-minded Josiah. Though she uses stereotypical characters like Josiah, Holley makes him more than a mere whipping boy for feminist ideas by repeatedly showing Samantha's genuine, warm affection for him, even while she roundly criticizes his ideas. And in such instances as the discussion about the gender of the courthouse "figger of liberty" (Selection 33), Holley allows Josiah to miss the point and claim victory, Samantha to remain smug about her verbal wit while tending the tea kettle, and the reader to discern the real point while being amused at both of them. Such uses of characterization, wit, and irony give more dimension to subjects and situations than the genre of humor often allows and offers the persona of Samantha as a woman of genuine good nature who would not be mistaken (even by antisuffragists) for a termagent wife who browbeats the long-suffering husband.

And she also displays that good nature (and didactic bent) when she confronts the Mrs. Flamm's of the world. Mrs. George Washington Flamm in *Samantha at Saratoga* represents the cosmopolitan genteel scatterbrain who has to go to the watering spa in stylish splendor. Her only criticism of the Statue of Liberty, that defective Goddess, is that she should really have a tapered waist, a skirt looped over a bustle, and a flowered hat on her head. Samantha protests that if she were thus gussied, Liberty couldn't lift her torch over her head and enlighten the world (Selection 15).

The extremes of the feminist view are also discouraged. A wild-eyed feminist appears with characteristically short hair, flailing vituperative barbs at those tyrants who oppress women. She is the man-hating radical bent upon immediate, militant tactics that would eventually give women dominance over men by rescinding male voting rights (Selection 13). Samantha listens attentively, remembers that after all Josiah is a man, and argues with innate mother-wit for a moderate approach that insures equality and eradicates subordination of either "sect." She also avoids any threat to the stability or sanctity of the family by pointing out in that interview with Victoria Woodhull that liberal divorce reforms and any overtones of free love are misguided.

Various townsmen, particularly elders in the Meetin' House, side with Josiah on the "woman question" and provide rationales for women's place. But in all her books, Holley insures that the male argument is in blatant, glaring contradiction to perceivable reality. Occasionally, Samantha will appeal to a politician to exert his position to "do the right thing." Though some are educable, like Horace Greeley, still they are politicians whose position is likely to vary according to pressure from interest groups, and Samantha knows that the liquor trade wields the most powerful lobby.

So, on the "woman question" Samantha sets herself squarely in the reasonable middle and makes foolish the masculine argument for female submission, the sentimental female argument for adherence to that defined role, and the radical feminists whose views and tactics might threaten the sanctity of home and family. In her sketches on women's social position, suffrage, temperance, powerlessness before the law and the church, the double standard, female symbols in public life, and traditional roles, Samantha's (and Holley's) stand on women's sphere becomes quite clear.

Holley exposes the contradiction between a democracy based on consent of the governed and the disenfranchisement of half of the members constituting that democracy. The government, because it denies the basic right of the vote to women, perpetuates women's powerlessness before the law. Common law provides that a woman's property, her body, her children, even her clothing belong to her husband, and she has no recourse under the law to take exception. She is not allowed equal education, equal job and professional opportunities, or equal pay for work done. Samantha illustrates women's place in the land of liberty in several ways and then proposes solutions: the vote, economic independence, freedom to speak publicly against wrongs.

In *Sweet Cicely* (1885), Samantha shows how helpless women are to change their condition, exercise their own principles, or influence society in any significant direct manner. The Cicely saga also illustrates the link Samantha nearly always draws between suffrage and temperance. Cicely is a sweet young mother whose good husband is brought to ruin and murder through the temptation of drink. After his death, she is helpless to do anything to save her young son from future temptations because she cannot vote. She cannot even control the estate to which she had brought considerable property. She is encouraged to influence society through training her son. The executor, though he knows of her strong feelings against liquor, nevertheless rents her property for saloons because it is financially advantageous. Thus she is powerless to insure that even her own property dealings will be consistent with her principles. And in a story that accumulates grievance upon grievance,

Samantha tells of the Burpy women who have suffered humiliation, imprisonment, and poverty – all legal according to the workings of the law.

Basic rights, therefore, are withheld from women by the government. Holley's characters give personality to the four predominant antisuffragist arguments delineated by Aileen Kraditor in her book *The Ideas of Woman Suffrage 1890–1920.* Kraditor argues that, like the suffragists, the antisuffragists had no one ideology. Unlike the suffragists, the rationale representing antisuffragism was not characterized by mass activity. There were, however, four standard arguments made by antisuffragists that, significantly, also appear in folksy form in the Samantha books.

One argument held sacred the sentimental vision of Home and Mother. Women were destined from birth to become full-time wives and mothers. The theological argument, Kraditor maintains, was merely pronouncement that God had ordained man and woman to perform different functions. Women were intended for home, men for the world. Advocates of this argument maintained that this division did not indicate superiority or inferiority. Quite to the contrary, if she remained in her proper sphere, woman was insured supremacy therein.[10]

The biological argument was based on two assumptions: souls as well as bodies have sexual attributes; women are physically incapable of undertaking various duties concomitant with voting. Consistent with the first assumption, femininity is identified with emotionalism and illogicality. Women's intuition is a higher faculty than male logic. However, though their method of arriving at truths is superior to men, it is nevertheless useless in the political realm. Consistent with the second assumption, antisuffragists argued that "the weakness, nervousness, and proneness to fainting" of the fragile sex would be out of place in voting booths and conventions.[11]

The sociological argument proclaimed that indeed men and women should occupy different spheres, but their respective spheres were equal. Social peace and welfare of the human race depended upon women staying at home, having children, and staying out of politics. Female suffrage represented a threat to the very structure of society, the basic unit of which was seen to be the family rather than the individual. The man voted as political representative of his family. Women were not deprived of the privilege to vote as were idiots, aliens, and criminals: women were exempt from the burden of being involved in the dirtiness of politics.[12]

Samantha's antisuffragists say it in the following ways. Since those who make the laws — men — also interpret the law, women inevitably become angel designates who can confidently look to men as their legal representatives. The male response to female dissatisfaction is to describe the consequences of voting which would outrage and destroy women's modesty by placing them in the same street with a man every election day. Man's sacred privilege is to protect woman's weakness. Josiah assures Samantha that he votes as her representative (a declaration from which she takes little comfort). Women are weak, helpless angels, "seraphones," sweet, delicate, coo'n' doves who can't rastle with difficult questions. The angels of our homes are too ethereal, too dainty to mingle with rude crowds. Women should have husbands instead of rights; voting would only lower women in the opinion of men. (Samantha replies that since women are already the lowest class in society, they could hardly consider this a threat.) It is flyin' in the face of the Bible not to marry and "stay to home." It is the Law of Nater for the female of the species to stay at home. Since women are naturally frivolous and weak-minded, they probably wouldn't even know how to fold the ballots right and would instead be leanin' over to the next booth to find out what kind of trimmin' the other lady had on her dress. Women can influence the world through their sons; it is unwomanly to suggest the vote. Women must leave to men the difficult task of interpretation. Entering the public sphere " . . . would endanger her life, her spirtual, her mental and her moral growth. It would shake the permanency of the sacred home relationship to its downfall. It would hasten anarchy, and . . . sizm."[13]

In order to claim their rights heretofore withheld, women clearly must have the vote. The two major suffragist arguments were one based on justice and one based on expediency. Kraditor claims that while the earlier suffrage movement held primarily to the natural rights argument, there was a shift in the later movement to an essentially pragmatic argument of expedience. The early suffragists, therefore, had stressed the natural inalienable rights of the common humanity shared by men and women while later arguments underscored the differences between men and women, seeing the vote as primarily a means to the ultimate goal of reform. The suffrage movement was, then, linked to temperance and to the general progressive movement as a means of influencing public morality.

Though Samantha argues for equality of the sexes because it is a natural human right, the vote itself is primarily advocated on grounds of expediency. It is a means to justice and social purity. The licensing of liquor is undermining the family structure. If women could vote, the family would remain inviolate because the whiskey trade would be smashed. Contrary to those who say suffrage would mean aproned men confined in kitchens amid suds and babies, Samantha maintains that suffrage is the way to insure that traditional morality and the sanctity of the home will be guaranteed. Liquor threatens both.

Samantha (and Holley) accepts the concept of women as moral and cultural guardians, and argues that women will be better wives and mothers when they can actively participate in making society a healthier place in which to rear their children. The truly benevolent natures and duties of women in caring for the sick and nurturing the young will be given more significance when the bad men are turned out of office by right-thinking women.

In only one book, *Samantha Among the Colored Folks*, does Holley propose a limited suffrage based on educational qualifications and general intelligence. The assumption clearly is that all white women and some black women would measure up. The fact that she articulates limited suffrage only in her work specifically concerning the race question shows that there are indeed limits to her concept of human equality. The "Southern Question" in the later suffrage movement involved issues of states' rights and maintenance of white supremacy. Though Holley is humanely sympathetic to the plight of the emancipated but generally uneducated black man, she sees temporary solutions in colonization and at least implicitly nods in the direction of southern women whose interests lie in keeping whites in power.

Like the suffragists of the 1890s, Holley was optimistic about what female suffrage could accomplish, and she was essentially conservative in ideology. The argument that women who vote would be better wives certainly implies no radical change in sex roles. Though she considered herself "megum" in all things, Samantha was rejecting only the frivolous, overdone, and sentimental characteristics of the genteel tradition. The morality and conservatism were still hers. Like the suffragists, who were primarily white, middle-class Anglo-Saxon Protestants, she encouraged social reform, not social revolution. The basic structure of society was not attacked, merely women's lack of participation in it.

In *Samantha Among the Brethren* (1890), Holley exposed the rights withheld from women by the church and the incredible reasoning that accompanied the blanket denial of those rights. The 1888 General Conference of the Methodist Episcopal Church had refused to seat four duly elected women delegates on the grounds that admission of women was not in accord with the constitutional provisions of the church embodied in the Restrictive Rules. A special investigative commission was appointed, but it eventually reported adversely on the admission of women delegates. In a publisher's appendix to *Brethren* six of the arguments — three for and three against admission — are cited.[14] Holley obviously just added her keen good humor to some already laughable arguments. Samantha describes a situation in which the Meetin' House is in disrepair and the women set out to fix it up. Through this narrative, she obliterates the argument that women are too weak to sit on the conference and exposes the lengths to which women who are economically dependent on men must go in order to secure the necessary monies. Women are reduced to self-sacrifice and even deceit, Holley implies, because they are unpaid labor dependent on the generosity of husbands or fathers in a society that values both money and independence.

Holley's point is clear. If women are to reclaim from the Church the rights and privileges denied them, they must have voting power on governing conferences; they must maintain some measure of economic independence, and they must be allowed to speak publicly without fear of being labeled "unwomanly." In the religious sphere as in the secular sphere, women have not been accorded equal human rights — ironic in terms of democracy, demonic in terms of salvation.

Thus, Marietta Holley transformed moralizing tracts into humorous sketches. However, her sketches involving problems of drinking, white slave traffic, race, imperialism, conflict between capital and labor, and insensitivity to and oppression of the poor are almost never humorous. She doesn't hesitate to eliminate even small children through violent death in order to make a moral point about injustice. One insensitive rich man loses his adored daughter to disease in the very tenement house he failed to repair. A wealthy industrialist who had refused to take safety precautions to reduce deaths caused by his trolleys loses his son in a trolley accident. Both men reform. Even Samantha's own granddaughter is killed by the inaccurate bullet of bigoted southern whites who want to keep the blacks down. These stories and the many stories involving the consequences of the liquor trade are dim reminders of what Holley's work would have been without her humor. They are sentimental, melodramatic episodes of didactic moralizing that seek to manipulate emotions and point the way to justice and reform.

Fortunately, her treatment of women's sphere, suffrage, the double standard, fashions, rural life, corruptions in government, and so forth do not fall victim to the same moribund moralizing. Though Holley turns again and again to the issue of suffrage, there are numerous sketches and images of women that relate to symbolic representations of women and to role assumptions about women.

In *Samantha at the World's Fair* Josiah Allen's Wife admires the achievements of women as exhibited by the Woman's Building. Josiah articulates male expectations of the extent of female productivity. He had anticipated seeing light and triflin' things like gauzes, artificial flowers, and tattin', but instead he saw that he had vastly underrated women's creative talents. Josiah, who had assumed that it wouldn't take long "to see all that wimmen has brung here," was astonished to learn that women had designed the building, decorated the interior with carved panels, and written the books shelved in the library (see Selection 29, n2). In noticing the many statues on the fairgrounds, Samantha remarked that she felt "dretful well, to see how much my sect wuz thought on in stun." Then she describes various statues symbolic of Truth, Liberty, Diligence, Tradition, etc. She finds that abstract properties are assigned to male and female in complete accord with assumptions about male and female roles. Samantha would probably be disappointed to know that Columbia, the female figure that used to be cosymbol with Uncle Sam, has met a quiet and apparently unnoticed demise.

In the later suffrage movement, the conservative ideology which supported women's sphere as in the home was reconciled with the ideology of social reform because some, such as Jane Addams, perceived the workings of the government as essentially "enlarged House-keeping" that required the experience of the nation's housekeepers.[15] Though she never makes an explicit connection to a specific suffrage argument of reform as housekeeping, Samantha does, significantly, use Columbia as symbol of the United States in *Samantha at the Centennial*. Columbia is the housekeeping metaphor: " . . . (she) has got her high heeled shoes on, as you may say, and is showin' off, tryin' to see what she can do. She has been keepin' house for a hundred years, and been a addin' to her house every year, and repairin' of it and gettin' housen stuff together, and now she is havin' a regular house warmin', to show off, what a housekeeper she is."[16]

Furthermore, Samantha is optimistic that things will go better for women now that "Justice is beginnin' to peek out and notice that 'male and female created He them.' Bein' so blind, and believin' jest what wuz told her, Justice had got it into her head that it read: 'Male created He them.' "[17]

Because Justice has been so blind and because the accounts have been "writ down by males and translated by 'em," the deeds of women have been ignored and/or forgotten. In a sketch about the wives of the Old Testament prophets, Samantha points to the function of woman as healer and nurturer, comforter and guardian, workhorse and hostess that remains constant over historical time in society's eyes. (Selection 28). Furthermore, the efforts and sacrifices of these faithful "help-meets" are not acknowledged in any historically significant way because their contribution was not in the political, religious, *public* sphere and because from a male point of view things are as they were created to be. Besides, men write the books. She understands (and understates) that women were probably overlooked because "it's sort o' naterel to stand up for your own sect."

So, Holley took the "woman question" and walked clear around it to see all sides as it was being enacted in late-nineteenth-century America. There is a strong temporal attachment to the issues of suffrage, temperance, and the holdover Victorian female virtues of piety, purity, submissiveness, and domesticity.[18] The use of Columbia as symbol of America is likewise dated because for some reason Columbia has fallen away or returned to the closet while Uncle Sam still wants you.

But though certain issues and symbols reflect a specific historical time, others that have persisted seem strikingly modern. Or at least modern feminists use language, imagery, and reversals that are amazingly akin to those of Holley. The story of the nurturing wives of the prophets obviously transcends a fixed historical time period. Samantha's use of the term "Revolutionary 4 Mothers" was no doubt shocking both because the term "forefathers" was so universally used and accepted and because any alternative that excluded the male gender was unthinkable (Selection 19). Holley points to the fact that women are assumed to be included in the term "man." Men, of course, would not automatically and unquestioningly feel included in the term "4 Mothers" and in fact have written history so that only our male ancestors really did anything worthwhile anyway. The current pressure for genderless terms (such as "chairperson") reflects the same concern that women be recognized as distinct people who should not automatically be subsumed under male titles.

Generally, an institution or a building is genderless. But Samantha jolts Josiah by referring to the Meetin' House as "she." His protest that it should be "he" because it "stands to reason" is only immediately acceptable to other "he's" (Selection 23). Holley would not have gone so far as to call God "she"; however, it is obviously but a short jump to the current "Our Mother who arte in Heaven." Holley questioned not the Deity, "Himself," but the interpretation of divine word so as to subordinate women in the social sphere and exclude them in the hierarchical structure of His institutional church. Nevertheless, the shock value of calling the Meetin' House a "she" was undoubtedly not lost upon an audience that would have considered a change in God's gender both blasphemous and sacrilegious.

In a sketch that elucidates via role reversal, Holley captures an image bearing noticeable resemblance to the caption of a recent British family-planning poster showing a man pregnant: "If it were you, how would you feel?" In "A Male Magdalene" (Selection 16), Samantha attacks the irrational double standard by simply reversing the traditional tale of the fallen woman. Nelt Chawgo, "that young he-hussy," is a lost man, a "ruined feller." He was ruined by Angerose Wilds who had deceived him by promising marriage, had used him, and then had deserted him. Samantha urges that neither Angerose nor Nelt is guiltless, nor should either bear the entire blame. There should be no double standard of conduct. She claims that men and women do and should perform different functions in society, but that qualities of soul and character and basic humanity have no sex identification. Women should not be above or below men — they should sit side by side as equals.

In *My Opinions and Betsey Bobbet's*, Samantha said in the preface that she had been persuaded by a deep inward voice that she must write about "Wimmen's Rights." She resolved to "set her shoulder blades to the wheel" and write what that voice of the heart knew must be authored. The cover page announces that *Opinions* is "designed as a beacon light, to guide women to life liberty and the pursuit of happiness, but which may be read by members of the sterner sect, without injury to themselves or the book."

For the mother-wit who exposed as preposterous many of the arguments against suffrage, current objections to the Equal Rights Amendment would be an enticing challenge. One wonders how Samantha would "rastle" with objections that passage of the ERA would mean unisex public bathrooms, women fighting beside men in the trenches of war, and the destruction of the family unit. Or, she would once again tackle the always current scriptural argument of fundamentalists who object that the ERA would be flyin' in the face of the Bible, which clearly shows woman's place to be subordinate to man's. Certainly, the current women's movement would elicit both her support and criticism, just as the earlier movement did. She had in common with modern feminists a sympathy for and commitment to ideas and projects that encouraged and demanded equal status as human beings. She would probably be distraught at current divorce rates, permissive sexual mores, the instability of the family structure, and militant feminist tactics. But my hunch is that Samantha would set her shoulder blades to the wheel and "resoom" the struggle, though of course, "eloquence is dretful tuckerin'."

<hr />

A different version of this introductory essay was published in the *Journal of Popular Culture*, VIII:4 (Spring, 1975). For most of the biographical information on Marietta Holley, I am indebted to Margaret Wyman Langworth's article in vol. II of the series on *Notable American Women 1607–1950*, edited by Edward T. James, Janet Wilson James, and Paul S. Boyer, and to an unpublished Ph.D. dissertation entitled "Marietta Holley" by Katherine G. Blyley, University of Pittsburgh, 1936, Ch. I, pp. 2–37.

NOTES

1. Ann Douglas, *The Feminization of American Culture* (New York, 1977), p. 11.

2. Quoted by Blyley from Holley's posthumously published autobiography, *The Story of My Life*, 1931, Chapter 1.

3. Blyley, p. 28. Blyley was able to interview Holley's longtime gardener and others who provided first-hand accounts of her daily habits.

4. Neil Burgess was a popular comedian who often dramatized humorous works. Among those he chose were Frances Whitcher's Widow Bedott and Holley's *Betsey Bobbet*. According to Blyley, Burgess agreed to pay a weekly royalty to Holley for the use of names of characters in the book and for the plot material which he was to adapt into a dramatic version. The author insisted that there be nothing "off color" in the adaptation. With Burgess playing Samantha, the Providence premiere was highly successful. In 1878 he moved the play to New York City, but he broke his contract by changing Samantha from a dignified philosopher to a grotesque termagent. The version, renamed *Vim*, ran for 200 performances at Bijou in 1883 and was revived periodically in both New York and Boston down to 1888.

5. *Notable Women*, p. 203. Although sales records are not available from Funk & Wagnalls publishers, there is further evidence of her popularity. In *Golden Multitudes*, Frank Luther Mott cites as best-sellers books believed to have had a total sale equal to 1 percent of the population of the continental United States for the decade in which it was published. Best-sellers in the decade 1880–89 required a sale of at least 500,000 to make the list. Better-sellers don't quite match that number but are believed to be 1 percent of the population. *Samantha at Saratoga* made the better-seller list for that decade.

6. *Notable Women*, p. 203; Blyley, pp. 2–37. A recent article evaluates Holley's value as a propagandist. See Shelley Armitage, "Marietta Holley: The Humorist as Propagandist," *Rocky Mountain Review*, 34:4 (Fall, 1980), 193–201.

7. Mabel Wagnalls, "A Glimpse of Marietta Holley," *Ladies Home Journal* (Nov., 1903), 61.

8. Marietta Holley, *My Opinions and Betsey Bobbet's* (Hartford, 1973), p. 24.

9. Marietta Holley, *The Widder Doodle's Love Affair* (New York, 1893), p. 43.

10. Aileen Kraditor, *The Ideas of the Woman Suffrage Movement, 1890–1920* (New York, 1971), pp. 12–26. Two general survey accounts of the campaign for suffrage are Eleanor Flexner, *A Century of Struggle* (Cambridge, Mass., 1959) and Andrew Sinclair, *The Emancipation of the American Woman* (New York, 1965), originally published as *The Better Half*. For documents pertaining to the suffrage movement, see Mari Jo Buhle and Paul Buhle, eds., *The Concise History of Woman Suffrage: Selections from the Classic Work of Stanton, Anthony, Gage, and Harper* (Urbana, Ill., 1978). See also Section III, "Woman and Government," in Kraditor, ed., *Up From the Pedestal* (New York, 1968).

11. Kraditor, ed., *Up From the Pedestal*.

12. *Ibid.*

13. Marietta Holley, *Samantha Among the Brethren* (New York, 1890), p. 20.

14. See headnote to Section V for specifics on these arguments.

15. Kraditor, *Ideas*, pp. 38–57. Samantha uses the housekeeping metaphor in *Samantha on the Race Problem* as follows: "I know the law is there. [She refers to the law passed by men that made the age of consent for children the venerable old age of seven.] But let wimmen have a chance to vote; let a few mothers and grandmothers get holt of that statute-book, and see where that law would be."

Sez I eloquently, "No spring cleanin' and scourin' wuz ever done by females so thorough as they would cleanse out them old law books and let a little of God's purity and justice shine into their musty old pages" (p. 238).

16. Marietta Holley, *Samantha at the Centennial* (Hartford, 1887), p. 496.

17. Marietta Holley, *Samantha Among the Colored Folks* (New York, 1894), pp. 317–18.

18. These four virtues were described by Barbara Welter in "The Cult of True Womanhood: 1820–1860," *American Quarterly* (Summer, 1966), 151–174. They seem appropriate to mention in this context because Samantha emphasizes all but submissiveness as admirable ideals. She does not, however, equate piety with subordination in church affairs nor purity with exclusively female mandates. She is proud of her domestic skills (and boasts of them periodically) but though she argues for suffrage on the grounds that the family and domestic sphere can be saved because of the votes of moral women, she is obviously not relegated to a nonpublic existence.

Welter's article was representative of a predominant theme in writings on women's history, often based on published didactic literature regarding woman's place and the home, which cited the changing status of nineteenth-century women that in fact diminished them when compared to their eighteenth-century mothers. Women became victims of an ideology of domesticity that served man's view of the social order. Nancy Cott, in *The Bonds of Womanhood* (New Haven, 1977), sees three successive interpretations of "woman's sphere," with Welter's perspective representing the first. The second, she contends while apologizing for the injustices of over-simplification, "observed that women made use of the ideology of domesticity for their own purposes, to advance their educational opportunities to gain influence and satisfaction, even to express hostility to men." This perspective was generally based on the published writings of women authors. The third, drawing primarily from diaries, letters, and other "private documents of non-famous women," turns tables on the first by viewing "woman's sphere as the basis for a subculture among women that formed a source of strength and identity and afforded supportive sisterly relations; this view implied that the ideology's tenacity owed as much to women's motives as to the imposition of men's or 'society's' wishes." See Cott's discussion, "On 'Woman's Sphere' and Feminism," 197–206.

Among those who show "true womanhood' to have been less mono-
lithic than Welter's assessment are Carroll Smith-Rosenberg, whose article "The Female World of Love and Ritual: Relations Between
Women in Nineteenth-Century America," *Signs*, 1:1 (1975), 1–29, describes long-lived, intimate same-sex relationships among eighteenth-
and nineteenth-century women that were casually accepted by American society. Though women possessed little status or power in the
larger world, the continuity of female closeness and support networks
signified their value, dignity, status, and power within the specifically
female world.

A forthcoming book (working title, *"Liberty, A Better Husband":
The Single Woman in America, 1780–1860)* should expand and revise
still more our understanding of options for the nineteenth-century
woman. Lee Chambers-Schiller discusses the "cult of single blessedness"
and argues that the assumption that single women were denigrated is
false. There was more flexibility in the social mores than has been
thought and in fact many women chose to live single lives (as mission-
aries, teachers, artists, scientists, writers) and were socially approved.

I

The Woman Question

" . . . What is the world comin' to!
Angle worms will be risin' up next and
demandin' to not be trod on."
— Zephaniah Beezum, groaning
over wimmin's rights

The selections in this section deal with the question of "wimmin's rights" in general. There is a strong, though not exclusive, emphasis on the need for the vote, but for Samantha "wimmin's rights" includes equal pay for equal work, taxation with representation, the right to speak in public, freedom from economic dependence on men (wife slavery), and a mother's equal right to her children. At the very least, she chides, women should be treated as well as idiots and lunatics with whom they are classed. In her constant effort to educate Josiah, Samantha offers "A Allegory of Wimmin's Rights" and once again does battle with Betsey Bobbet in "Wimmin's Speah."

Meanwhile, threatened by women's demands for rights and outraged at the plight of their British brethren at the hands of the Militant Suffragettes, the Jonesville men (in "The Creation Searchin' Society") meet to voice their displeasure and suggest some ways to "stop them women's disgraceful doin's."

"Female Delicacy"

1 "A Allegory on Wimmen's Rights"

About a couple of weeks after the quiltin', Thomas Jefferson said to Josiah, one Saturday mornin',

"Father, can I have the old mare to go to Jonesville to-night?"

"What do you want to go to Jonesville for?" said his father, "you come from there last night."

"There is goin' to be a lecture on wimmin's rights; can I have her, father?"

"I s'pose so," says Josiah, kinder short, and after Thomas J. went out, Josiah went on —

"Wimmin's rights, wimmin's rights, I wonder how many more fools are goin' a caperin' round the country preachin' 'em up — I am sick of wimmin's rights, I don't believe in 'em."

This riled up the old Smith blood, and says I to him with a glance that went clear through to the back side of his head —

"I know you don't, Josiah Allen — I can tell a man that is for wimmin's rights as fur as I can see 'em. There is a free, easy swing to thier walk — a noble look to thier faces — thier big hearts and soles love liberty and justice, and bein' free themselves they want everybody else to be free. These men haint jealous of a woman's influence — haint afraid that she won't pay him proper respect if she haint obleeged to — and they needn't be afraid, for these are the very men that wimmin look up to, and worship, — and always will. A good, noble, true man is the best job old natur ever turned off her hands, or ever will — a man, that would wipe off a baby's tears as soft as a woman could, or "die with his face to the foe."

"They are most always big, noble-sized men, too," says I, with

From *My Opinions and Betsey Bobbet's* (Hartford, 1891), pp. 85–98.

another look at Josiah that pierced him like a arrow. (Josiah don't weigh quite one hundred by the steelyards.)

"I don't know as I am to blame, Samantha, for not bein' a very hefty man."

"You can let your sole grow, Josiah Allen, by thinkin' big, noble-sized thoughts, and I believe if you did, you would weigh more by the steelyards."

"Wall, I don't care, Samantha, I stick to it, that I am sick of wimmin's rights; if wimmin would take care of the rights they have got now, they would do better than they do do."

Now I love to see folks use reason if they have got any — and I won't stand no importations cast on to my sect — and so I says to him in a tone of cold and almost freezin' dignity —

"What do you mean, Josiah?"

"I mean that women hain't no business a votin'; they had better let the laws alone, and tend to thier housework. The law loves wimmin and protects 'em."

"If the law loves wimmin so well, why don't he give her as much wages as men get for doin' the same work? Why don't he give her half as much, Josiah Allen?"[1]

Josiah waved off my question, seemin'ly not noticin' of it — and continued with the doggy obstinacy of his sect —

"Wimmin haint no business with the laws of the country."

"If they haint no business with the law, the law haint no business with them," says I warmly. "Of the three classes that haint no business with the law — lunatics, idiots, and wimmin — the lunatics and idiots have the best time of it," says I, with a great rush of ideas into my brain that almost lifted up the border of my head-dress. "Let a idiot kill a man; 'What of it?' says the law; let a luny steal a sheep; again the law murmurs in a calm and gentle tone, 'What of it? they haint no business with the law and the law haint no business with them.' But let one of the third class, let a woman steal a sheep, does the law soothe her in these comfortin' tones? No, it thunders to her, in awful accents, 'You haint no business with the law, but the law has a good deal of business with you, vile female, start for State's prisen; you haint nothin' at all to do with the law, only to pay all the taxes it tells you to — embrace a license bill that is ruinin' your husband — give up your innocent little children to a wicked father if it tells you to — and a few other little things, such as bein' dragged off to prison by it — chained up for life, and hung, and et cetery.' "[2]

Josiah sot motionless — and in a rapped eloquence I went on in the allegory way.

" 'Methought I once heard the words,' sighs the female, 'True government consists in the consent of the governed;' did I dream them, or did the voice of a luny pour them into my ear?'

" 'Haint I told you,' frouns the law on her, 'that that don't mean wimmin — have I got to explain to your weakened female comprehension again, the great fundymental truth, that wimmin haint included and mingled in the law books and statutes of the country only in a condemnin' and punishin' sense, as it were. Though I feel it to be bendin' down my powerful manly dignity to elucidate the subject further, I will consent to remind you of the consolin' fact, that though you wimmin are, from the tender softness of your natures, and the illogical weakness of your minds, unfit from ever havin' any voice in makin' the laws that govern you; you have the right, and nobody can ever deprive you of it, to be punished in a future world jest as hard as a man of the strongest intellect, and to be hung in this world jest as dead as a dead man; and what more can you ask for, you unreasonable female woman you?'

"Then groans the woman as the great fundymental truth rushes upon her —

" 'I can be hung by the political rope, but I can't help twist it.'

" 'Jest so,' says the law, 'that rope takes noble and manly fingers, and fingers of principle to twist it, and not the weak unprincipled grasp of lunatics, idiots, and wimmin.'

" 'Alas!' sithes the woman to herself, 'would that I had the sweet rights of my wild and foolish companions, the idiots and lunys. But, says she, venturing with a beating heart, the timid and bashful inquiry, 'are the laws always just, that I should obey them thus implicitly? There is old Creshus,[3] he stole two millions, and the law cleared him triumphantly. Several men have killed various other men, and the law insistin' they was out of their heads (had got out of 'em for the occasion, and got into 'em agin the minute they was cleared) let 'em off with sound necks. And I, a poor woman, have only stole a sheep, a small-sized sheep too, that my offspring might not perish with hunger — is it right to liberate in a triumphin' way the two million stealer and the

man murderer, and inkarcerate the poor sheep stealer? and my children was *so* hungry, and it was such a small sheep,' says the woman in
pleadin' accents.

" 'Idiots! lunatics! and wimmin! are they goin' to speak?' thunders
the law. 'Can I believe my noble right ear? can I bein' blindfolded trust
my seventeen senses? I'll have you understand that it haint no woman's
business whether the laws are just or unjust, all you have got to do is
jest to obey 'em, so start off for prison, my young woman.'

" 'But my house-work,' pleads the woman; 'woman's place is home:
it is her duty to remain at all hazards within its holy and protectin'
precincts; how can I leave its sacred retirement to moulder in State's
prison?'

" 'House-work!' and the law fairly yells the words, he is so filled with
contempt at the idee. 'House-work! jest as if house-work is goin' to
stand in the way of the noble administration of the law. I admit the
recklessness and immorality of her leavin' that holy haven, long enough
to vote — but I guess she can leave her house-work long enough to be
condemned, and hung, and so forth.'

" 'But I have got a infant,' says the woman, 'of tender days, how can
I go?'

" 'That is nothing to the case,' says the law in stern tones. 'The
peculiar conditions of motherhood only unfits a female woman from
ridin' to town with her husband, in a covered carriage, once a year,
and layin' her vote on a pole. I'll have you understand it is no hind-
rance to her at all in a cold and naked cell, or in a public court room
crowded with men.'

" 'But the indelikacy, the outrage to my womanly nature?' says the
woman.

" 'Not another word out of your head, young woman,' says the law,
'or I'll fine you for contempt. I guess the law knows what is indelikacy,
and what haint; where modesty comes in, and where it don't; now start
for prison bareheaded, for I levy on your bunnet for contempt of me.'

"As the young woman totters along to prison, is it any wonder that
she sithes to herself, but in a low tone, that the law might not hear her,
and deprive her also of her shoes for her contemptas thoughts —

" 'Would that I were a idiot; alas! is it not possible that I may become even now a luny? — then I should be respected.' "

As I finished my allegory and looked down from the side of the
house, where my eyes had been fastened in the rapped eloquence of

thought, I see Josiah with a contented countenance, readin' the almanac, and I said to him in a voice before which he quailed —

"Josiah Allen, you haint heard a word I've said, you know you
haint."

"Yes I have," says he, shettin' up the almanac; "I heard you say wimmin ought to vote, and I say she hadn't. I shall always say that she is too
fraguile, too delikate, it would be too hard for her to go to the pole."

"There is one pole you are willin' enough I should go to, Josiah
Allen," and I stopped allegorin', and spoke with witherin' dignity and
self respect — "and that is the hop pole."[4] (Josiah has sot out a new hop
yard, and he proudly brags to the neighbors that I am the fastest picker
in the yard.) "You are willin' enough I should handle them poles!" He
looked smit and conscience struck, but still true to the inherient principles of his sect, and thier doggy obstinacy, he murmured —

"If wimmin know when they are well off, they will let poles and 'lection boxes alone, it is too wearin for the fair sect."

"Josiah Allen," says I, "you think that for a woman to stand up
straight on her feet, under a blazin' sun, and lift both her arms above
her head, and pick seven bushels of hops, mingled with worms and
spiders, into a gigantic box, day in, and day out, is awful healthy, so
strengthenin' and stimulatin' to wimmin, but when it comes to drop-
pin' a little slip of clean paper into a small seven by nine box, once a
year in a shady room, you are afraid it is goin' to break down a
woman's constitution to once."

He was speechless, and clung to Ayer'es almanac[5] mechanically (as it
were) and I continued —

"There is another pole you are willin' enough for me to handle, and
that is our cistern pole. If you should spend some of the breath you
waste — in pityin' the poor wimmin that have got to vote — in byin' a
pump, you would raise 25 cents in my estimation, Josiah Allen. You
have let me pull on that old cistern pole thirteen years, and get a ten
quart pail of water on to the end of it, add I guess the political pole
wouldn't draw much harder than that does."

"I guess I will get one, Samantha, when I sell the old critter. I have
been a calculatin' to every year, but things will kinder run along."

"I am aware of that," says I in a tone of dignity cold as a lump of cold
ice. "I am aware of that. You may go into any neighborhood you
please, and if there is a family in it, where the wife has to set up
leeches,[6] make soap, cut her own kindlin' wood, build fires in winter,

set up stove-pipes, dround kittens, hang out clothes lines, cord beds, cut up pork, skin calves, and hatchel flax[7] with a baby lashed to her side — I haint afraid to bet you a ten cent bill, that that womans husband thinks that wimmin are too feeble and delicate to go the pole."

Josiah was speechless for pretty near half a minute, and when he did speak it was words calculated to draw my attention from contemplatin' that side of the subject. It was for reasons, I have too much respect for my husband to even hint at — odious to him, as odious could be — he wanted me to forget it, and in the gentle and sheepish manner men can so readily assume when they are talkin' to females he said, as he gently fingered Ayer's almanac, and looked pensively at the dyin' female revivin' at a view of the bottle —

"We men think too much of you wimmin to want you to lose your sweet, dignified, retirin' modesty that is your chieftest charm. How long would dignity and modesty stand firm before the wild Urena of public life? You are made to be happy wives, to be guarded by the stronger sect, from the cold blast and the torrid zone. To have a fence built around you by manly strength, to keep out the cares and troubles of life. Why, if I was one of the fair sect, I would have a husband to fence me in, if I had to hire one."

He meant this last, about hirin' a husband, as a joke, for he smiled feebly as he said it, and in other and happier times stern duty would have compelled me to laugh at it — but not now, oh no, my breast was heavin' with too many different sized emotions.

"You would hire one, would you? a woman don't lose her dignity and modesty a racin' round tryin' to get married, does she? Oh no," says I, as sarcastic as sarcastic could be, and then I added sternly, "If it ever does come in fashion to hire husbands by the year, I know of one that could be rented cheap, if his wife had the proceeds and avails in a pecuniary sense."

He looked almost mortified, but still he murmur'd as if mechanically. "It is wimmen's place to marry and not to vote."

"Josiah Allen," says I, "Anybody would think to hear you talk that a woman couldn't do but just one of the two things any way — marry or vote, and had got to take her choice of the two at the pint of the bayonet. And anybody would think to hear you go on, that if a women could live in any other way, she wouldn't be married, and you couldn't get her to." Says I, looking at him shrewdly, "if marryin' is such a dreadful nice thing for wimmen I don't see what you are afraid of.[8]

You men act kinder guilty about it, and I don't wonder at it, for take a bad husband, and thier haint no kind of slavery to be compared to wife slavery. It is jest as natural for a mean, cowardly man to want to abuse and tyranize over them that they can, them that are dependent on 'em, as for a noble and generous man to want to protect them that are weak and in thier power. Figurin' accordin' to the closest rule of arithmetic, there are at least one-third mean, dissopated, drunken men in the world, and they most all have wives, and let them tread on these wives ever so hard, if they only tread accordin' to law, she can't escape. And suppose she tries to escape, blood-hounds[9] haint half so bitter as public opinion on a women that parts with her husband, chains and handcuffs haint to be compared to her pride, and her love for her children, and so she keeps still, and suffers agony enough to make four first class martyrs. Field slaves have a few hours for rest at night, and a hope, to kinder boy them up, of gettin' a better master. But the wife slave has no hope of a change of masters, and let him be ever so degraded and brutal is at his mercy day and night. Men seem to be awful afraid that wimmen wont be so fierce for marryin' anybody, for a home and a support, if they can support themselves independent, and be jest as respectable in the eyes of the world. But," says I,

"In them days when men and wimmen are both independent — free and equal, they will marry in the only true way — from love and not from necessity. They will marry because God will join thier two hearts and hands so you cant get 'em apart no how. But to hear you talk Josiah Allen, anybody would think that there wouldn't another woman marry on earth, if they could get rid of it, and support themselves without it." And then I added, fixin' my keen grey eyes upon his'en. "You act guilty about it Josiah Allen." "But," says I, "just so long as the sun shines down upon the earth and the earth answers back to it, blowin' all out full of beauty — Jest so long as the moon looks down lovin'ly upon old ocien makin' her heart beat the faster, jest so long will the hearts and souls God made for each other, answer to each other's call. God's laws can't be repealed, Josiah Allen, they wasn't made in Washington, D.C."

I hardly ever see a man quail more than he did, and to tell the truth, I guess I never had been quite so eloquent in all the 14 years we had lived together — I felt so eloquent that I couldn't stop myself and I went on.

"When did you ever see a couple that hated each other, or didn't care for each other, but what their children, was either jest as mean as pusley — or else wilted and unhappy lookin' like a potato sprout in a dark suller? What that potato sprout wants is sunshine, Josiah Allen. What them children wants is love. The fact is love is what makes a home — I don't care whether its walls are white, stone, marble or bass wood. If there haint a face to the winder a waitin' for you, when you have been off to the store, what good does all your things do you, though you have traded off ten pounds of butter? A lot of folks may get together in a big splendid house, and be called by the same name, and eat and sleep under the same roof till they die, and call it home, but if love don't board with 'em, give me an umbrella and a stump. But the children of these marriages that I speak of, when they see such perfect harmony of mind and heart in their father and mother, when they have been brought up in such a warm, bright, happy home — they can't no more help growin' up sweet, and noble, and happy, than your wheat can help growin' up straight and green when the warm rain and the sunshine falls on it. These children, Josiah Allen, are the future men and wimmens who are goin' to put their shoulder blades to the wheel and roll this world straight into millenium." Says Josiah,

"Wimmen are too good to vote with us men, wimmen haint much more nor less than angels any way."

When you have been soarin' in eloquence, it is always hard to be brought down sudden — it hurts you to light — and this speech sickened me, and says I, in a tone so cold that he shivered imperceptibly.

"Josiah Allen, there is one angel that would be glad to have a little wood got for her to get dinner with, there is one angel that cut every stick of wood she burnt yesterday, that same angel doin' a big washin' at the same time," and says I, repeatin' the words, as I glanced at the beef over the cold and chilly stove, "I should like a handful of wood Josiah Allen."

"I would get you some this minute Samantha," says he gettin' up and takin' down his plantin' bag, "but you know jest how hurried I be with my spring's work, can't you pick up a little for this forenoon? you haint got much to do have you?"

"Oh no!" says I in a lofty tone of irony, "Nothin' at all, only a big ironin', ten pies and six loaves of bread to bake, a cheese curd to run up, 3 hens to scald, churnin' and moppin' and dinner to get. Jest a easy mornin's work for a angel."

"Wall then, I guess you'll get along, and to-morrow I'll try to get you some."

I said no more, but with lofty emotions surgin' in my breast, I took my axe and started for the wood-pile.

NOTES

1. Samantha illustrates the economic dependence of her rural women neighbors in a later selection, "On Economics," when the women of the Meetin' House try to raise money to refurbish the church and contribute to the minister's salary. See Section V, "Rights Denied by the Church."

Women in the early nineteenth century often worked at spinning and weaving, teaching, or domestic service. In 1833 women working at home earned as little as $1.25 per week; women and children in factories earned $1 to $3 per week, minus board for lodgings provided by the company. By the turn of the century more women had become service, garment, and textile manufacturing workers; the number of working women had grown from approximately 4 million in 1890 to 17.5 million in 1910, and wages ranged from $2 to $6 a week. For specific information on women's wages see Connie Brown and Jane Seitz, " 'You've Come a Long Way, Baby': Historical Perspectives," *Sisterhood is Powerful* (New York, 1970), pp. 6–8, 21. Also, Edith Abbott, *Women in Industry* (New York, reprint edition, 1969), pp. 262–316, and Rosalyn Baxandall, Linda Gordon, Susan Reverby, eds., *America's Working Women* (New York, 1976).

In 1870 in New York women worked by the piece, selling shirts for 6¢ each. The Annual Report of the Massachusetts Bureau of Labor, published in 1884 and based on the census of 1880, showed 38,881 female workers, 20,000 of whom were employed in occupations other than domestic service. Based on a sample of 1,032 of the "working girls of Boston," the occupations were as follows: Personal Service (matrons and nurses, restaurant employees, carpet sewers, laundry employees, telegraph operators, etc.) – 83; Trade (bookkeepers, clerks, cashiers, saleswomen, etc.) – 123; Manufactures (heavily represented by clothing and canning industries) – 826. The average weekly income for a year in personal service was $5.25, in trade $4.81, in manufacture $5.22, or a general average of $5.17 per week. See the report reprinted in Nancy Cott, *Roots of Bitterness* (New York, 1972), pp. 311–21; also see pp. 333 – 37 for 1894 report on comparison of educated women's wages with men's wages in professions, technical, and other white-collar jobs.

Today, 42 percent of the U.S. work force are women, nearly one-half of all married women are in the labor force, 80 percent of women in the work force are in female-dominated jobs (clerical, sales, service, etc.) Women earn approximately 59¢ for every dollar earned by men, and the issue of equal pay for equal work has expanded to include the concept of comparable worth, which calls into question the practice of paying men in male-dominated jobs more than women in female-dominated jobs.

2. The license bill refers to the selling of liquor, which Samantha consistently links to bad family fortunes. See "On the Sufferings of the Burpy Women" for examples of husbands ruined by drink.

The argument that women are held accountable by laws they had no voice in drafting, that they are taxed without representation, and that they are stripped of legal means to protect the very children they are charged with influencing is repeated often in Holley's work. The reference to giving up one's innocent children underscores women's lack of rights even to the offspring they bear. Even a proven drunkard husband still had sole rights to his children if he chose to exercise them. In case of divorce, the children were "rightfully" in the husband's custody. See n8 for more information on the Married Women's Property Act and the "civil death" marriage entailed.

In the American colonies both men and women who broke the law were put in stocks, whipped, ducked or publicly hanged. Jails served mainly as a way-station for those awaiting trial or punishment. After 1815, however, many American states built penitentiary institutions for the "dangerous class" of vagrants, thieves and prostitutes. There were three major categories of crimes — against person, property, or public order — and only the last included a significant number of women. These crimes included drunkenness, vagrancy, streetwalking, and petty larceny. Women convicted of such crimes were often remanded to local jails. For crimes such as murder, arson, manslaughter, or burglary, women served terms in penitentiaries.

A subcategory of crimes against the public order — sometimes called crimes against decency or chastity — applied exclusively to women. The nineteenth-century female convicted of offenses against chastity or decency carried the lifetime label "fallen woman." The conditions in prisons holding both male and female prisoners, including the sexual exploitation of women prisoners by male guards and overcrowded, poorly-ventilated cells in prisons not designed for women, inspired a reform movement for separate women's prisons. For a comprehensive account of this subject, see Estelle B. Freedman, *Their Sisters' Keepers: Women's Prison Reform in America, 1830–1930* (Ann Arbor, 1981).

3. Croesus was King of Lydia from 560–546 B.C. One legend claims that Croesus, whose wealth had been acquired by trade, hoped to escape his conqueror, Cyrus of Persia, by burning himself with his wealth on a funeral pyre but was captured before he could do so. According to Herodotus, he was condemned by Cyrus but was miraculously saved after the fire had been lighted and he lived to become Cyrus's friend and counsellor. At any rate, the wealth of Croesus became proverbial, his gold staters and silver shekels among the most

famous coins of antiquity, and his name is now generic for a very rich man.

4. Holley is probably using this image to play on the word "poll" more than to reflect prevailing custom. Samantha refers in other books to the boy who brings in the milk, and it is probable that folks such as the Allens would have had some help in the fields so that attending the hops pole wouldn't have been women's work. But this image is consistent with others Holley uses regarding the physical strength required by women to do their daily chores, on the one hand, and the male argument that women are too fragile to vote or too weak to sit on the Methodist Conference, on the other.

5. *Ayer's American Almanac*, published yearly beginning in 1852 by Dr. J.C. Ayer & Co., Practical and Analytical Chemists, Lowell, Massachusetts, was advertised for the use of "farmers, planters, mechanics and all families." The cover always featured a picture (of chemical paraphernalia, winged woman with wreath and trumpet, etc.) with the inscription "Heal the Sick." Basically, the almanac was an extended advertisement for Ayer's medicinal compounds and home remedies such as his Hair Vigor (restores natural hair color, eradicates dandruff, and sometimes promotes new hair growth), Sarsaparilla (compound to fight scrofula and attendant problems), Cherry Pectoral, Cathartic Pills, and Ague Cure. The disease and its symptoms are described, then one of Ayer's medicines is prescribed along with directions for its use and testimonials from readers to its effectiveness.

Also included was the standard almanac fare such as monthly calendars with moon phases, sunrises, sunsets, and important historical events, aphorisms, and witticisms. The 1873 almanac offered these quips which would well have found favor with Josiah: "Young women should graduate A.B. (a bride): the next degree is A.M. (a mother)." "A lady says the female suffrage question, simmered down, is just a quarrel with the Almighty that they are not men." "Female agitation does not stop at the right of suffrage. As the party season flourishes, she insists on her right to bare arms."

6. The process of preparing leeches for bleeding as a medicinal procedure. Leeches were kept in a diluted water solution so that they were alive but not fed. Thus, they were hungry when applied to the skin.

7. To hatchel flax is part of the process of getting flax ready for spinning. After it's been retted or rotted, the flax is put through a break (flax-break) which breaks away the outside fiber of the flax. Then it's put into a hatchel, which combs the inside fiber.

8. Feminists often referred to the assertions of Sir William Blackstone (English common law), which pronounced the "civil death" of women in marriage, when arguing for women's rights and the vote. Blackstone wasn't literally transplanted from England to America, and laws relating to women were often devised in a piecemeal fashion, dif-

ferent in different states or regions. (Even today laws regarding divorce, alimony, child support, names, credit, etc., vary by state or region). Still, the American laws were broadly based on English common law and in that law Blackstone classed women with minors and idiots. By marriage the husband and wife became one person in the law and that person was the husband. Thus in the nineteenth century when a woman married, she gave up control over her body, her property, her wages, even her personal possessions (her dresses, her egg money — see Selection 19 wherein Samantha describes the humiliating trials of Abigail Burpy Flanders). She was not allowed to testify in court, sue, contract, hold title to property, sign papers as a witness, or establish businesses. A wife's will had to be signed by her husband to be legal. Husbands had control of children after a divorce and were generally able to secure a divorce on broader grounds than were women. Divorce involved public proceedings and punishment of the guilty party. Divorce laws were finally changed to give the innocent party custody of the children.

The Woman's Property Act of 1848 in New York State "gave the wife full control over her real and personal property at the time of her marriage, and excepting it from her husband's debts. The wages earned by a wife were still, however, the property of her husband" (Sinclair, pp. 87–88).

The 1855 marriage document of Henry B. Blackwell and Lucy Stone (reprinted in Kraditor, *Up From the Pedestal*, pp. 149–50) specifically protests against the laws which give to the husband the custody of the wife's person, exclusive control and guardianship of their children, sole ownership of her personal and real property, the right to the product of her industry, a larger and more permanent interest of the widower in the property of a deceased wife than they give to the widow. Lastly, they protest "against the whole system by which 'the legal existence of the wife is suspended during marriage,' so that in most states, she neither has a legal part in the choice of her residence, nor can she make a will, nor sue or be sued in her own name, nor inherit property." They declared their view that marriage should be an "equal and permanent partnership, and so recognized by law."

9. Given the lack of a legal, separate existence for married women, the taking of the master's name, the giving over of control even to one's body, the economic dependence on one's guardian-husband, the link between slavery and wifehood was often underscored by feminists. The reference here to escape and blood-hounds likens the public humiliation of divorce or abandonment with the physical imprisonment of runaway slaves who, after the Fugitive Slave Act of 1850, could be pursued into free territories, captured, and returned to their masters.

2 "Wimmen's Speah"

One bright, beautiful day, I had got my mornin's work all done up, and had sot doun to double some carpet yarn, and Josiah sot behind the stove, blackin' his boots, when Betsey come in for a mornin's call. She hadn't sot but a few minutes when says she,

"I saw you was not doun to the lecture night before last, Josiah Allen's wife. I was sorry that I attended to it, but my uncle's people where I was visitin' went, and so I went with them. But I did not like it, I do not believe in wimmin's havin' any rights. I think it is real bold and unwomanly in her to want any rights. I think it is not her speah, as I remarked last night to our deah New Preacher. As we was a coming out, afteh the lecture, the fringe of my shawl ketched on to one of the buttons of his vest, and he could not get it off — and I did not try to, I thought it was not my place — so we was obleeged to walk close to-gatheh, cleah through the hall, and as I said to him, afteh I had enquired if he did not find it very lonesome here, says I, 'It is not wimmin's speah to vote,' and says I, 'do you not think it is woman's nature naturally to be clingin'?" 'I *do*,' says he, 'Heaven *knows* I *do*.' And he leaned back with such a expression of stern despaih on to his classic features, that I knew he felt it strongly. And I said the truth. I do not believe wimmin ought to vote."

"Nor I nuther," says Josiah, "she haint got the rekrisite strength to vote, she is too fraguile."

Jest at this minute the boy that draws the milk came along, and Josiah, says he to me, "I am in my stockin' feet, Samantha, can't you jest step out and help Thomas Jefferson on with the can?"

Says I, "If I am too fraguile to handle a paper vote, Josiah Allen, I am too fraguile to lift 100 and 50 pounds of milk."

He didn't say nothin', but he slipped on his rubbers and started out,

From *My Opinions and Betsey Bobbet's* (Hartford, 1891), pp. 222–43.

and Betsey resumed, "It is so revoltin' to female delicacy to go to the poles and vote; most all of the female ladies that revolve around in the high circles of Jonesville aristocracy agree with me in thinkin' it is real revoltin' to female delicacy to vote."

"Female delicacy!" says I, in a austeer tone. "Is female delicacy a plant that withers in the shadder of the pole, but flourishes in every other condition only in the shadder of the pole?" says I in a tone of witherin' scorn. "Female delicacy flourishes in a ball room, where these sensitive creeters with dresses on indecently low in the neck, will waltz all night with strange men's arms round their waists," says I. "You have as good as throwed it in my face, Betsey Bobbet, that I haint a modest woman, or I would be afraid to go and vote; but you ketch me with a low neck dress on, Betsey Bobbet, and you will ketch me on my way to the Asylum, and there haint a old deacon, or minister, or presidin' Elder in the Methodist church, that could get me to waltz with 'em, let alone waltzin' with promiscuus sinners. And," says I in the deep, calm tone of settled principle, "if you don't believe it, bring on your old deacons and ministers, and presidin' Elders, and try me."

"You are gettin' excited, Samantha," says Josiah.

"You jest keep blackin' your boots, Josiah Allen, I haint a talkin' to you. Betsey, is it any worse for a female woman to dress herself in a modest and Christian manner, with a braige viel over her face, and a brass mounted parasol in her hand, and walk decently to the pole and lay her vote on it, than to be introduced to a man, who for all you know may be a retired pirate, and have him walk up and hug you by the hour, to the music of a fiddle and a base violin?"

"But if you vote you have got to go before a board of men, and how tryin' to delicacy that would be."

"I went before a board of men when I joined the meetin' house, and when I got the premium for my rag carpet, and I still live and call myself a respectable character, but," says I in a vain of unconcealed sarcasm "if these delicate ball characters are too modest to go in broad daylight armed with a umbrell before a venerable man settin' on a board, let 'em have a good old female board to take thier votes."

"Would it be lawful to have a female board?" says Betsey.

"Wimmen can be boards at charity schools — poor little paupers, pretty hard boards they find 'em some times — and they can be boards at fairs, and hospitals, and penitentarys, and picnics, and African missions, and would it be any worse to be a board before these delicate

wimmen," says I, almost carried away with enthusiasm, "I would be a
board myself."

"Yes you would make a pretty board," says Josiah, "you would make
quite a pile of lumber." I paid no attention to his sarkastic remark, and
Betsey went on.

"It would be such public business Josiah Allen's wife for a woman to
recieve votes."

"I dont know as it would be any more public business, than to sell
Episcopal pin cushiens, Methodist I scream, or Baptist water melons,
by the hour to a permiscuus crowd."

"But," says Betsey, "twould devouh too much of a female's time, she
would not have time to vote, and perform the other duties that are in-
cumbient upon her."

Says I, "Wimmen find time for thier everlastin' tattin' and croshain'.
They find plenty of time for thier mats, and their tidys, their flirta-
tions, thier feather flowers, and bead flowers, and hair flowers, and
burr flowers, and oriental paintins, and Grecian paintins, and face
paintins. They spend more time a frizzin' thier front hair than they
would, to learn the whole constitution by heart; and if they get a new
dress they find plenty of time to cut it all up into strips, jest to pucker it
up and set it on agin. They can dress up in thier best and patrol the
streets as regular as a watchman, and lean over the counter in dry good
stores till they know every nail in 'em by heart. They find plenty of time
for all this, and to go to all the parties they can hear of, and theatres
and conserts, and shows of all kinds, and to flirt with every man they
can lay hold of, and to cover their faces with their fans and giggle; but
when it comes to an act as simple and short as puttin' a letter into the
post office, they are dreadul short on it for time."

But says Betsey, "The study that would be inevitable on a female in
ordeh to make her vote intelligably, would it not be too wearing on
her?"

"No! not a single bit; s'posin these soft, fashionable wimmen should
read a little about the nation she lives in, and the laws that protects her
if she keeps 'em, and hangs and imprisons her if she breaks 'em? I don't
know but it would be as good for her, as to pore over novels all day
long," says I; "these very wimmen that think the President's bureau is a
chest of draws where he keeps his fine shirts, and the tariff is a wild
horse the senators keep to ride out on, — these very wimmen that can't
find time to read the constitution, let 'em get on to the track of a love-

sick hero and a swoonin' heroine, and they will wade through half a dozen volumes, but what they will foller 'em clear to Finis to see 'em married there," says I, warmin' with my subject, "Let there be a young woman hid in a certain hole, guarded by 100 and 10 pirates, and a young man tryin' to get to her, though at present layin' heavily chained in a underground dungeon with his rival settin' on his back, what does a woman care for time or treasure, till she sees the pirates all killed off with one double revolver, and the young woman lifted out swoonin' but happy, by the brave hero?" Says I, in a deep camp meetin' voice, "If there had been a woman hid on the Island of Patmos, and Paul's letters to the churches had been love letters to her, there wouldn't be such a thick coat of dust on bibles as there is now."[1]

"But if wimmen *don't* read about the laws they'll know as much as some other folks do. I have seen men voters," says I, and I cast a stern glance onto Josiah as I spoke, "whose study into national affairs didn't wear on 'em enough to kill 'em at all. I have seen voters," says I with another cuttin' look at him, "that didn't know as much as their wives did." Josiah quailed a very little as I said this, and I continued on — "I have seen Irish voters, whose intellects wasn't tiresome to carry round, and whose knowledge concernin' public affairs wasn't so good as it was about rum, and who would sell their votes for a drink of whiskey, and keep it up all day, votin' and drinkin' and then drinkin' and votin', and I guess wimmen won't do any worse."[2]

Betsey almost quailed before my lofty glance and voice, but continued on cleavin' to the subject — "How awful and revolting it would sound to hear the faih and softeh sex talking about tariffs and caurkusses."

"I don't know," says I, "but I had as lives hear 'em talk about caurkusses, as to hear 'em backbitin' thier neighbors and tearin' the charicters of other wimmen into bits, or talkin' about such little things as wimmen will; why in a small place, a woman can't buy a calico apron without the neighborhood holdin' a inquest over it. Some think she ort to have it, some think it is extravagant in her, and some think the set flower on it is too young for her, and then they will all quarrel agin whether she ort to make it with a bib or not." Says I, "the very reason why men's talk as a general thing is nobler than wimmen's, is because they have nobler things to think about." Says I, "Betsey Bobbet, when did you ever know a passel of men to set down and spend a whole afternoon talkin' about each other's vest, and mistrustin' such a feller painted; fill a woman's mind with big, noble sized thoughts, and she won't talk such little back bitin' gossip as she does now."

"Josiah Allen's wife," says Betsey, "I shall always say it is not woman's speah to vote."

"No," says Josiah, "it hain't; wimmen would vote for the handsomest men, and the men that praised thier babys, they wouldn't stand up onto principal as men do, and then, how they would clog up the road 'lection day, tryin' to get all the news they could, wimmen have got such itchin' ears."

"Itchin' ears!" says I, "principle!" says I, in low but awful deep tones of voice, "Josiah Allen, it seems to me, that I wouldn't try to stand up onto principle agin, till the pantaloons are wore out you hired a man with to vote your ticket." He begun to look sheepish at once, and I continued in still more awful accents, "talk bout itchin' ears, Josiah Allen! here you have sot all the mornin' blackin' your boots, you have rubbed them boots till you have most rubbed holes through 'em, jest for an excuse to set here and hear me and Betsey Bobbet talk. And it haint' the first time nuther, for I have known you Josiah Allen, when I have had female visitors, to leave your work and come in and lay on that lounge behind the stove till you was most sweltered, pretendin' you was readin'."

"I *wuz* a readin'." says Josiah drawin' on his boots.

"I have ketched you laughin' over a funeral sermon, and a President's message, what is there highlarious in a funeral sermon Josiah Allen? What is there exhileratin' in a President's message?"

"Wall," says he, "I guess I'll water the steers."

"I should think you had better," says I coolly, and after he went out, Betsey resumed,

"Josiah Allen's wife, I still say it is not woman's speah to vote," and she continued, "I have got a few verses in my pocket, which I composed that night aftah I returned from the lecture, which embody into them the feelings of my soul concerning woman's speah. I went to my chamber, and let down my back haih, and took out my teeth, I always feel more free somehow, and poetic, with my hair down and my teeth out, and there I wrote these stanzeys, and seeing it is you, I will read them to you."

My firm and cast iron principles forbid my wishin' in a reckless way that I wasn't myself, and I was in my own house, and horspitality for-

bid my orderin' her in stern accents, not to read a word of 'em, so I sub-
mitted, and she read as follows:

WIMMEN'S SPEAH;
Or whisperin's of nature to
BETSEY BOBBET.

Last night as I meandered out
To meditate apart,
Secluded in my parasol,
Deep subjects shook my heart.
The earth, the skies, the prattling brooks,
All thundered in my ear,
"It is matrimony! it is matrimony
That is a woman's speah."

Day with a red shirred bonnet on,
Had down for China started,
Its yellow ribbons fluttered o'er
Her head, as she departed;
She seemed to wink her eyes on me,
As she did dissapeah;
And say, "It is matrimony, Betsey,
That is a woman's speah."

A rustic had broke down his team;
I mused almost in teahs,
"How can a yoke be borne along
By half a pair of steers?"
Even thus in wrath did nature speak,
"Heah! Betsey Bobbet, heah!
It is matrimony! it is matrimony
That is a woman's speah."

I saw a paih of roses
Like wedded pardners grow;
Sharp thorns did pave thier mortal path,
Yet sweetly did they blow;
They seemed to blow these *glorious* words,
Into my *willing* eah;
"It is matrimony! it is matrimony
That is a woman's speah."

Two gentle sheep upon the hills;
How sweet the twain did run,

As I meandered gently on
And sot down on a stun;
They seemed to murmur sheepishly,
"Oh Betsey Bobbet deah,
It is matrimony! it is matrimony
That is a women's speah."

Sweet was the honeysuckles breath
Upon the ambient aih;
Sweet was the tendah coo of doves,
Yet sweeter husbands aih.
All nature's voices poured these words
Into my *willing* eah;
"B. Bobbet, it is matrimony
That is a woman's speah."

"The above are my sentiments," says she, as she folded up the paper.

"I am a married woman," says I, "and I hain't got nothin' to say aginst marryin', especially when Josiah's back is turned, I don't believe in bein' underhanded. But there are a great many widows and unmarried wimmen in the world, what are they to do?"

"Let them take heed to these glorious and consoling words,

" 'It is matrimony, it is matrimony,
That is a woman's speah.' "

"Shet up about your speah's," says I, gettin wore out, "You may sing it Betsey Bobbet, and ministers may preach it, and writers may orate about it, that it is women's only speah to marry, but what are you goin' to do? Are you goin' to compel men to marry all the wimmen off?" says I, with a penetratin' look onto Betsey.

"I have seen wimmen that was willin' to marry, but the men wasn't forthcomin', what are they to do? What are the wimmen to do whose faces are as humbly as a plate of cold greens?" Says I, in stern tones, "Are men to be pursued like stricken dears by a mad mob of humbly wimmen? Is a woman to go out into the street and collar a man and order him to marry her? I am sick of this talk about its bein' a woman's only speah to marry. If it is a woman's only speah to marry, the Lord will provide her with a *man*, it stands to reason he will. One that will suit her too, one that will come jest as nateral for her to leave all of the rest of the world and foller, as for a sunflower to foller on after the sun. One that she seems to belong to, jest like North and South America, joined by nature unbeknown to them ever sense creation. She'll know him if she ever sees him, for their two hearts will suit each other jest like the two halves of a pair of shears. These are the marriages that Heaven signs the certificates of, and this marryin' for a home, or for fear of bein' called a old maid, is no more marriage in the sight of God, no more true marriage, than the blush of a fashionable woman that is bought for ten cents an ounce and carried home in her pocket, is true modesty."

Here was a pause, durin' which Betsey quailed some, and I then resumed again, in the same lofty tones and I don't know but a little loftier, "There is but one thing that makes marriage pure and holy in the sight of God."

"And what is that?" says Betsey in an enquirin' tone.

"Love," says I, in a full clear tone, "Love, such as angels feel for one another, love, such as Samantha Smith felt for Josiah Allen, though *why* I loved him, Heaven knows, I don't. But I couldn't help it, and I would have lived single till them days we read of, if I hadn't. Though for what reason I loved him — " I continued mewsin'ly, and almost lost in deep retrospectin', — "I don't know. I don't believe in rehearsin' privacies and braggin' about such things, but in the name of principle I speak. A richer man wanted me at the same time, a man that knew half as much agin, at least, as Josiah. I no need to have wet the ends of my fingers in dishwater if I had married the other one, but I couldn't do it, I loved Josiah, *though why*" — and agin I plunged down into deep abstraction as I murmured to myself. — "though *why* I did, I don't know."

"In them days," says I, risin' up agin out of my revery, "In them days to come, when men and wimmen are independent of each other, marriage will be what it ought to be, for folks won't marry unless God unites their hearts so close they can't get 'em apart nohow. They won't be tackled together by any old rotten ropes of interest and accomidation, that are liable to break in to pieces any minute, and in them days, the hands of divorce writers won't be so lame as they be now."

"I cannot comprehend" says Betsey "how wimmen's votin', will change the reprehensible ideah of marryin' for a home, or for fear of being ridiculed about, if it will, I cannot see."

"Cant you see daylight Betsey Bobbet, when the sun is mountin' up into the clear horizeon?" Says I in a eloquent voice, "it stands to reason that a woman wont marry a man she dont love, for a home, if she is capable of makin' one for herself. Where's the disgrace of bein' a old maid, only wimmen are kinder dependent on men, kinder waitin' to have him ask her to marry him, so as to be supported by him? Give a woman as many fields to work in as men have, and as good wages, and let it be thought jest as respectable for 'em to earn *thier* livin' as for a man to, and that is enough. It riles me to hear 'em talk about wimmen's wantin' to wear the breeches; they don't want to; they like calico better than broadcloth for stiddy wear, they like muslin better than kersey mear for handsome, and they have a nateral hankerin' after the good opinion and admiration of the other sect, but they can do better without that admiration than they can without vittles."

"Yes," says Betsey "men do admire to have wimmen clingin' to 'em, like a vine to a stately tree, and it is indeed a sweet view."

"So 'tis, so 'tis," says I, "I never was much of a clinger myself. Still if females want to cling, I haint no objection. "But," says I, in reasonable tones, "as I have said more'n a hundred times, if men think that wimmen are obleeged to be vines, they ought to feel obleeged to make trees of themselves, for 'em to run up on. But they wont; some of 'em, they will not be trees, they seem to be sot against it. And as I have said what if a vine haint no tree convenient to cling to? or if she has, what if the tree she clings to happens to fall through inherient rotteness at the core, thunder and lightnin' or etcetery? If the string breaks what is to become of the creeper if it can't do nothin' but creep? Says I, "it is all well enough for a rich woman to set in a velvet gown with her feet on the warm hearth and wonder what makes the poor drunkard's wife down in the street, shiver. Let her be out once with her bare feet in the snow, and she'd find out. It haint the rich, happy, comfortable clingers I am talkin' in behalf of, but the poor shiverers outside who haint nothin' to cling to,"

"Women's speah"—began Betsey.

"Women's speah," says I interuptin' her in a magestic tone before which Betsey quailed imperceptably. "Women's speah is where she can do the most good; if God had meant that wimmen should be nothin' but men's shadders, He would have made gosts and fantoms of 'em at once. But havin' made 'em flesh and blood, with braens and souls, I believe He meant 'em to be used to the best advantage. And the talk about wimmen havin' to fight, and men wash dishes, if wimmen vote, is all shear nonsense. In the Baptist church where wimmen vote, I dont see as they act different from other wimmen, and I dont see as the Baptist men act any more sheepish than common men." Says I, "it is jest as ridiculous to say it would make a woman act coarse and rampage round to vote, as to say that kissin' a pretty baby, or lovin' books and music and pictures, makes a man a hen huzzy."

Says I, carried away with powerful emotions, "you may shet a lion up for years, in a room full of cambric needles and tattin shettles, and you can't get him to do anything but roar at 'em, it haint a lion's nature to do fine sewin," says I. "And you may tie up a old hen as long as you please, and you cant break her of wantin' to make a nest, and scratch for her chickens." Says I — wavin' my right hand, slow and magesticly — "you may want a green shade onto the front side of your house, and to that end and effect you may plant a acorn, and set out a rose bush, but all the legeslaters in creation cant make that acorn tree blow out with red posy's, no more can they make that rose bush stand up straight as a giant. And thier bein' planted by the side of each other — on the same ground and watered out of the same waterin' jug — dont olter thier natural turn. *They will both help shade the winder*, but do it in their own way which is different. And men and wimmen votin' side by side, would no more alter their natural dispositions than singin' one of Watts'es hymns together would. One will sing base, and the other air, so long as the world stands."

"Josiah Allen's wife," says Betsey, "I think your views are uronieus. We cannot think alike about clinging, we also diffeh in our views about caurkusses. When I consideh that 'lections and caurkusses come once every yeah, then comes home the solemn feelin', how wearin' it would be for a female to drop all her domestic labohs and avocations, and be present at them. Josiah Allen's wife, let us sposen the case, sposen a women is a washin', or churnin' buttah, how could she leave this laboh to go and vote?" I was so wore out, that says I, "we *will* sposen the case, sposen a women is a fool, how can she talk common sense?" Says I, with so impatient a gesture that I broke off a thread, and had to tie it on agin "you are goin' over the same old ground agin of a woman's time," says I, "wimmen can drop all thier domestic labors and go to fares — town fares, and county fares, and state fares if she can get to 'em. She will be on the ground in time to see the first punkin and bed-quilt carried on to it, and she will stay to see the last horse, trot his last trot; she can find time for picnics and pleasure exertions, and celebrations, and 4th of July — that last, all day — and it would take about half a minute to vote." "But," says I, in the most grand and noble tone I had used yet, "Men haint took by the coat collar and dragged off to caurkusses and 'lections, they dont go unless they are a mind to, and I dont suppose wimmen would be drove there like a flock of sheep. They wouldn't want to go; only, when some great law was up concerning right and wrong, or her own intrinsick interests, as givin a mother a equal right to her children, a right she earnt naturally, a deed God himself stamped with the great seals of fear and agony. Or bein' taxed without representation; which breaks the old constitution right into, in the middle, every time it is done. Or concernin' equal pay, for equal labor. I spose every female clerk and teacher and operator, who have half starved on about one third what men get for doin' the same work would be on hand. Like wise concerning Temperance, I spose every drunkards wife and mother and girl would go to the pole, that could get there.[3] Poor things, under the Legislator they have enjoyed the right of sufferin'; sposen it lets 'em enjoy the right of suffragin' a spell, mebby they would find it as easy if not easier."

Jest at this minute we see the new Local Preacher, comin' down the road in a open buggy, and Betsey said to once she must be goin, for her folks would be a worryin' after her." Says I, as she hurried to the door,

"Mebby you will get a ride."

"Oh no," says she, "I had a great deal rather walk afoot, I think there is nothing like walking afoot for strengthenin' the mussles."

I am glad she felt so, for I see he didn't ask her to ride. But as she said, health is a blessing, and it is a treat indeed to have strong mussles.

NOTES

1. In the Preface to *My Opinions and Betsey Bobbet's* Samantha declares her inability to write a book because she's unacquainted with what had become the conventions of sentimental fiction. Holley satirizes the female sentimental poet in the form of Betsey Bobbet and in this passage and elsewhere gets in a lick against the tomfoolery of the sentimental novel. In the Preface, Samantha admitted: "I don't know no underground dungeons. I haint acquainted with no haunted houses, I never see a hero suspended over a abyss by his gallusses, I never beheld a heroine swoon away, I never see a Injun tommy hawked, nor a ghost; I never had any of these advantages; I can't write a book."

In "Wit, Sentimentality, and the Image of Women in the Nineteenth Century," *American Studies*, XXII:2, Nancy Walker argues that most of the women humorists of the nineteenth century satirized the popular image of the "woman writer as soggy sentimentalist," an image considered an insult by women of wit. She asserts that Holley "went further than most of her fellow humorists in demolishing the image of the sentimental female writer," but that with "varying degrees of acidity" women humorists ["Fanny Fern," Caroline Kirkland, Frances Whitcher, Gail Hamilton] "mocked the notion that women were humorless creatures, incapable of the insight and perspective which underlay the witty utterance. Almost every nineteenth-century female humorist felt the need to create and demolish this image as if exorcising a demon which would have prevented her from writing humor."

2. The great Irish immigration was in the 1840s. This antiforeign bias with attendant stereotypes regarding the behavioral characteristics of certain national groups became more typical of suffragist arguments from the mid-1880s on when millions of Poles, Italians, Russians, etc. immigrated. See Chapter 6, "The 'New Immigration' and Labor," in Kraditor, *The Ideas of the Woman Suffrage Movement 1890–1920*. In his overview of the nineteenth-century women's movement, William Chafe discusses the appeal to nativism in *The American Woman* (New York, 1972), pp. 14–15.

3. Many claims were made for the resulting effects of woman's suffrage. In *Up From the Pedestal*, pp. 285–87, six predictions (1852, 1891, 1898, 1903, and 1914) of the results of women's enfranchisement are reprinted. Among them is a song sung at an 1876 woman suffrage convention whose verses claim vast change in "politics, morals, religion and trade." There will be no more lying, cheating, fraud or drunken husbands; women will be equal partners with men, and oppression, war, and slavery will disappear. Others claimed that the "brutal business" of prizefighting would be stopped and Tammany would not have returned to power in New York if women could vote. The claim that we could end wars if women voted was a frequent one. Women with the ballot would act as a cohesive force for positive social change.

After the suffrage amendment was passed, major parties did in fact court women voters in the first half of the 1920s. The strong women's lobby affecting congressional passage of maternity and infancy legislation (Shepphard-Towner Bill) showed that women could have bloc influence. Other bills concerning consumer protection, child labor, merit system in civil service, and citizenship requirements for married women also passed. However, it later became clear that the threatened clout had not materialized; women did not vote as a bloc. Women didn't vote in great numbers and when they voted, there was a lack of evidence that they voted differently from men. William Chafe discusses this issue in his chapter, "Women and Politics" in *The American Woman*.

3 "The Creation Searchin' Society"

It was only a few days after we got home from New York that Josiah come into the house dretful excited. He'd had a invitation to attend a meetin' of the Creation Searchin' Society.

"Why," sez I, "did they invite you? You are not a member?"

"No," sez he, "but they want me to help 'em be indignant. It is a indignation meetin'."

"Indignant about what?" I sez.

"Fur be it from me, Samantha, to muddle up your head and hurt your feelin's by tellin' you what it's fur." And he went out quick and shet the door. But I got a splendid dinner and afterwards he told me of his own accord.

I am not a member, of course, for the president, Philander Daggett, said it would lower the prestige of the society in the eyes of the world to have even one female member. This meetin' wuz called last week for the purpose of bein' indignant over the militant doin's of the English Suffragettes.[1] Josiah and several others in Jonesville wuz invited to be present at this meetin' as sort of honorary members, as they wuz competent to be jest as indignant as any other male men over the tribulations of their sect.

Josiah said so much about the meetin', and his Honorary Indignation, that he got me curious, and wantin' to go myself, to see how it wuz carried on. But I didn't have no hopes on't till Philander Daggett's new young wife come to visit me and I told her how much I wanted to go, and she bein' real good-natered said she would make Philander let me in.

He objected, of course, but she is pretty and young, and his nater bein' kinder softened and sweetened by the honey of the honeymoon, she got round him. And he said that if we would set up in a corner of the gallery behind the melodeon, and keep our veils on, he would let

From *Samantha on the Woman Question* (New York, 1913), pp. 176–92.

her and me in. But we must keep it secret as the grave, for he would lose all the influence he had with the other members and be turned out of the Presidential chair if it wuz knowed that he had lifted wimmen up to such a hite, and gin 'em such a opportunity to feel as if they wuz equal to men.

Well, we went early and Josiah left me to Philander's and went on to do some errents. He thought I wuz to spend the evenin' with her in becomin' seclusion, a-knittin' on his blue and white socks, as a woman should. But after visitin' a spell, jest after it got duskish, we went out the back door and went cross lots, and got there ensconced in the dark corner without anybody seein' us and before the meetin' begun.

Philander opened the meetin' by readin' the moments of the last meetin', which wuz one of sympathy with the police of Washington for their noble efforts to break up the Woman's Parade,[2] and after their almost Herculaneum labor to teach wimmen her proper place, and all the help they got from the hoodlum and slum elements, they had failed in a measure, and the wimmen, though stunned, insulted, spit on, struck, broken boneded, maimed, and tore to pieces, had succeeded in their disgustin' onwomanly undertakin'.

But it wuz motioned and carried that a vote of thanks be sent 'em and recorded in the moments that the Creation Searchers had no blame but only sympathy and admiration for the hard worked Policemen for they had done all they could to protect wimmen's delicacy and retirin' modesty, and put her in her place, and no man in Washington or Jonesville could do more. He read these moments, in a real tender sympathizin' voice, and I spoze the members sympathized with him, or I judged so from their linements as I went forward, still as a mouse, and peeked down on 'em.

He then stopped a minute and took a drink of water; I spoze his sympathetic emotions had het him up, and kinder dried his mouth, some. And then he went on to state that this meetin' wuz called to show to the world, abroad and nigh by, the burnin' indignation this body felt, as a society, at the turrible sufferin's and insults bein' heaped onto their male brethren in England by the indecent and disgraceful doin's of the militant Suffragettes, and to devise, if possible, some way to help their male brethren acrost the sea. "For," sez he, "pizen will spread. How do we know how soon them very wimmen who had to be spit on and struck and tore to pieces in Washington to try to make 'em keep their place, the sacred and tender place they have always held enthroned as angels in a man's heart—"

Here he stopped and took out his bandanna handkerchief, and wiped his eyes, and kinder choked. But I knew it wuz all a orator's art, and it didn't affect me, though I see a number of the members wipe their eyes, for this talk appealed to the inheriant chivalry of men, and their desire to protect wimmen, we have always hearn so much about.

"How do we know," he continued, "how soon they may turn aginst their best friends, them who actuated by the loftiest and tenderest emotions, and determination to protect the weaker sect at any cost, took their valuable time to try to keep wimmen down where they ort to be, *angels of the home,* who knows but they may turn and throw stuns at the Capitol an' badger an' torment our noble lawmakers, a-tryin' to make 'em listen to their silly petitions for justice?"

In conclusion, he entreated 'em to remember that the eye of the world wuz on 'em, expectin' 'em to be loyal to the badgered and woman endangered sect abroad, and try to suggest some way to stop them woman's disgraceful doin's.

Cyrenus Presly always loves to talk, and he always looks on the dark side of things, and he riz up and said, "he didn't believe nothin' could be done, for by all he'd read about 'em, the men had tried everything possible to keep wimmen down where they ort to be, they had turned deaf ears to their complaints, wouldn't hear one word they said, they had tried drivin' and draggin' and insults of all kinds, and breakin' their bones, and imprisonment, and stuffin' 'em with rubber tubes, thrust through their nose down into their throats. And he couldn't think of a thing more that could be done by men, and keep the position men always had held as wimmen's gardeens and protectors, and he said he thought men might jest as well keep still and let 'em go on and bring the world to ruin, for that was what they wuz bound to do, and they couldn't be stopped unless they wuz killed off."

Phileman Huffstater is a old bachelder, and hates wimmen. He had been on a drunk and looked dretful, tobacco juice runnin' down his face, his red hair all towsled up, and his clothes stiff with dirt. He wuzn't invited, but had come of his own accord. He had to hang onto the seat in front of him as he riz up and said:

"He believed that wuz the best and only way out on't, for men to rise up and kill off the weaker sect, for their wuzn't never no trouble of any name or nater, but what wimmen wuz to the bottom on't, and the world would be better off without 'em." But Philander scorfed at him and reminded him that such hullsale doin's would put an end to the world's bein' populated at all.

But Phileman said in a hicuppin', maudlin way that "the world had better stop, if there had got to be such doin's, wimmen risin' up on every side, and pretendin' to be equal with men."

Here his knee jints kinder gin out under him, and he slid down onto the seat and went to sleep.

I guess the members wuz kinder shamed of Phileman, for Lime Peedick jumped up quick as scat and said, "It seemed the Englishmen had tried most everything else, and he wondered how it would work if them militant wimmen could be ketched and a dose of sunthin' bitter and sickenin' poured down 'em. Every time they broached that loathsome doctrine of equal rights, and tried to make lawmakers listen to their petitions, jest ketch 'em and pour down 'em a big dose of wormwood or sunthin' else bitter and sickenin', and he guessed they would git tired on't."

But here Josiah jumped up quick and said, "he objected," he said, "that would endanger the right wimmen always had, and ort to have of cookin' good vittles for men and doin' their housework, and bearin' and bringin' up their children, and makin' and mendin' and waitin' on 'em. He said nothin' short of a Gatlin gun could keep Samantha from speakin' her mind about such things, and he wuzn't willin' to have her made sick to the stomach, and incapacitated from cookin' by any such proceedin's."

The members argued quite awhile on this pint, but finally come round to Josiah's idees, and the meetin' for a few minutes seemed to come to a standstill, till old Cornelius Snyder got up slowly and feebly. He has spazzums and can't hardly wobble. His wife has to support him, wash and dress him, and take care of him like a baby. But he has the use of his tongue, and he got some man to bring him there, and he leaned heavy on his cane, and kinder stiddied himself on it and offered this suggestion:

"How would it do to tie females up when they got to thinkin' they wuz equal to men, halter 'em, rope 'em, and let 'em see if they wuz?"

But this idee wuz objected to for the same reason Josiah had advanced, as Philander well said, "wimmen had got to go foot loose in order to do the housework and cookin'."

Uncle Sime Bentley, who wuz awful indignant, said, "I motion that men shall take away all the rights that wimmen have now, turn 'em out of the meetin' house, and grange."

But before he'd hardly got the words out of his mouth, seven of the members riz up and as many as five spoke out to once with different exclamations:

"That won't do! we can't do that! Who'll do all the work! Who'll git up grange banquets and rummage sales, and paper and paint and put down carpets in the meetin' house, and git up socials and entertainments to help pay the minister's salary, and carry on the Sunday School? and tend to its picnics and suppers, and take care of the children? We can't do this, much as we'd love to."

One horsey, sporty member, also under the influence of liquor, riz up, and made a feeble motion, "Spozin' we give wimmen liberty enough to work, leave 'em hand and foot loose, and sort o' muzzle 'em so they can't talk."

This seemed to be very favorably received, 'specially by the married members, and the secretary wuz jest about to record it in the moments as a scheme worth tryin', when old Doctor Nugent got up, and sez in a firm, decided way:

"Wimmen cannot be kept from talking without endangerin' her life; as a medical expert I object to this motion."

"How would you put the objection?" sez the secretary.

"On the ground of cruelty to animals," sez the doctor.

A fat Englishman who had took the widder Shelmadine's farm on shares, says, "I 'old with Brother Josiah Hallen's hargument. As the father of nine young children and thirty cows to milk with my wife's 'elp, I 'old she musn't be kep' from work, but h'I propose if we can't do anything else that a card of sympathy be sent to hold Hengland from the Creation Searchin' Society of America, tellin' 'em 'ow our 'earts bleeds for the men's sufferin' and 'ardships in 'avin' to leave their hoccupations to beat and 'aul round and drive females to jails, and feed 'em with rubber hoses through their noses to keep 'em from starvin' to death for what they call their principles."

This motion wuz carried unanimously.

But here an old man, who had jest dropped in and who wuz kinder deef and slow-witted, asked, "What it is about anyway? what do the wimmen ask for when they are pounded and jailed and starved?"

Hank Yerden, whose wife is a Suffragist, and who is mistrusted to have a leanin' that way himself, answered him, "Oh, they wanted the lawmakers to read their petitions asking for the rights of ordinary citizens. They said as long as their property wuz taxed they had the right of representation. And as long as the law punished wimmen equally with men, they had a right to help make that law, and as long as men claimed wimmen's place wuz home, they wanted the right to guard that home. And as long as they brought children into the world they wanted the right to protect 'em. And when the lawmakers wouldn't hear a word they said, and beat 'em and drove 'em round and jailed 'em, they got mad as hens, and are actin' like furiation and wild cats. But claim that civil rights wuz never give to any class without warfare."

"Heavens! what doin's!" sez old Zephaniah Beezum, "what is the world comin' to! Angle worms will be risin' up next and demandin' to not be trod on." Sez he, "I have studied the subject on every side, and I claim the best way to deal with them militant females is to banish 'em to some barren wilderness, some foreign desert where they can meditate on their crimes, and not bother men."

This idee wuz received favorably by most of the members, but others differed and showed the weak p'ints in it, and it wuz gin up.

Well, at ten P.M., the Creation Searchers gin up after arguin' pro and con, con and pro, that they could not see any way out of the matter, they could not tell what to do with the wimmen without danger and trouble to the male sect.

They looked dretful dejected and onhappy as they come to this conclusion, my pardner looked as if he wuz most ready to bust out cryin'. And as I looked on his beloved linement I forgot everything else and onbeknown to me I leaned over the railin' and sez:

"Here is sunthin' that no one has seemed to think on at home or abroad. How would it work to stop the trouble by givin' the wimmen the rights they ask for, the rights of any other citizen?"

I don't spoze there will ever be such another commotion and upheaval in Jonesville till Michael blows his last trump as follered my speech. Knowin' wimmen wuz kep' from the meetin', some on 'em thought it wuz a voice from another spear. Them wuz the skairt and horrow struck ones, and them that thought it wuz a earthly woman's voice wuz so mad that they wuz by the side of themselves and carried on fearful. But when they searched the gallery for wimmen or ghosts, nothin' wuz found, for Philander's wife and I had scooted acrost lots and wuz to home a-knittin' before the men got there.

And I d'no as anybody but Philander to this day knows what, or who it wuz.

And I d'no as my idee will be follered, but I believe it is the best way out on't for men and wimmen both, and would stop the mad doin's of the English Suffragettes, which I don't approve of, no indeed! much as I sympathize with the justice of their cause.

NOTES

1. Emmeline Pankhurst, daughters Christobel and Sylvia, the Pethick-Lawrences, Annie Kenney, and Lady Constance Lytton were prime movers in England's Women's Social and Political Union, formed on October 10, 1903. For eleven years the group, known as the Militant Suffragettes, waged a campaign for the vote. Speeches, petitions, and peaceful demonstrations gave way to bloody riots wherein suffragettes were thrown to the pavement and otherwise assaulted by both policemen and unsympathetic onlookers. As rational discourse proved ineffective in creating change, their tactics became more violent, involving rock-throwing, window-smashing, arson, and bombings. Suffragettes endured beatings, imprisonment, hunger and thirst strikes, and brutal forced feedings.

One militant, Emily Wilding Davison, became convinced that only the sacrifice of a human life would move the conscience of the country. On June 4, 1913, with the W.S.P.U. colors sewn in her coat, she threw herself under the hoofs of the King's horse on the Derby course in full view of the King and Queen.

In 1918 women over 30 who could fulfill certain property requirements were granted the vote. By 1928 all women over 21 attained voting rights. For a documentary account of their struggle, see Midge Mackensie, *Shoulder to Shoulder* (New York, 1975).

2. The day before Woodrow Wilson's inauguration in March, 1913, approximately 10,000 women marched on Pennsylvania Avenue in Washington, D.C. The women had been given a permit to march, but inadequate police protection allowed an angry mob to break it up.

II

The "Nater of the Sect":
Social Status and Role Assumptions

"If God had meant wimmen should be nothin'
but men's shadders, He would have made gosts
and fantoms of 'em at once."
— Samantha

Many arguments for the allotted sphere of women rested on the
"nature" of the sex. Josiah, time and time again, belies his lightweight
status by choosing inappropriate examples from the natural world
(ostriches), by praising men injudiciously while classing "wimmen" as
weak-minded, simple "creeters," and by offering a *tour de force* of illogic when trying to explain evident contradictions. The following selections illustrate Samantha's observations that women have a "sort of
silent hankerin'" or aptitude for martrydom" and that they are not "naturally" angels. They also show Josiah's opinions of "wimmen" as they
collide with Samantha's common sense.

Beginning with "An Unmarried Female," we are introduced to
Samantha's female foil, Betsey Bobbet, the ugly spinster who has accepted the male definition of "women's speah." In her conversations
with Samantha, Betsey exemplifies the pathetic consequences of "layin'
holt" of marriage as your only theme, of gushy sentimentality, of a
clinging vine all a'tangle. Her ideas, as well as those of the Debatin'
Society men who enthusiastically uphold the impropriety of public
speaking by women, serve as targets for Samantha's puncturing barbs.

"Betsey Bobbet"

4 On Being Remembered in Stone

"Samantha, goin' to funerals, or hearin' about 'em, puts folks to thinkin'."

"Yes, it duz, Josiah;" and sez I, in quite a solemn axent, "it stands us all in hand to be prepared."

Sez he, "I wuzn't thinkin' of that side of the subject, Samantha; but it brings back to me that old thought and fear that has been growin' on me for years more or less. Samantha," sez he, "I worry, and have worried for years, for fear that you will some time be left a relict with nuthin' to lean on."

I glanced up at him, and the thought come to me instinctively that it would be the ondoin' of us both if I should try to lean heavy on him now, for my weight is great, and he is small-boneded, and I knew that he would crumple right down under the weight of 200 pounds heft.

But I didn't speak my thoughts—oh, no; I merely looked at him real affectionate, and I took up a sock I wuz mendin' for him (we wuz in our own room), and I attackted it as socks should be attackted if you lay out to make 'em good and sound. And he went on still more confidential and confidin', and told me several things he thought I had ort to do if I wuz ever left a relict of him.

It wuz real touchin', and I wuz considerable affected by it—not to tears—no; I thought I wouldn't shed any tears if I could help it, for darnin' is close work, and it calls for all the eyesight you have got; and then I had on a new gray lawn dress that I felt would spot easy; so I restrained my emotions with a almost marble composure, and anon I sez to him as he wuz a goin' on in that affectin' way, and sez I:

"I may be took first, Josiah Allen."

And he admitted that that might be the case, though he couldn't bear to think on't, he said, it gin him such awful feelin's.

From *Samantha on the Race Problem* (Minneapolis, 1892), pp. 326–33.

He said he had never been able to think on't with any composure. But after a while he talked more diffuse on the subject, and owned up that he had thought on't; and sez he, in a still more confidin' and affectionate way:

"For years, Samantha, I have had it in my head what I would put on your tombstun if I should live to stand up under the hard, hard blow of havin' to rare one up over you.

"I have thought I should have it read as follers, and to wit, namely:

" 'Here lies Samantha, wife of Deacon Josiah Allen, Esquire, of Jonesville. Deacon in the Methodist Church, salesman in the Jonesville cheese factory, and a man beloved and respected by every one who knows him but to love him, and names him but to praise.'

"Its endin' in poetry, Samantha, wuz jest what I knew wuz touchin', dumb touchin', and would be apt to please you; and it is always a man's aim to write the obituarys of his former deceased pardner in a way that would suit her and be pleasin' to her."

Sez I calmly, "Yes, I should know a man wrote that if I read it in the darkest night that ever rolled, and I wuz blindfolded."

"Wall," sez he anxiously, "don't it suit you? Don't you think it is uneek, sunthin' new and strikin'?"

"Oh, no," sez I, "no, it hain't nuthin' new at all; but mebby it is strikin'—or that is," sez I, "it depends on who is struck."

"Wall," sez he, "it is dumb discouragin', after a man racks his brains to try to get up sunthin' strong and beautiful, to think a woman can't be tickled and animated with it."

Sez I calmly, "I hain't said that I wuzn't suited with it." And sez I with still more severe axents, for I see he looked disappointed, "I will say further, Josiah, that it meets my expectations fully; it is jest what I should expect a male pardner to write."

"Wall," sez he, lookin' pleaseder and more satisfieder, "I thought you would appreciate it after you thought it over for a spell."

"I do, Josiah," sez I, turnin' over the sock I wuz a mendin' and attacktin' a new weak spot in the heel, "I do appreciate it fully."

Josiah looked real tickled and sort o' proud, and I kep' on in calm axents and a darnin' too, for the hole wuz big, and night wuz a descendin' down onto us. And I could hear Aunt Mela's preparations for supper down below, and I wanted to get the sock done before I went down-stairs. So I sez, sez I:

"I have thought about it sometimes too, Josiah, and I have got it kinder fixed out in my mind what I would have on your tombstun — if I lived through it," sez I with a deep sithe.

"What wuz it?" sez he in a contented tone, for he knows I love him. "It is poetry, hain't it?"

"Yes," sez I calmly, "I laid out to end it with a verse of poetry; it wuz to run as follers: 'Here lies Josiah Allen, husband of Samantha Allen, and — ' "

"Hold on!" sez Josiah, gettin' right up and lookin' threatenin'. "Hold on right there where you be; no such words as them is a goin' on my tombstun while I have a breath left in my body. Husband of — Josiah, husband of — I won't have no such truck as that, and I can tell you that I won't."

"Be calm, Josiah," sez I, "be calm and set down," for he looked so bad and voyalent that I feared apperplexy or some other fit. Sez I, "Be calm, or you will bring sunthin' onto yourself."

"I won't be calm, and I don't care what I bring on, and I tell you I ruther bring it on than not, a good deal ruther. The idee! Josiah Allen, husband of — It has got to a great pass if a man has got down to that — to be a husband of — "

"Why," sez I, lookin' up into his face stiddily, as he stood over me in a wild and threatenin' attitude — and some wimmen would have been skairt and showed it out; but I wuzn't. Good land! don't I know Josiah Allen, and through him the hull race of mankind? I knew he wouldn't hurt a hair of my foretop, but he would like to skair me out of the idee, that I knew.

But sez I in a reasonable axent, "You had got it all fixed out 'Samantha, wife of Josiah — ' "

"Wall, that is the way!" sez he, hollerin' enough almost to crack my ear-pan — "that is the way every man has it on his pardner's headstun. Go through the hull land and see if it hain't; you can look on every stun."

Oh, how that "stun" rolled through my head! And sez I, "I am not deaf, Josiah Allen, neither am I in Shackville, or Loontown, or the barn. Do you want to raise a panick in your son's household? Moderate your voice or you will harm your own insides. I know it is the way every man has wrote it about their pardners, and it seemed so popular amongst men I thought I would try it."

"Wall, you won't try it on me!" he hollered as loud as ever. "You won't try it on me, and don't you undertake it. Why, ruther than to have them words rared up over me I would—I would ruther not die at all. 'Josiah Allen, husband of—' No, mom, you don't come no such game over me; you don't demean me down into a 'husband of—'!"

"Why," sez I, lookin' calmly into his face (for I see I must be calm), "don't you know how I have wrote my name for years and years, 'Josiah Allen's Wife'?"

"Wall, that wuz the way to write it; it wuz stylish," he yelled. Oh, how he yelled! Why, that "stylish" almost broke a hole through my ear-pan; the pan jest jarred, it wuz so voyalent.

Sez I, "Set down, Josiah, and less argue on it."

"I won't argue on it, it is too dumb foolish; I am goin' out to walk in the back garden before supper."

And he ketched down his hat and drawed it down over his ears enough to break 'em off if they hadn't been well sot on, and slammed the door so one of them panels is weak to this day—it wuz a little loose to start with.

And I went and stood in the winder with my hand over my eyes, and watched him all the while he wuz a walkin' up and down them walks, for I wuz most afraid he would totter and fall over, or mebby he would start off a bee-line for the crick and drown himself, he wuz so rousted up and agitated. And I hain't dasted to open my head sence on the sub-ject—I don't dast to, not knowin' what it would bring onto him. At the table they noticed my pardner's excited and riz up mean—they couldn't help it.

And Maggie asked him, "if he wuzn't feelin' well."

And I spoke right up, such is a female's devoted love for her compan-ion—I spoke right up and sez:

"We have been a talkin' over funerals and such, and your Pa got agitated."

I spoze I told the truth—I spoze I did; I didn't tell what the "such" wuz that he had been a talkin' about; I don't know as I wuz obleeged to.

5 On the Tuckerin' Nature of Pedestals

Well, Josiah went that day with Billy Huff, he santered off without any system or plan, and wouldn't take my pad though I offered it to him. But I guess they jest poked round miscelaneous, as you may say, seein' jest what they happened to run into. And in some of their travels they met Barzelia Trimble, a woman lecturer, she's young and good lookin' and smart as a whip, and I guess she made much of Josiah, 'tennyrate she gin him tickets to her lecture.

She said she'd met a man whose brother-in-law's cousin had bought a dog once of a neighbor of mine, and so feelin' so well acquainted with me she sent me the tickets, and did hope we would come. She said she felt that she knew us both so well that it would be a treat to her.

The way she come to see Josiah that day, Billy had met her at school where she lectured.

Josiah wuz very anxious that we should both go. He remembered the dog.

But I sez, "I thought you didn't believe in wimmen's lecturin' and havin' rights, Josiah."

"Well, I don't believe in 'em, but the tickets wuz gin to us, fifty cents right out of her pocket, and she'll expect us. She said it would make her feel more homelike to have us present."

"Well," sez I, "I don't know as I feel so very intimate with her, I never see the dog, but her idees on wimmen's rights is sensible, I've read about 'em."

And that kinder headed Josiah off onto a new tact; we had had a dretful good supper, and I believe Miss Trimble had made a sight on him, I believe she had flattered and pompeyed him and for the time bein' he felt soft in sperit towards the sex.

And 'tennyrate men's moods are like the onfathomable sea, some-

From *Samantha at the St. Louis Exposition* (New York, 1904), pp. 155–61.

times turbulent, throwin' up stunny arguments and sandy ones, and agin flowin' calm and smooth as ile, and this wuz one of the gently swashin' ones.

"Id'no," sez he, "and I told her so, what wimmen want rights for, or to vote; I never wanted wimmen to vote, I told her they wuz too good, they wuz too near angels to have rights. You know I've always said so, Samantha, and I wuz readin' a piece a day or two ago, writ by one of the first ministers in the country, and he said that wimmen hadn't ort to want any rights; they ort to be riz up on a pedestal and I say so too."

And I sez, "No, Josiah, I can't go into that with all the rest I have to do, and it seems onreasonable in that minister to want wimmen to climb up onto pedestals when they have to do their own housework."

"Well, I say it hain't onreasonable. You ort to be up on one, Samantha."

(How much Miss Trimble must have made on him. He wuz so oncommon clever, and he never wuz megum, poor creeter!) I didn't really want to get into an argument at that time o' day, but I see he wuz on the wrong tact, and I felt I must convince him, so I sez in reasonable axents:

"I jest as lives be on a pedestal as not, I'd kinder love to if I could set, I always did enjoy bein' riz up, if I had nothin' to do only to stay up there some time, but wimmen have to git round so much it wouldn't work. How could I take a tower histed up like the car of Juggernaut or a Pope in a procession. I couldn't get carriers for one thing, and I wouldn't give a cent to be carried round anyway with my dizzy spells, I should more'n as likely as not fall off. But that hain't the main reason I'm agin it, it is too tuckerin' a job for wimmen."

"Tuckerin' to be enthroned on a pedestal with the male sect lookin' up to you and worshippin' you. You call that tuckerin'?" sez he.

"Yes," sez I, "I do. How under the sun can I or any other woman be up on a pedestal and do our own housework, cookin', washin' dishes, sweepin', moppin', cleanin' lamps, blackin' stoves, washin', ironin', makin' beds, quiltin' bed quilts, gittin' three meals a day, day after day, biled dinners and bag puddin's and mince pies and things, to say nothin' of custard and pumpkin pies that will slop over on the level, do the best you can; how could you keep 'em inside the crust histin' yourself up and down? And cleanin' house time — "

"Mebby," sez I honestly, "it would come handy in whitewashin' or fixin' the stovepipe, but where would it be in cleanin' mop-boards, or puttin' down carpets, or washin' winders, or doin' a three weeks washin', or bilin' soap? or pickin' geese? They act like fury shot up on the barn floor. How could you git our old gander up on a pedestal? His temper is that fiery, to say nothin' of settin' or standin' on it and holdin' on to the old thing and pickin' it. And raisin' chickens and washin' old trousers and overalls, and cleanin' sullers and paintin' floors and paperin', and droudgin' round all the time, as a woman has to to keep her house comfortable.

"And pickin' black-caps and strawberries, and churnin' big churnin's of butter, and pickin' wool, to say nothin' of onexpected company comin', and no girl. Let a lot of company come to stay all day the relations on your side and the work not done, and me posin' like a statute, lookin' down on you and your sect, you'd feel like a fool and jaw, you know you would. I presoom you'd throw your boot-jack at me and threaten to part with me, and how mean that would be in you when I did it at your request. 'Tain't anything any woman would go into if she wuz let alone."

"And then think of the thrashers and silo fillers comin' in hungry as bears, what would they say? No dinner cookin' and I on a pedestal, why it would be the town's talk. Or you comin' home from Jonesville on a cold night fraxious as a dog and sayin' you should die off if you didn't have supper in ten minutes. How could I git it on time perched up there?

"I say it can't be done, and it is onreasonable for men to want it, and at the same time want wimmen to do her own housework. For these men, every one on 'em, would act like fury if their house wuzn't clean and their clothes in order, and meals on time. And you must know it would jest about kill a woman to be doin' all this and histin' herself up and down a hundred times a day, and mebby half dead with rumatiz too. Why, it would be worse for me than all the rest of my work, and you hadn't ort to ask it of me."

Josiah looked real huffy and sez, "I hain't the only man that's wantin' it done; men have always been sot on it. There's been more'n a wagon load of poetry writ on it and you know it. Men have always said a sight about it, I hain't alone in it," he snapped out.

"No," sez I honestly, "I've hearn it before. But you see it wouldn't work, don't you? And I believe I could convince every man if I could git to 'em and talk it over with 'em. And I don't see where the beauty on't would come in; of course a woman couldn't change her clothes and put on Greek drapery right in the midst of cleanin' the buttery shelves or moppin' off the back steps. And to see a woman standin' up on a pedestal with an old calico dress pinned up round her waist and a slat sunbunnet on and her pardner's rubber boots, and her sleeves rolled up, and her face red as blood with hard work, and her hands all swelled up with hot soap suds and lye, what beauty would there be in it? It always did seem onreasonable besides bein' so tuckerin' no woman could stand it for a day."

He looked mad as a hen and sez he, "They could manage it if their minds wuz strong enough."

Sez I, "It seems to me it would depend more on the strength of their legs, specially if the pedestal wuz a high one. I never could git up onto it at all if I should go into it without gittin' up on a chair and then on a table. No woman no matter how strong she wuz could git more than two meals a day under the circumstances."

Josiah looked worried and sez, "Well, mebby there has been too much said about it, mebby it would be jest as well to leave pedestals to statters."

And I sez, "It is as well agin. Wimmen couldn't stand it with all they have to do."

And so we ended by bein' real congenial in our two minds and thinkin' considerable alike, which is indeed a comfort to pardners.

6   On Looking to Nature for Woman's "Spear"

"Fear!" sez he; "I don't know the meanin' of that word only from what I've read about it in the dictionary. Men don't know what it is to be afraid, and that is why," sez he, "that I've always been so anxious to have wimmen keep in her own spear, where men could watch over her, humble, domestic, grateful.

"Nater plotted it so," sez he; "nater designs the male of creation to branch out, to venter, to labor, to dare, while the female stays to hum and tends to her children and the housework." Sez he, "In all the works of nater the females stay to hum, and the males soar out free.

"It is a sweet and solemn truth," sez he, "and female wimmen ort to lay it to heart. In these latter days," sez he, "too many females are a-risin' up, and vainly a-tryin' to kick aginst this great law. But they can't knock it over," sez he — "the female foot hain't strong enough."

He wuz a-goin' on in this remarkably eloquent way on his congenial theme, but I kinder drawed him in by remindin' him of Miss Sheldon's tent we see in the Transportation Buildin' — the one she used in her lonely journeyin' a-explorin' the Dark Continent. Sez I, "There is a woman that has kinder branched out."

"Yes," sez he, "but men had to carry her." Sez he, "Samantha, the Lord designed it that females should stay to hum and tend to their babies, and wash the dishes. And when you go aginst that idee you are goin' aginst the everlastin' forces of nater. Nater has always had laws sot and immovable, and always will have 'em, and a passel of wimmen managers or lecturers hain't a-goin' to turn 'em round.

"Nater made wimmen and sot 'em apart for domestic duties — some of which I have enumerated," sez he.

"Whilst the males, from creation down, have been left free to skirm-

From *Samantha at the World's Fair* (New York, 1893), pp. 606–13.

ish round and git a livin' for themselves and the females secreted in the holy privacy of the hum life."

Jest as he reached this climax we come in front of the Ostrich Farm, where thirty of the long-legged, humbly creeters are kept, and we hearn the keeper a-describin' the habits of the ostriches to some folks that stood round him.

And Josiah, feelin' dretful good-natered and kinder patronizin' towards wimmen, and thinkin' that he wuz a-goin' to be strengthened in his talk by what the man wuz a-sayin', sez to me in a dretful, over-bearin', patronizin' way, and some with the air as if he owned a few of the ostriches, and me, too, he kinder stood up straight and crooked his forefinger and bagoned to me.

"Samantha," sez he, "draw near and hear these interestin' remarks. I always love," sez he, "to have females hear about the works of nater. It has a tendency," sez he, "to keep her in her place."

Sez the man as we drew near, a-goin' on with his remarks — he wuz addressin' some big man — but we hearn him say, sez he —

"The ostrich lays about a dozen and a half eggs in the layin' season — one every other day — and then she sets on the eggs about six hours out of the twenty-four, the male bird takin' her place for eighteen hours to her six.

"The male bird, as you see, stays to hum and sets on the eggs three times as long as she duz, and takes the entire care of the young os-triches, while the female roams round free, as you may say."

I turned round and sez to Josiah, "How interestin' the works of Nater are, Josiah Allen, How it puts woman in her proper spear, and men, too!"[1]

He looked real meachin' for most a minute, and then a look of mad-ness and dark revenge come over his liniment. A tall, humbly male bird stood nigh him, as tall agin most as he wuz.

And as I looked at Josiah he muttered, "I'll learn him — I'll learn the cussed fool to keep in his own spear."

I laid holt of his vest, and sez I, "What do you mean, Josiah Allen, by them dark threats? Tell me instantly," sez I, for I feared the worst.

"Seein' this dum fool is so willin' to take work on him that don't be-long for males to do, I'll give him a job at it. I'll see if I can't ride some of the consarned foolishness out of him."

Sez I, "Be calm, Josiah; don't throw away your own precious life through madness and revenge. The ostrich hain't to blame, he's only actin' out Nater."

"Nater!" sez Josiah scornfully — "Nater for males to stay to hum and set on eggs, and hatch 'em, and brood young ones? Don't talk to me!"

He wuz almost by the side of himself.

And in spite of my almost frenzied appeals to restrain him, he lanched upon him.

You could ride 'em by payin' so much, and money seemed to Josiah like so much water then, so wild with wrath and revenge wuz he.

I see he would go, and I reached my hand up, and sez I, "Dear Josiah, farewell!"

But he only nodded to me, and I hearn him murmurin' darkly —

"Seein' he's so dum accommodatin' that he's took wimmen's work on him that they ort to do themselves, I'll give him a pull that will be apt to teach him his own place."

And he started off at a fearful rate; round and round that inclosure they went, Josiah layin' his cane over the sides of the bird, and the keeper a-yellin' at him that he'd be killed.

And when they come round by us the first time I heard him a-apos-throfizin' the bird —

"Don't you want to set on some more eggs? don't you want to brood a spell?" and then he would kick him, and the ostrich would jump, and leap, and rare round. But the third time he come round I see a change — I see deadly fear depictered in his mean, and sez he wildly —

"Samantha, save me! save me! I am lost!" sez he.

I wuz now in tears, and I sez wildly —

"I will save that dear man, or perish!" and I wuz jest a-rushin' into the inclosure when they come a-tearin round for the fourth time, and jest a little ways from us the ostrich give a wild yell and leap, and Josiah wuz thrown almost onto our feet.

As the keeper rushed in to pick him up, we see he held a feather in his hand.

He thought it wuz tore out by excitement, and Josiah clinched the feathers to save himself.

But Josiah owned up to me afterwards that he gin up that he wuz a-goin' to be killed, and that his last thought wuz as he swooned away — wuz how much ostrich feathers cost, and how sweet it would be to give me a last gift of dyin' love, by pickin' a feather off for nothin'.

NOTE

1. On one of her tours, Samantha discusses the question of "nater" with Horace Greeley (see Selection 11, n1). Horace claims: "Man is sometimes mistaken in his honest beliefs, but Nature makes her laws unerringly. Nature intended the male of every species to take the preeminence. Nature designed man to be at the head of all public affairs. Nature never makes any mistakes." Samantha counters: "Nature made queen bees Horace. Old Nature herself clapped the crown on 'em. You never heard of king bees, did you?" She then describes the "public duties" of queen bees, whose constituents are up early for work and home "stiddy" at night. Her public duties don't spoil her domestic habits; indeed, "where will you find more stiddy, industrious, equinomical orderly doin's through a whole nation than she has in hern?" Samantha is careful to point out that she doesn't approve of the practice of disposing of the lazy drone husbands just to keep from winterin' 'em, but every great nature has its peculiarities and "this is hern." She winds up her discourse, which soared in eloquence, as follows: "In my opinion there has a great many men set up in their high chairs that would have done well to pattern after this Executive Female" (from *My Opinions and Betsey Bobbet's*, pp. 384–85).

7 "An Unmarried Female"

I suppose we are about as happy as the most of folks, but as I was sayin, a few days ago to Betsey Bobbet a neighborin' female of ours—"Every Station house in life has its various skeletons. But we ort to try to be contented with that spear of life we are called on to handle." Betsey haint married and she don't seem to be contented. She is awful opposed to wimmens rights, she thinks it is wimmens only spear to marry, but as yet she can't find any man willin' to lay holt of that spear with her. But you can read in her daily life and on her eager willin' countenance that she fully realizes the sweet words of the poet, "while there is life there is hope."

Betsey haint handsome. Her cheek bones are high, and she bein' not much more than skin and bone they show plainer than they would if she was in good order. Her complexion (not that I blame her for it) haint good, and her eyes are little and sot way back in her head. Time has seen fit to deprive her of her hair and teeth, but her large nose he has kindly suffered her to keep, but she has got the best white ivory teeth money will buy; and two long curls fastened behind each ear, besides frizzles on the top of her head, and if she wasn't naturally bald, and if the curls was the color of her hair they would look well. She is awful sentimental, I have seen a good many that had it bad, but of all the sentimental creeters I ever did see Betsey Bobbet is the sentimentalest, you couldn't squeeze a laugh out of her with a cheeze press.

As I said she is awful opposed to wimmin's havein' any right only the right to get married. She holds on to that right as tight as any single woman I ever see which makes it hard and wearin' on the single men round here. For take the men that are the most opposed to wimmin's havin' a right, and talk the most about its bein' her duty to cling to man

From *My Opinions and Betsey Bobbet's* (Hartford, 1891), pp. 26 –37.

like a vine to a tree, they don't want Betsey to cling to them, they *won't
let* her cling to 'em. For when they would be a goin' on about how
wicked it was for wimmin to vote—and it was her only spear to marry,
says I to 'em "Which had you ruther do, let Betsey Bobbet cling to you
or let her vote?" and they would every one of 'em quail before that
question. They would drop their heads before my keen grey eyes—and
move off the subject.

But Betsey don't get discourajed. Every time I see her she says in a
hopeful wishful tone, "That the deepest men of minds in the country
agree with her in thinkin' that it is wimmin's duty to marry, and not to
vote." And then she talks a sight about the retirin' modesty and dignity
of the fair sect, and how shameful and revoltin' it would be to see wimmen throwin' 'em away, and boldly and unblushin'ly talkin' about law
and justice.

Why to hear Betsey Bobbet talk about wimmins throwin' their modesty away you would think if they ever went to the political pole, they
would have to take their dignity and modesty and throw 'em against
the pole, and go without any all the rest of their lives.

Now I don't believe in no such stuff as that, I think a woman can be
bold and unwomanly in other things besides goin' with a thick veil over
her face, and a brass mounted parasol, once a year, and gently and
quietly dropping a vote for a christian president, or a religeous and noble minded pathmaster.

She thinks she talks dreadful polite and proper, she says "I was came-
ing" instead of "I was coming," and "I have saw" instead of "I have
seen," and "papah" for paper, and "deah" for dear. I don't know much
about grammer, but common sense goes a good ways. She writes the
poetry for the Jonesville Augur, or "Augah," as she calls it. She used to
write for the opposition paper, the Jonesville Gimlet, but the editer of
the Augur, a long haired chap, who moved into Jonesville a few months
ago, lost his wife soon after he come there, and sense that she has turned
Dimocrat, and writes for his paper stiddy. They say that he is a dreadful big feelin' man, and I have heard—it came right straight to me—his
cousin's wife's sister told it to the mother in law of one of my neighbor's
brother's wife, that he didn't like Betsey's poetry at all, and all he
printed it for was to plague the editer of the Gimlet, because she used
to write for him. I myself wouldn't give a cent a bushel for all the
poetry she can write. And it seems to me, that if I was Betsey, I
wouldn't try to write so much, howsumever, I don't know what turn

I should take if I was Betsey Bobbet, that is a solemn subject and one I don't love to think on.

I never shall forget the first piece of her poetry I ever see. Josiah Allen and I had both on us been married goin' on a year, and I had occasion to go to his trunk one day where he kept a lot of old papers and the first thing I laid my hand on was these verses. Josiah went with her a few times after his wife died, a 4th of July or so and two or three camp meetin's, and the poetry seemed to be wrote about the time *we* was married. It was directed over the top of it "Owed to Josiah," just as if she were in debt to him. This was the way it read.

"OWED TO JOSIAH."

Josiah I the tale have hurn,
With rigid ear, and streaming eye,
I saw from me that you did turn,
I never knew the reason why.
   Oh Josiah,
   It seemed as if I must expiah.

Why did you, Oh why did you blow
Upon my life of snowy sleet,
The fiah of love to fiercest glow,
Then turn a damphar on the heat?
   Oh Josiah,
   It seemed as if I must expiah.

I saw thee coming down the street,
She by your side in bonnet bloo;
The stuns that grated 'neath thy feet
Seemed crunching on my vitals too.
   Oh Josiah,
   It seemed as if I must expiah.

I saw thee washing sheep last night,
On the bridge I stood with marble brow,
The waters raged, thou clasped it tight,
I sighed, 'should both be drownded now —'
   I thought Josiah,
   Oh happy sheep to thus expiah."

I showed the poetry to Josiah that night after he came home, and told him I had read it. He looked awful ashamed to think I had seen it, and says he with a dreadful sheepish look.

"The persecution I underwent from that female can never be told, she fairly hunted me down, I had'nt no rest for the soles of my feet. I thought one spell she would marry me in spite of all I could do, without givin' me the benefit of law or gospel." He see I looked stern, and he added with a sick lookin' smile, "I thought one spell, to use Betsey's language, 'I was a gonah.' "

I did'nt smile — oh no, for the deep principle of my sect was reared up — I says to him in a tone cold enough to almost freeze his ears, "Josiah Allen, shet up, of all the cowardly things a man ever done, it is goin' round braggin' about wimmen' likin' em, and follerin' em up. Enny man that'l do that is little enough to crawl through a knot hole without rubbing his clothes." Says I, "I suppose you made her think the moon rose in your head, and set in your heels, I dare say you acted foolish enough round her to sicken a snipe, and if you make fun of her now to please me I let you know you have got holt of the wrong individual." Now, says I, "go to bed," and I added in still more freezing accents, "for I want to mend your pantaloons." He gathered up his shoes and stockin's and started off to bed, and we haint never passed a word on the subject sence. I believe when you disagree with your pardner, in freein' your *mind* in the first on't, and then not be a twittin' about it afterwards. And as for bein' jealous, I should jest as soon think of bein' jealous of a meetin'-house as I should of Josiah. He is a well principled man. And I guess he was'nt fur out o' the way about Betsey Bobbet, though I would'nt encourage him by lettin' him say a word on the subject, for I always make it a rule to stand up for my own sect; but when I hear her go on about the editor of the Augur, I can believe anything about Betsey Bobbet. She came in here one day last week, it was about ten o'clock in the mornin'. I had got my house slick as a pin, and my dinner under way, (I was goin' to have a biled dinner, and a cherry puddin' biled, with sweet sass to eat on it,) and I sot down to finish sewin' up the breadth of my new rag carpet. I thought I would get it done while I had'nt so much to do, for it bein' the first of March, I knew sugarin, would be comin' on, and then cleanin' house time, and I wanted it to put down jest as soon as the stove was carried out in the summer kitchen. The fire was sparklin' away, and the painted floor a shinin' and the dinner a bilin,' and I sot there sewin' jest as calm as a clock, not dreamin' of no trouble, when in came Betsey Bobbet.

I met her with outward calm, and asked her to set down and lay off her things. She sot down, but she said she couldn't lay off her things. Says she, "I was comin' down past, and I thought I would call and let you see the last numbah of the Augah, there is a piece in it concernin' the tariff that stirs men's souls, I like it evah so much."

She handed me the paper, folded so I could'nt see nothin' but a piece of poetry by Betsey Bobbet. I see what she wanted of me and so I dropped my breadths of carpetin' and took hold of it and began to read it.

"Read it audible if you please," says she, "Especially the precious remahks ovah it, it is such a feast for me to be a sitting, and heah it reheahsed by a musical vorce."

Says I, "I spose I can rehearse it if it will do you any good," so I began as follers:

"It is seldem that we present to the readers of the Augur (the best paper for the fireside in Jonesville or the world) with a poem like the following. It may be by the assistance of the Augur (only twelve shillings a year in advance, wood and potatoes taken in exchange) the name of Betsey Bobbet will yet be carved on the lofty pinnacle of fame's towering pillow. We think however that she could study such writers as Sylvanus Cobb, and Tupper with profit both to herself and to them.   EDITOR OF THE AUGUR."

Here Betsey interrupted me, "The deah editah of the Augah had no need to advise me to read Tuppah, for he is indeed my most favorite authar, you have devorhed him havn't you Josiah Allen's wife?"

"Devoured who?" says I, in a tone pretty near as cold as a cold icicle.

"Mahten, Fahyueah, Tuppah, that sweet authar," says she.

"No mom," says I shortly, "I hain't devoured Martin Farquhar Tupper, nor no other man, I hain't a cannibal."

"Oh! you understand me not, I meant, devorhed his sweet, tender lines."

"I haint' devoured his tenderlines, nor nothin' relatin' to him," and I made a motion to lay the paper down, but Betsey urged me to go on, and so I read.

GUSHINGS OF A TENDAH SOUL.

Oh let who will,
Oh let who can,
Be tied onto
A horrid male man.

Thus said I 'ere,
My tendah heart was touched,
Thus said I 'ere
My tendah feelings gushed.

But oh a change
Hath swept ore me,
As billows sweep
The "deep blue sea."

A voice, a noble form,
One day I saw;
An arrow flew,
My heart is nearly raw.

His first pardner lies
Beneath the turf,
He is wandering now,
In sorrows briny surf.

Two twins, the little
Deah cherub creechahs,
Now wipe the teahs,
From off his classic feachahs.

Oh sweet lot, worthy
Angel arisen,
To wipe the teahs,
From eyes like hisen.

"What think you of it?" says she as I finished readin'.

I looked right at her most a minute with a majestic look. In spite of her false curls, and her new white ivory teeth, she is a humbly critter. I looked at her silently while she sot and twisted her long yeller bunnet strings, and then I spoke out,

"Hain't the Editor of the Augur a widower with a pair of twins?"

"Yes," says she with a happy look.

Then says I, "If the man hain't a fool, he'll think you are one."

"Oh!" says she, and she dropped her bunnet strings, and clasped her long bony hands together in her brown cotton gloves, "oh, we ahdent soles of genious, have feelin's, you cold, practical natures know nuthing of, and if they did not gush out in poetry we should expiah. You may as well try to tie up the gushing catarack of Niagarah with a piece of welting cord, as to tie up the feelings of an ahdent sole."

"Ardent sole!" says I coldly. "Which makes the most noise, Betsey Babbet [sic], a three inch brook or a ten footer? which is the tearer? which is the roarer? deep waters run stillest. I have no faith in feelins' that stalk round in public in mournin' weeds. I have no faith in such mourners," says I.

"Oh Josiah's wife, cold, practical female being, you know me not; we are sundered as fah apart as if you was sitting on the North pole, and I was sitting on the South pole. Uncongenial being, you know me not."

"I may not know you, Betsey Bobbet, but I do know decency, and I know that no munny would tempt me to write such stuff as that poetry and send it to a widower, with twins."

"Oh!" says she, "what appeals to the tendah feeling heart of a single female woman more, than to see a lonely man who has lost his relict? And pity never seems so much like pity as when it is given to the deah little children of widowehs. And," says she, "I think moah than as likely as not, this soaring soul of genious did not wed his affinity, but was united to a weak women of clay."

"Mere women of clay!" says I, fixin' my spektacles upon her in a most searchin' manner, "where will you find a woman, Betsey Bobbet, that hain't more or less clay? and affinity, that is the meanest word I ever heard; no married woman has any right to hear it. I'll excuse you, bein' a female, but if a man had said it to me, I'd holler to Josiah. There is a time for everything, and the time to hunt affinity is before you are married; married folks hain't no right to hunt it," says I sternly.

"We kindred souls soah above such petty feelings, we soah fah above them."

"I hain't much of a soarer," says I, "and I don't pretend to be, and to tell you the truth," says I, "I am glad I hain't."

"The Editah of the Augah," says she, and she grasped the paper offen the stand and folded it up, and presented it at me like a spear, "the Editah of this paper is a kindred soul, he appreciates me, he undahstands me, and will not our names in the pages of this very papah go down to posterety togathah?"

Then says I, drove out of all patience with her, "I wish you was there now, both of you, I wish," says I, lookin' fixedly on her, "I wish you was both of you in posterity now."

8   On Soothin', Clingin', and Cooin'

She [Betsey] took out her work, and says she, "I have come to spend the day. I saw thier deah Pa bringin' the deah little twins in heah, and I thought maybe I could comfort the precious little motherless things some, if I should come over heah. If there is any object upon the earth, Josiah Allen's wife, that appeals to a feelin' heart, it is the sweet little children of widowers. I cannot remember the time when I did not want to comfort them, and thier deah Pa's. I have always felt that it was woman's highest speah, her only mission to soothe, to cling, to smile, to coo. I have always felt it, and for yeah's back it has been a growin' on me. I feel that you do not feel as I do in this matter, you do not feel that it is woman's greatest privilege, her crowning blessing, to soothe lacerations, to be a sort of a poultice to the noble, manly breast when it is torn with the cares of life."

This was too much, in the agitated frame of mind I then was.

"Am I a poultice Betsey Bobbet, do I look like one? — am I in the condition to be one?" I cried turnin' my face, red and drippin' with perspiration towards her, and then attacked one of Josiah's shirt sleeves agin. "What has my sect done" says I, as I wildly rubbed his shirt sleeves, "That they have got to be lacerator soothers, when they have got everything else under the sun to do?" Here I stirred down the preserves that was a runnin' over, and turned a pail full of syrup into the sugar kettle. "Everybody says that men are stronger than women, and why should they be treated as if they was glass china, liable to break all to pieces if they haint handled careful. And if they have got to be soothed," says I in an agitated tone, caused by my emotions (and by pumpin' 6 pails of water to fill up the biler), "Why don't they get men to sooth'em? They have as much agin time as wimmen have; evenin's they don't have anything else to do, they might jest as well be a soothin'

From *My Opinons and Betsey Bobbet's* (Hartford, 1891), pp. 62–68.

each other as to be a hangin' round grocery stores, or settin' by the fire whittlin'.'"

I see I was frightenin' her by my delerious tone and I continued more mildly, as I stirred down the strugglin' sugar with one hand—removed a cake from the oven with the other—watched my apple preserves with a eagle vision, and listened intently to the voice of the twins, who was playin' in the woodhouse.

"I had jest as soon soothe lacerations as not, Betsey, if I hadn't everything else to do. I had jest as lives set down and smile at Josiah by the hour, but who would fry him nut cakes? I could smoothe down his bald head affectionately, but who would do off this batch of sugar? I could coo at him day in and day out, but who would skim milk—wash pans—get vittles—wash and iron—and patch and scour—and darn and fry—and make and mend—and bake and bile while I was a cooin', tell me?" says I.

Betsey spoke not, but quailed, and I continued—

"Women haint any stronger than men, naturally; thier backs and thier nerves haint made of any stouter timber; their hearts are jest as liable to ache as men's are; so with thier heads; and after doin' a hard day's work when she is jest ready to drop down, a little smilin' and cooin' would do a woman jest as much good as a man. Not what," I repeated in the firm tone of principle "Not but what I am willin' to coo, if I only had time."

A pause enshued durin' which I bent over the washtub and rubbed with all my might on Josiah's shirt sleeve. I had got one sleeve so I could see streaks of white in it, (Josiah is awful hard on his shirt sleeves), and I lifted up my face and continued in still more reesonable tones, as I took out my rice puddin' and cleaned out the bottom of the oven, (the pudden had run over and was a scorchin' on), and scraped the oven bottom with a knife,

"Now Josiah Allen will go out into that lot," says I, glancein' out of the north window "and plough right straight along, furrow after furrow, no sweat of mind about it at all; his mind is in that free calm state that he could write poetry."

"Speaking of poetry, reminds me," said Betsey, and I see her hand go into her pocket; I knew what was a comin', and I went on hurriedly, wavin' off what I knew must be, as long as I could. "Now, I, a workin' jest as hard as he accordin' to my strength, and havin' to look 40 ways to once, and 40 different strains on my mind, now tell me candidly,

Betsey Bobbet, which is in the best condition for cooin', Josiah Allen or me? but it haint expected of him," says I in agitated tones, "I am expected to do all the smilin' and cooin' there is done, though you know," says I sternly, "that I haint no time for it."

"In this poem, Josiah Allen's wife, is embodied my views, which are widely different from yours."

I see it was vain to struggle against fate, she had the poetry in her hand. I rescued the twins from beneath a half a bushel of beans they had pulled over onto themselves — took off my preserves which had burnt to the pan while I was a rescuin', and calmly listened to her, while I picked up the beans with one hand, and held off the twins with the other.

"There is one thing I want to ask your advice about, Josiah Allen's wife. This poem is for the Jonesville Augah. You know I used always to write for the opposition papah, the Jonesville Gimlet, but as I said the othah day, since the Editah of the Augah lost his wife I feel that duty is a drawing of me that way. Now do you think that it would be any more pleasing and comforting to that deah Editah to have me sign my name Bettie Bobbet — or Betsey, as I always have?" And loosin' herself in thought she murmured dreamily to the twins, who was a pullin' each other's hair on the floor at her feet —

"Sweet little mothahless things, you couldn't tell me, could you, deahs, how your deah Pa would feel about it?"

Here the twins laid holt of each other so I had to part 'em, and as I did so I said to Betsey, "If you haint a fool you will hang on to the Betsey. You can't find a woman nowadays that answers to her true name. I expect," says I in a tone of cold and almost witherin' sarcasm, "that these old ears will yet hear some young minister preach about Johnnie the Baptist, and Minnie Magdalen. Hang on to the Betsey; as for the Bobbet," says I, lookin' pityingly on her, "that will hang on for itself."

I was too well bread to interrupt her further, and I pared my potatoes, pounded my beefsteak, and ground my coffee for dinner, and listened. This commenced also as if she had been havin' a account with Love, and had come out in his debt.

OWED TO LOVE

Ah, when my deah future companion's heart with grief is rife,
With his bosom's smart, with the cares of life,

Ah, what higher, sweeter, bliss could be,
Than to be a soothing poultice unto he?

And if he have any companions lost — if they from earth have risen,
Ah, I could weep tears of joy — for the deah bliss of wiping away hisen;
Or if he (should happen to) have any twins, or othah blessed little ties,
Ah, *how willingly* on the altah of duty, B. Bobbet, herself would
  sacrifice.

I would (all the rest of) life to the cold winds fling,
And live for love — and live to cling.
Fame, victuals, away! away! our food shall be,
His smile on me — my sweet smile on he.

There was pretty near twenty verses of 'em, and as she finished she
said to me —

"What think you of my poem, Josiah Allen's wife?"

"Says I, fixin' my sharp grey eyes upon her keenly, "I have had more
experience with men than you have, Betsey;" I see a dark shadow set-
tlin' on her eyebrow, and I hastened to apologise — "you haint to blame
for it, Betsey — we all know you haint to blame."

She grew calm, and I proceeded, "How long do you suppose you
could board a man on clear smiles, Betsey — you jest try it for a few
meals and you'd find out. I have lived with Josiah Allen 14 years, and I
ought to know somethin' of the natur of man, which is about alike in all
of 'em, and I say, and I contend for it, that you might jest as well try to
cling to a bear as to a hungry man. After dinner, sentiment would have
a chance, and you might smile on him. But then," says I thoughtfully,
"there is the dishes to wash."

Jest at that minute the Editor of the Augur stopped at the gate, and
Betsey, cathin' up a twin on each arm, stood up to the winder, smilin'.

He jumped out, and took a great roll of poetry out from under the
buggy seat — I sithed as I see it. But fate was better to me than I de-
served. For Josiah was jest leadin' the horse into the horse barn, when
the Editor happened to look up and see Betsey. Josiah says he
swore — says he "the d — — — !" I won't say what it was, for I belong to
the meetin' house, but it wasn't the Deity though it begun with a D. He
jumped into the buggy agin, and says Josiah,

"You had better stay to dinner, my wife is gettin' a awful good one —
and the sugar is most done."

Josiah says he groaned, but he only said—

"Fetch out the twins."

Says Josiah, "You had better stay to dinner—you haint got no women folks to your house—and I know what it is to live on pancakes," and wantin' to have a little fun with him, says he, "Betsey Bobbet is here."

Josiah says he swore agin, and agin says he, "fetch out the twins." And he looked so kind o' wild and fearful towards the door, that Josiah started off on the run.

Betsey was determined to carry one of the twins out, but jest at the door he tore every mite of hair offen her head, and she, bein' bald naturally, dropped him. And Josiah carried 'em out, one on each arm, and he drove off with 'em fast. Betsey wouldn't stay to dinner all I could do and say, she acted mad. But one sweet thought filled me with such joyful emotion that I smiled as I thought of it—I shouldn't have to listen to any more poetry that day.

9 "A Song"

Composed not for the stong minded females, who madly and indecently insist on rights, but for the retiring and delicate minded of the sex, who modestly murmer, "we will not have any rights, we scorn them." Will some modest and bashful sisteh set it to music, that we may timidly, but loudly warble it; and oblige, hers 'till deth, in the glorious cause of wimmen's only true speah. BETSEY BOBBET.

> Not for strong minded wimmen,
> Do I now tune up my liah;
> Oh, not for them would I kin-
> dle up the sacred fiah.
> Oh, modest, bashful female,
> For you I tune up my lay;
> Although strong minded wimmen sneah,
> We'll conqueh in the fray.
>> CHORUS. — Press onward, do not feah, sistehs,
>> Press onward, do not feah;
>> Remembeh wimmen's speah, sistehs,
>> Remembeh wimmen's speah.
>
> It would cause some fun if poor Miss Wade
> Should say of her boy Harry,
> I shall not give him any trade,
> But bring him up to marry;
> And would cause some fun, of course deah maids,
> If Miss Wades'es Harry,
> Should lose his end and aim in life,
> And find no chance to marry.
>> CHORUS. — Press onward, do not feah, sistehs, &c.

From *My Opinions and Betsey Bobbet's* (Hartford, 1891), pp. 184–5.

Yes, wedlock is our only hope,
All o'er this mighty nation;
Men are brought up to other trades,
But this is our vocation.
Oh, not for sense or love, ask we;
We ask not to be courted,
Our watch-word is to married be,
That we may be supported.
      CHORUS. — Press onward, do not feah, sistehs, &c.

Say not, you're strong and love to work;
Are healthier than your brotheh,
Who for a blacksmith is designed;
Such feelins you must smotheh;
Your restless hands fold up, or gripe
Your waist into a span,
And spend your strength in looking out
To hail the coming man.
      CHORUS. — Press onward, do not feah, sistehs, &c.

Oh, do not be discouraged, when
You find your hopes brought down;
And when you meet unwilling men,
Heed not their gloomy frown;
Yield not to wild dispaih;
Press on and give no quartah,
In battle all is faih;
We'll win for we had orteh.
      CHORUS. Press onward, do not feah, sistehs,
               Press onward, do not feah;
               Remembeh wimmen's speah, sistehs,
               Remembeh wimmen's speah.

10 "A Serenading Episode, &c."

These verses of Betsey's come out in the last week's *Gimlet*, and I call it foolish stuff. Though (on measurin' 'em in a careless way with a yard-stick) I found the lines was pretty nigh of a equal length, and so I s'pose it would be called poetry.

A WIFE'S STORY.

Oh Gimlet! back again I float,
　　With broken wings, a weary bard;
I cannot write as once I wrote,
　　I have to work so very hard;
So hard my lot, so tossed about,
My muse is fairly tuckered out.

My muse aforesaid once hath flown,
　　But now her back is broke, and breast;
And yet she fain would crumple down;
　　On Gimlet pages she would rest,
And sing plain words as there she's sot —
Haply they'll rhyme, and haply not.

I spake plain words in former days,
　　No guile I showed, clear was my plan;
My gole it matrimony was;
　　My earthly aim it was a man.
I gained my man, I won my gole;
Alas! I feel not as I fole.

Yes, ringing through my maiden thought
　　This clear voice rose: "Oh come up higher."
To speak plain truth, with candor fraught,
　　To married be was my desire.

From *My Wayward Pardner or Trials with Josiah* (Hartford, 1881), pp. 355–65.

Now, sweeter still this lot shall seem,
To be a widder is my theme.

For toil hath claimed me for her own,
    In wedlock I have found no ease;
I've cleaned and washed for neighbors round,
    And took my pay in beans and pease;
In boiling sap no rest I took,
Or husking corn, in barn, and shock.

Or picking wool from house to house,
    White-washing, painting, papering;
In stretching carpets, boiling souse;
    E'en picking hops, it hath a sting,
For spiders there assembled be,
Mosquitoes, bugs, and e t c.

I have to work, oh! very hard;
    Old Toil, I know your breadth and length;
I'm tired to death, and, in one word,
    I have to work beyond my strength,
And mortal men are very tough
To get along with, — hasty, rough.

Yes, tribulation's doomed to her
    Who weds a man, without no doubt.
In peace a man is singuler;
    His ways they are past findin' out.
And oh! the wrath of mortal males —
To pont their ire, earth's language fails.

And thirteen children in our home
    Their buttons rend, their clothes they burst,
Much bread and such do they consume;
    Of children they do seem the worst.
And Simon and I do disagree;
He's prone to sin continuallee.

He horrors has, he oft doth kick,
    He prances, yells, — he will not work.
Sometimes I think he is too sick;
    Sometimes I think he tries to shirk.
But 'tis hard for her, in either case,
    Who B. Bobbet was in happier days.

Happier? Away! such thoughts I spurn.
  I count it true, from spring to fall,
'Tis better to be wed, and groan,
  Than never to be wed at all.
I'd work my hands down to the bone
Rather than rest a maiden lone.

This truth I will not, cannot shirk,
  I feel it when I sorrow most:
I'd rather break my back with work,
  And haggard look as any ghost, —
Rather than lonely vigils keep,
I'd wed and sigh, and groan and weep.

Yes, I can say, though tears fall quick,
  Can say, while briny tear-drops start,
I'd rather wed a crooked stick
  Than never wed no stick at all.
Sooner than laughed at be, as of yore,
  I'd rather laugh myself no more.

I'd rather go half-clad and starved,
  And mops and dish-cloths madly wave,
Than have the words "B. Bobbet" carved
  On headstun rising o'er my grave.
Proud thought! now, when that stun is risen,
'Twill bear two names — my name and hisen.

Methinks 'twould colder make the stun
  If but one name, the name of she,
Should linger there alone — alone.
  How different when the name of he
Does also deck the funeral urn;
Two wedded names, — his name and hurn.

And sweeter yet, oh blessed lot!
  Oh state most dignified and blest!
To be a widder, calmly sot,
  And have both dignity and rest.
Oh, Simon! strangely sweet 'twould be
To be a widder unto thee.

The warfare past, the horrors done,
  With maiden's ease and pride of wife,

The dignity of wedded one,
  The calm and peace of single life, —
Oh, strangely sweet this lot doth seem;
A female widder is my theme.

I would not hurt a hair of he,
Yet, did he from earth's toils escape,
I could most reconciled be,
Could sweetly mourn, e'en without crape,
Could say, without a pang of pain,
That Simon's loss was Betsey's gain.

I've told the plain tale of my woes,
With no deceit, or language vain,
Have told whereon my hopes are rose,
Have sung my mournful song of pain.
And now I e'en will end my tale,
I've sung my song, and wailed my wail.

I have made a practice of callin' that Poetry, bein' one that despises envy and jealousy amongst female authoresses. No, you never ketch me at it, bein' one that would sooner help 'em up the ladder than upset 'em, and it is ever my practice so to do. But truth must be spoke if subjects are brung up. Uronious views must be condemned by Warriors of the Right, whether ladders be upset or stand firm on their legs — poetesses also.

I felt that this poetry attacted a tender subject, a subject dearer to me than all the world besides — the subject of Josiah. Josiah is a man.

And I say it, and I say it plain, that men hain't no such creeters as she tries to make out they be. Men are first-rate creeters in lots of things, and are as good as wimmen be any day of the week.

Of course, I agree with Betsey, that husbands are tryin' in lots of things; they need a firm hand to the hellum to guide 'em along through the tempestuous waves of married life, and get along with 'em. They are lots of trouble, but then I think they pay after all. Why, I wouldn't swap my Josiah for the best house and lot in Jonesville, or the crown of the Widder Albert. I love Josiah Allen. And I don't know but the very trouble he has caused me makes me cling closer to him. You know the harder a horse's head beats aginst burdock burs the tighter the burdocks will cling to its mane. Josiah makes me sights of trouble, but I cling to him closely.

I admit that men are curious creeters, and very vain, and they hain't willin' to let well enough alone. They over-do, and go beyond all sense and reason. A instance of these two strong traits of their's has jest occurred and took place, which, as a true historian relatin' solemn facts, I will relate in this epistol.

Yes, men are tejus creeters a good deal of the time. But then agin, so be wimmen, jest as tejus, and I don't know but tejuser. I believe my soul, if I had got to be born agin, I had jest as lieves be born a man as a woman, and I don't know but I drather.

No, I don't think one sect ort to boast over the other one. They are both about equally foolish and disagreeable, and both have their goodnesses and nobilities, and both ort to have their rights.

Now, I hain't one to set up and say men hadn't ort to vote, that they don't know enough, and hain't good enough, and so forth and so on. No, you don't ketch me at it. I am one that stands up for justice and reason.

Now, the other day a wild-eyed woman, with short hair, who goes round a lecturin' on wimmen's rights, come to see me, a tryin' to inviggle me into a plot to keep men from votin'. Says she, "The time is a drawin' near when wimmen are a goin' to vote, without no doubt."

"Amen!" says I. "I can say amen to that with my hull heart and soul."

"And then," says she, "when the staff is in our own hands, less we wimmen all put in together and try to keep men from votin'."

"Never!" says I, "never will you get into such a scrape as that," says I. "Men have jest exactly as good a right to vote as wimmen have. They are condemned, and protected, and controlled by the same laws that wimmen are, and so of course are equally interested in makin' 'em. And I won't hear another word of such talk. You needn't try to inviggle me into no plot to keep men from votin', for justice is ever my theme, and also Josiah."

Says she, bitterly, "I'd love to make these miserable sneaks try it once, and see how they would like it, to have to spend their property, and be hauled around, and hung by laws they hadn't no hand in makin'."

But I still says, with marble firmness, "Men have jest as good a right to vote as wimmen have. And you needn't try to inviggle me into no such plans, for I won't be inviggled."

And so she stopped invigglin', and went off.

And then again in Betsey's poetry (though as a neighbor and a female author I never would speak a word aginst it, and what I say I say as a warrior, and would wish to be so took) I would say in kindness, and strictly as a warrior, that besides the deep undercurrent of foolishness that is runnin' through it, there is another thought that I deeply condemn. Betsey sot out in married life expectin' too much. Now, she didn't marry in the right way, and so she ort to have expected tougher times than the usual run of married females ort to expect; more than the ordinary tribulations of matrimony. But she didn't; she expected too much.

And it won't do to expect too much in this world, anyway. If you can only bring your mind down to it, it is a sight better to expect nothing, and then you won't be disappointed if you get it, as you most probable will. And if you get something it will be a joyful surprise to you. But there are few indeed who has ever sot down on this calm hite of filosify.

Folks expect too much. As many and many times as their hopes have proved to be uronious, they think, well now, if I only had that certain thing, or was in that certain place, I should be happy. But they hain't. They find when they reach that certain gole, and have clim up and sot down on it, they'll find that somebody has got onto the gole before 'em, and is there a settin' on it. No matter how spry anybody may be, they'll find that Sorrow can climb faster than they can, and can set down on goles quicker. Yes, they'll find her there.

It hain't no matter how easy a seat anybody sets down in in this world, they'll find that they'll have to hunch along, and let Disappointment set down with 'em, and Anxiety, and Weariness, and et cetery, et cetery.

Now, the scholar thinks if he can only stand up on that certain hite of scientific discovery, he will be happy, for he will know all that he cares about or wants to. But when he gets up there, he'll see plain; for the higher he is riz above the mists of ignorance that floats around the lower lands, the clearer his vision; and he will see another peak right ahead of him, steeper and loftier and icier than the last, and so on ad infinitum, ad infinity.

11   On Membership in the Creation Searchin' Society

. . . We got to the school-house where it [Debatin' Society] was held, in good season, and got a good seat, and I loosened my bunnet strings and went to knittin'. But, as I said, they was determined (some on 'em) that I should hold up one of the sides of the arguments; but of course, as could be expected in such a interestin' and momentous affair, in which Jonesville and the world at large was so deeply interested, there was them that it galled, to see a woman git up so high in the world. There was them that said it would have a tendency to onsettle and break up the hull fabric of society for a woman to take part in such hefty matters as would be argued here. Some said it was a revolutionary idee, and not to be endured for half a moment of time; and they brought up arguments from the Auger — wrote by its Editor — to prove out that wimmen ortn't to have no such privileges and honors. They said, as sick as the Editor was now, it would kill him if he should hear that the "Creation Searchin' Society" — that he had labored so for — had demeaned itself by lettin' a woman take part in it. They said as friends of the Editor, *they* wouldn't answer for the shock on his nervous and other system. Neither would they answer for the consequences to Jones-ville and the world — the direful consequences, sure to flow from liftin' a female woman so far above her spear.

Their talk was scareful, very, and some was fearfully affected by it; but others was jest as rampant on the other side; they got up and defied 'em. They boldly brought forward my noble doin's on my tower; how I had stood face to face with that heaven-honored man of peace, Horace Greely[1] — heaven-honored and heaven-blest now — how he had confided in me; how my spectacles had calmly gazed into hisen, as we argued in deep debate concernin' the welfare of the nation, and wimmen. How I

From *Samantha at the Centennial* (Hartford, 1884), pp. 32–52.

had preserved Grant from perishin' by poetry; how I had labored with Victory and argued with Theodore.[2] They said such doin's had rose me up above other wimmen; had lifted me so far up above her common spear, as to make me worthy of any honors the nation could heap onto me; made me worthy even to take a part in the "Jonesville Creation Searchin' and World Investigatin' Society."

"I let 'em fight it out, and didn't say a word. They fit, and they fit; and I sot calmly there on my seat a knittin' my Josiah's socks, and let 'em go on. I knew where I stood in my own mind; I knew I shouldn't git up and talk a word after they got through fightin'. Not that I think it is out of character for a woman to talk in public; nay, verily. It is, in my opinion, no more wearin' on her throat, or her morals, to git up and talk to a audience for their amusement and edification, in a calm and collected voice, than it is for her to key up her voice and sing to 'em by the hour, for the same reason. But everybody has their particular fort, and they ort in my opinion to stick to their own forts and not try to git on to somebody else'es.

Now, influencin' men's souls, and keepin' their morals healthy by words of eloquence, is some men's forts. Nailin' on good leather soles to keep their body's healthy, is another man's fort. One is jest as honorable and worthy as the other, in my opinion, if done in the fear of God and for the good of mankind, and follerd as a fort ort to be follerd. But when folks leave their own lawful forts and try to git on to somebody else'es fort, that is what makes trouble, and makes crowded forts and weak ones, and mixes things. Too many a gettin' on to a fort at one time, is what breaks it down. My fort haint talkin' in public,[3] and I foller it up from day to day, as a fort ort to be follerd. So I was jest as cool as a cewcumber, outside and inside, and jest as lives see 'em go on makin' consummit idiots of themselves as not, and ruther.

It was enough to make a dog snicker and laugh (if he hadn't deep principle to hold him back, as I had,) to see 'em go on. The President Cornelius Cork, and Solomon Cypher talked the most. They are both eloquent and almost finished speakers; but Solomon Cypher havin' had better advantages than the President, of course goes ahead of him as an oriter. A nephew of hisen, P. Cypher Bumpus, old Philander Bumpus'es only boy, (named after his father, and uncle Cypher,) has been there to his uncle's givin' him lessons all winter, in elocution and dramatic effects. Solomon has give him his board for tutorin' him.

I s'pose P. Cypher Bumpus can't be beat on elocution; he's studied hard, and took lessons of some big elocutionists, and they say he can holler up as loud, and look as wild as the biggest of 'em, and dwindle his voice down as low, and make as curious motions as the curiousest of 'em. Besides, he has took up lots in his own head. He is very smart, naturally, and has stood by his uncle Solomon all winter, like a Major. And considerin' Solomon's age, and his natural mind — which haint none of the best — and his lameness, I never see a man make such headway as Solomon Cypher has. He can make eloquent and impressive gestures, very.

Cornelius Cork, the President, they say has been a tryin to learn himself; has tried to take gestures and motions up in his own head; but bein' a poor man and not bein' able to hire a teacher, of course he don't make much headway; don't git along nigh so well. He haint got but one gesture broke in so he can handle it to any advantage, and that is: pointin' his forefinger at the audience, with the rest of his hand shet up; dartin' it out sometimes, as if it was a bayonet he was goin' to run through their hearts; and sometimes holdin' it back, and takin' a more distant and deliberate aim with it, as if it was a popgun he kep' by him to shoot down congregations with. That is all he has got at present; but truly, he does the best he can, with what he has to do with. It don't scare the audience so much I s'pose as he thinks it ort to, and he probable gits discouraged; but he ort to consider that he can't show off much in gestures, while Solomon Cypher is livin'. A kerosine lamp can't show off to any advantage when the sun gits up. But the President done well as I said, with what he had to do with. He pinted that forefinger almost threatningly in every direction, from Zenith to Nathan, as he went on to say: he hadn't no personal objections to Josiah Allen's wife, *"fur frummit."*

Cornelius Cork bein' a poor man, and shackled with the support of four maiden sisters of his own, and a mother-in-law and a grandmother-in-law of his wife's, besides a large family of children of their own, haint never felt able to own a dictionary, and so he pronounces by ear, and makes mistakes. But considerin' his circumstances and shackles, I don't think he ort to be run down for it. It makes it very bad, sometimes, for Solomon Cypher, for he bein' so took up with gestures and motions, and bein' one easy led astray by them that are in high office, he follers on blindly after the President and uses lots of words he wouldn't dremp of usin', if he hadn't heerd the President use 'em. It makes it bad for Solomon, very.

The President repeated the words again, with dignity and emphasis: *"fur frummit."* He trusted he realized too well whose tower it was, that bein' gone off on, had lifted Jonesville fur up above surroundin' nations; had lifted it high up on fame's towerin' pillow, and shed a lurid light on the housen thereof. He trusted he was too familiar with that noble book of hern, of which he had read the biggest heft, and was calculatin' to tackle the rest of it if he lived long enough. And he had said, and he said still, that such a book as that, was liable to live and go down to Posterity, if Posterity didn't git shiftless and hang off too long. And if anybody said it wasn't liable to, he called 'em "traitor, to the face; traitor to Jonesville; traitor to Josiah Allen's wife; traitor to Josiah."

His face got red as blood, and he sweat considerable, he talked so hard, and got so excited, and pointed that forefinger so powerful and frequent at the audience, as if he was — in spirit — shootin' 'em down like wild turkeys.

Jest as quick as he collected breath enough, he went on to say that though nobody could go ahead of him in honorin' that esteemable woman, still he sot principle up in his mind above any other female; higher even than Josiah Allen's wife. It was solid principle he was upholdin'; the principle of the male sex not bein' infringed upon; that was his stand. Says he, "For a female woman to talk in public on such momentous and weighty subjects — subjects that weigh I don't know what they wont weigh but this I know: every one will be hefty; — for a female woman to talk on those deep and perhaps awful subjects as they are a bein' brung up, would have a dangerous tendency to make a woman feel as if she was equal to man. It would have a tendency to infringe on him; and if there is anything a man can't, nor wont stand, it is infringin'. And it would also bring her into too close contract with him; and so, on them grounds, as a Latin author observes in a similar case: 'I deny her the right *in tato toto.*'"

That was Latin, and I s'pose he thought it would scare me, but it didn't a mite; for I don't s'pose he knew what it meant no more'n I did. I bound off my heel with composure. But the excitement was fearful; no sooner would them on one side make a motion, than them on the other side would git up and make a different motion. You know when sheep go to jumpin' over the fence, if one goes, they all want to go. There was the awfulest sight of motions made, I ever see; everybody was jumpin' up and makin' 'em. Why, one spell, I had to lay holt of

Josiah Allen and hold him down by main strength, or he'd been up a makin' 'em; he wanted to, and tried to, but I laid holt of him and argued to him. Says I:

"Let 'em fight it out; don't you make a single motion, Josiah Allen."

And Josiah, feelin' clever, consented not to, and sot still, and I went to knittin' again. But it was a scene of almost fearful confusion, and excitement. No sooner had the President sot down, sayin' he denied me the right "*in tato toto*," than Simon Slimpsey got up (with difficulty) and says he, in a almost thick tone:

"I think taint best to give her the potato."

He had been a drinkin' and didn't know what he was sayin'. He sot down again right off—had to—for he couldn't stand up. But as he kinder fell back on his seat, he kep' a mutterin' that "she did'nt ort to have the potato give her; she didn't know enough to plant the tater, or hoe it—she hadn't ort to have it."

Nobody minded him. But Solomon Cypher jumped up, and says he, smitin' his breast with his right hand:

"I motion she haint no right to talk." And again he smote his breast almost severely.

"I motion you tell on what grounds you make the motion!" says the Editor of the Gimlet, jumpin' up and throwin' his head back nobly.

"I motion you set down again," says the President,—takin' aim at him as if he was a mushrat—"I motion you set down and give him a chance to git up and tell why he made the motion."

So the Editor of the Gimlet sot down, and Solomon Cypher riz up:

"I stand on this ground," (says he, stampin' down his right foot) "and on this ground I make my motion:" (says he, stampin' down his left one, and smitin' himself a almost dangerous blow in the breast) "that this society haint no place for wimmen. Her mind haint fit for it; '*fur frummit*,' as my honored friend, the President observes,—'*fur frummit*.' There is deep subjects a goin' to be brung up here, that is all *my* mind can do, to rastle with and throw 'em; and for a female woman's mind to tackle 'em, it would be like settin' a pismire to move a meetin' house. Wimmen's minds is weak."

Here he smote himself a fearful blow right in the pit of his stomach, and repeated the words slowly and impressively:

"Wimmen's minds is weak. But this haint the main reason why I make my motion. My main reason is, that I object, and I always will—while I have got a breath left in my body—object to the two sexes a

comin' — as my honored friend the President says — 'in such close contract with each other, as they would have to if wimmen took any part
with men in such public affairs. Keep separate from each other! that is
my ground, and that is my motion. Keep wimmen off as fur as you can,
if you would be safe and happy. Men has their place," says
he, — stridin' forred a long step with his right foot, and stretchin' up his
right arm nobly towards the sky as fur as he could with safety to his
armpit — "and wimmen has hern!" — steppin' back a long step with his
left foot, and pintin' down with his left hand, down through a hole in
the floor, into the cellar — "and it is necessary for the public safety,"
says he, — a smitin' his breast, first with his right hand and then with his
left — "that he keep hisen, and she hern. As the nation and individuals
are a goin' on now, everything is safe." (Here he stopped and smiled.)
"The nation is safe." (Another smile.) "And men and wimmen are safe,
for they don't come in contract with each other." (Here he stopped and
smiled three times.) "But if wimmen are ever permitted in the future to
take any part in public affairs; if they are every permitted to come in
contract with man, and bring thereby ruin, deep, deadly ruin onto
Jonesville and the world, I want Jonesville and the world to remember
that I have cleared *my* coat-skirts in the matter. I lift 'em out of the
fearful and hazardous enterprise."

He had an old-fashioned dress coat on, with long skirts, that come
most to the floor, and as he said this, he lifted 'em up with a almost
commandin' air, as if he was a liftin' 'em out of black mud. He lifted
'em right up, and they stood out in front of his arms, some like wings;
and, as he stood lookin' round the audience, in this commandin' and
imposin' position, he repeated the words in a more lofty and majestic
tone:

"I clear *my* coat-skirts of the hull matter. You *see* me clear 'em. None
of the bloody ruin can be laid onto *my* coat-skirts."

It was a thrillin' moment. It had a terribly depressin' effect on a great
many lovers of justice and wimmen's votin', who was present. They see
the dangers hedgin' in the enterprise, as they never see 'em before.
They see the power of the foe they was fightin' ag'inst, and trembled
and quailed before him. But though I realized well what was a goin' on
before me, though I knew what a deadly blow he was a givin' to the
cause, I held firm, and kep' a cool mean, and never thought for half a
moment of givin' up my shield. And then I knew it wasn't so much his
words — although they was witherin' — as his lofty majesty of bearin',

that influenced the almost breathless audience. He stood in that commandin' posture, I have described, for I should judge, nearly one moment and a half, and then he repeated the words:

"For I say unto you," — and here he dropped his coat-skirts suddenly,
and struck himself in the breast a sudden and violent blow with his
thumb, — the fingers all standin' out straight, like the bones of a fan —
"for I say unto you; and if these are the last words you shall ever hear
from my humble but perfectly honorable mouth, — remember, Jonesville and the world, that I died a sayin', beware of the female pole."

I never in my hull life heerd a pole sound so faint and sickly as that
pole did. It dwindled away almost to nothin', and he kinder shet his
eyes up and sallied away, as if he was a goin to die off himself. It skairt
some of the wimmen most to death, it was so impressive; but I knew it
was all the effect of high trainin'; I knew he would come to in a minute,
and he did. Pretty soon he kinder repeated the words, in a sickly tone:

"Remember, I died a sayin': beware of the female pole. Beware.
beware!!"

And oh, how skairt them wimmen was again; for he straightened
right up and yelled out them two bewares, like a couple of claps of
thunder; and his eyes kep' a growin' bigger and bigger, and his voice
grew louder and louder, till it seemed as if it would raise the very ruff
— though it had jest been new shingled, (cost the deestrick 20 dollars,)
— and he looked round the audience as wise as any owl I ever laid eyes
on, and struck himself a very fearful blow with his thumb, right on his
stomach, and says he:

"Beware of bein' infringed upon!" — and then followed another
almost dangerous blow — "Beware of that terrible and fearful day,
when men and wimmen shall come in contract with each other."

He stopped perfectly still, looked all round the house with that wise
and almost owl-like look on him, and then in a slow, impressive, and
eloquent manner, he raised his hands and struck his breast bone with
both thumbs and sot down. Some of the speakers seemed to be real en-
vious of his gestures, but they ort to have considered that it was all in
knowin' how; it was all in practice. He'd probably studied on every
motion for days and days, and they hadn't ort to have begreched 'em so
to him. But if he hadn't never studied on elocution and impressive ges-
turin'; if he hadn't looked a mite like an owl for solemnity and wisdom,
his talk would have been dretful impressive and scareful to some, he
painted it all out in such high colors, what a terrible and awful thing it

would be for the two sects to ever come in "contract with each other." I s'pose he meant contact, — I haint a doubt of it.

Why, to have heerd him go on, if there had been a delegate present to the "Creation Searchin' Society," from the moon — or any other world adjacent to Jonesville — he wouldn't have had any idee that men and wimmen had ever got any nearer to each other than from half to three-quarters of a mile. I s'pose I never could have made that foreigner believe, if I had talked myself blind, that, for all Solomon Cypher showed such deadly fear of men comin' in "contract" with wimmen, he had lived with one forty years; drinked out of the same dipper; slept together Sundays in the same pew of the same meetin' house; and brought up a big family of children together, which belonged to both on 'em.

Howsumever, them was the facts of the case; but I let him go on, for principle held me down, and made me want to know how it would end; whether freedom, and the principles of our 4 fathers would triumph, or whether they would be quirled up like caterpillers, and be trod on.

I knew in my mind I shouldn't git up and talk, not if they voted me in ten times over, for reasons that I give more formally; and besides them reasons, I was lame, and had ruther set and knit, for Josiah needed his socks; and I have always said, and I say still, that a woman ort to make her family comfortable, before she tackles the nation, or the heathen, or anything.

So they kep' on a fightin', and I kep' on a knittin'; and upheld by principle, I never let on but what I was dyin' to git up and talk. They got awful worked up on it; they got as mad as hens, every one on 'em, all but Josiah. He sot by me as happy as you please, a holdin' my ball of yarn. He acted cleverer than he had in some time; he was awful clever and happy; and so was I; we felt well in our 2 minds, as we sot there side by side, while the fearful waves of confusion and excitement, and Cornelius Cork and Solomon Cypher, was a tostin' to and fro about us.

And oh, how happyfyin' and consolin' and satisfyin' to the mind it is, when the world is angry and almost mad at you, to set by the side of them you are attached to by links considerable stronger than cast iron. In the midst of the wildest tempests, you feel considerable safe, and some composed. No matter if you don't speak a word to them, nor they to you, their presence is sufficient; without 'em, though you may be surrounded by admirin' congregations, there is, as the poet says, "a goneness;" the biggest crowds are completely unsatisfactory, and dwindle down to the deepest lonesomeness. Though the hull world should be a holdin' you up, you would feel tottlin' and lonesome, but the presence of the one beloved, though he or she — as the case may be — may not be hefty at all, still is large enough to fill a meetin' house, or old space himself without 'em; and truly, when heart leans upon heart, (figgeratively speakin') there is a rest in it that feather beds cannot give, neither can they take away. My companion Josiah's face shines with that calm, reposeful happiness, when he is in my society, and I — although I know not why I do — experience the same emotions in hisen.

Finally, at half past eleven — and they was completely tuckered out on both sides — the enemies of wimmen's suffragin' and justice, kinder all put together and brought in a motion, Solomon Cypher bein' chief bearer and spokesman of the procession. They raised him up to this prominent position, because he was such a finished speaker. The motion was clothed upon in eloquent and imaginative language. Solomon Cypher never got it up alone. Cornelius Cork, and the Editor of the Auger, and probable two or three others had a hand in it, and helped git it up. It had a almost thrillin' effect on the audience; though, by jest readin' it over, nobody can git any clear idee how it sounded to hear Solomon Cypher declaim it forth with appropriate and impressive gestures, and a lofty and majestic expression onto him. This was the motion:

"Be it resolved over, and motioned at, and acted upon by us, 'Creation Searchers and World Investigators,' that wimmen's body and mind, are both of 'em, as much too weak and feeble to tackle the subjects that will be brung up here, as a span of pismires are, to lay to and move a meetin' house."

After he had finished makin' the motion, he stood a moment and a half lookin' round on the audience with a smile on his lips, while such is the perfect control he has got by hard practice over his features, that at the same time his mouth was a smilin', there was a severe and even gloomy expression on the upper part of his face, and an empty and vacant look in his eyes. Then he smote himself meaningly and impressively in the pit of his stomach, and sot down. And then, as it was considerable still for a moment, I spoke calmly out of my seat to the Editor of the Gimlet, who happened to be a standin' near, and thanked him and the others on his side, for their labors in my behalf, and told 'em I hadn't no idee of takin' part in their Debatin'-school (I called it so before I thought), and hadn't had, none of the time. And then, with a calm and collected mean onto me, I knit in the middle of my needle, and Josiah wound up my ball of yarn, and we started for home . . .

NOTES

1. Horace Greeley (1811–72), editor and political leader, is perhaps most popularly remembered for his injunction to "Go West, young man." He was an "egalitarian who hated and feared all kinds of monopoly, landlordism, and class dominance. . . . He opposed capital punishment, urged freedom of speech and of the mails for abolitionists, advocated restriction of liquor-selling and supported cooperative shops and labor unions." (*Dictionary of American Biography*, p. 529) While he didn't believe in woman's suffage, he did sympathize with other parts of the woman's rights crusade. Greeley ran against Grant in the 1872 presidential election and lost resoundingly. His wife died that October; he became the "worst beaten man ever to run for high office" in November; he lost the editorship of the Tribune and died on November 29, insane. Holley takes some liberties, since the first edition of *My Opinions and Betsey Bobbet's*, wherein Samantha discusses the issue of nature with Greeley, was published in 1873.

2. See Selection 12. This reference is to Victoria Woodhull and Theodore Tilton.

3. Like her character, Marietta Holley's "fort" was not public speaking. See introduction for comments on her shyness.

III

"Megumness" and the Double Standard

> "The idee of thinkin' that the same sin when
> committed by a man and a woman ort to be laid
> entirely onto the party that is in the law classed
> with lunaticks and idiots." Sez she, "That hain't
> good logic. If a woman is a fool she hadn't ort to
> be expected to have her brain tapped and run
> wisdom and morality, and if she is a lunatick she
> might be expected to cut up and act."
> —W.C.T.U. lecturer in "The Male Magdalene"

Whether the subject is corsets, pantaloons, free love, or wild-eyed feminists, Samantha consistently advocates "megumness" and denigrates extremes in any direction. She also dutifully exposes the injustice of double standards of behavior and morality and argues again that one must walk all the way 'round a subject to see it clearly. Having done so, she contends, one should conclude that what is right or wrong for women is likewise right or wrong for men.

"Miss Flamm's Ideal Goddess"

12 "Interview with Theodore and Victory"

The young black African opened the door and says he, "Josiah Allen's wife, and Betsey Bobbet, mom." He had asked us our names jest before he opened it.

Miss Woodhull[1] was a standin' pretty near the door, a talkin' with 3 wimmin as we went in. But she come forward immediatly and put out her hand. I took it in mine, and shook it a very little, mebby 3 or 4 times back and forth. But she must have felt by that cool, cautious shake, that I differed from her in her views, and had come to give her a real talkin' to.

One of the wimmen she was a talkin' to, had jest about as noble a lookin' face as I ever see, with short white curls a fallin' all round it. The beholder could see by the first glance onto that face, that she hadn't spent all the immortal energies of her soul in makin' clover leaf tattin', or in cuttin' calico up into little pieces, jest to sew 'em togather agin into blazin' stars and sunflower bedquilts. It was the face of an earnest noble woman, who had asked God what He wanted her to do, and then hadn't shirked out of doin' it. Who had gripped holt of life's plough, and hadn't looked back because the furrows turned over pretty hard, and the stumps was thick.

She knew by experience that there was never any greensward so hard to break up, as old prejudices and customs; and no stumps so hard to get round as the ridicule and misconceptions of the world. What made her face look so calm then, when she was doin' all this hard work? Because she knew she was makin' a clearin' right through the wilderness that in the future was goin' to blossom like a rosa. She was givin' her life for others, and nobody ever did this since the days of Jesus, but what somethin' of his peace is wrote doun on thier forwards. That is the way Elizabeth Cady Stanton[2] looked to me, as Miss Woodhull in-

From *My Opinions and Betsey Bobbet's* (Hartford, 1891), pp. 313–35.

troduced me and Betsey to her, and to the two other ladies with her.

One of the other wimmen I fell in love with at first sight, and I suppose I should have been jest so partial to her if she had been as humbly as one of the Hotentots in my old Olney's Geography, and I'll tell you why, because she was the sister of H.W. Beecher. As a general thing I don't believe in settin' folks up, because they happen to have smart relations. In the words of one of our sweetest and noblest writers, "Because a man is born in a stable it don't make him a horse." Not as a general thing, it don't.

But not once in 100 years does Nature turn out such a man as H.W.B. It takes her longer than that to get her ingregiences and materials together to make such a pure sweet nature, such a broad charity, and such a intellect as hisen. Why, if the question had been put to me before I was born, whether I would be born his sister, or the twin sister of the queen of England, I'd never give a second thought to Miss Victoria Albert, not but what I respect the Widder Albert deeply, I think she is a real nice woman. But I had ruther be his sister than to be the sister of 21 or 22 other kings. For he is a king not make by the layin' on of earthly hands, he is God's own annointed, and that is a royalty that can't be upset. So as I remarked I s'pose Isabella Beecher Hooker[3] would have looked pretty good to me any way.

The other lady was smart and sensible lookin', but she was some like me, she wont never be hung for her beauty. This was Susan B. Anthony.[4] Betsey Bobbet sot down on a chair pretty nigh the door, but I had considerable talk with Susan. The other two was awful long discussin' some question with Miss Woodhull.

Susan said in the course of her remarks that "she had made the 'Cause of Wimmen's Rights,' her husband, and was going to cleave to it till she died."

I told her I was deeply interested in it, but I couldn't marry myself to it, because before gettin' acquainted with it, I had united myself to Josiah."

We had considerable reasonable and agreeable talk, such as would be expected from two such minds as mine and hern, and then the three ladies departed. And Miss Woodhull came up to me agin kinder friendly, and says she,

"I am glad to meet you Josiah Allen's wife," and then she invited me to set down. As I turned round to get a chair I see through a door into another room where sot several other wimmen — some up to a table, and all dreadful busy readin' papers and writin' letters. They looked so business-like and earnest at thier work, that I knew they could not have time to backbite thier neighbors, and I was glad to see it. As I took my seat I see a awful handsome gentleman settin' on a sofa — with long hair put back behind his ears, — that I hadn't ketched sight of before. It was Theodore Tilton, and Miss Woodhull introduced him to Betsey and me. He bowed to Betsey, but he came forward and took my hand in his'en. I couldn't refuse to take it, but I looked up in his handsome face with a look about two thirds admiration, and one of sorrow. If the handsomest and best feathered out angel, had fell right over the walls of heaven into our dooryard at Jonesville, I couldn't have give it a more piercin', and sort of pitiful look than I did him. I then turned and silently put my umberell in the corner and sot down. As I did so, Miss Woodhull remarked to Mr. Tilton,

"She is a Strong Wimen's Righter, she is one of us."

"No, Victory; I haint one of you, I am Josiah Allen's wife." Then I sithed. And says I, "Victory you are in the right on it, and you are in the wrong on it," and says I, "I come clear from Jonesville to try to set you right where you are wrong." Says I, almost overcome with emotion. "You are younger than I Victory, and I want to talk with you jest as friendly as if I was your mother in law."

Says she, "Where do you think I am in the right, and where do you think I am in the wrong?"

Says I, "You are right in thinkin' what a solemn thing it is to bring up children as they ought to be. What an awful thing it is to bring the little creeters into the world without their votin' on the subject at all, and then neglect 'em, and abuse 'em, and make their poor little days awful long in the world, and then expect them to honor you for it. You are right in your views of health, and wimmin's votin' and etcetery — but you are wrong Victory, and I don't want you to get mad at me, for I say it with as friendly feelins' as if I was your mother in law, — you are wrong in this free love business, you are wrong in keepin' house with two husbands at the same time."

"Two husbands! it is false; I was divorced from him, and my husband and I found him perishing in the streets, and we took him home and took care of him 'till he died. Which would the Lord have done Josiah Allen's wife, passed by on the other side, or took pity on him?

"I don't know what the Lord would have done, Victory, but I believe I should have sent him to a good horsepittle or tarven, and hired
him took care of. I never could stand it to have another husband in the
same house with me and Josiah. It would seem so kind o' curious, somethin' in the circus way. I never could stand it never."

"There have been a good many things Josiah Allen's wife that you
have not been required to stand, God and man united you to a good
husband whom you love. But in your happiness you should'nt forget
that some other woman has been less fortunate. In your perfect happiness, and harmony—"

"Oh!" says I candidly, "I don't say but what Josiah and me have had
our little spats, Victory. Josiah will go in his stockin' feet considerable
and—"

But she interrupted of me with her eyes a flashin',

"What would you say to livin' with a man that forgot every day of his
life that he was a man, and sunk himself into a brute. Leaving his
young wife of a week for the society of the abandoned? What would
you say to abuse, that resulted in the birth of a idiot child? Would you
endure such a life? Would you live with the animal that he had made
himself? I married a man, I never promised God nor man that I would
love, honor and obey the wild beast he changed into. I was free from
him in the sight of a pure God, long enough before the law freed me."

I let her have her say out, for Josiah Allen's wife is one to let every
man or mouse tell thier principles if they have got any. And if I was
conversin' with the overseer of the bottomless pit (I don't want to speak
his name right out, bein' a Methodist), I would give him a chance to get
up and relate his experience. But as she stopped with her voice kinder
choked up, I laid my brown cotton glove gently onto her shoulder, and
says I,

"Hush up, Victory," says I, "wimmen must submit to some things,
they can pray, and they can try to let thier sorrows lift 'em nearer to
heaven, makin' angels of 'em."

Here Mr. Tilton spoke up and says he, "I don't believe in the angels
exclusively, I don't see why there shouldn't be he angels, as well as she
ones."

I was tickled, and I looked at him approvin'ly, and says I,

"Theodore you are the first man with one exception that I ever see
that felt that way, and I respect you for it." Says I, "men as a general

thing think that wimmen have got to do up all the angel business there is done. Men seem to get the idee that they can do as they are a mind to and the Lord will wink at 'em. And there are lots of things that the world thinks would be awful coarse in a woman, but is all right in a man. But I don't believe a man's cigar smoke smells any sweeter to the Lord than a woman's would. And I don't believe a coarse low song, sounds any sweeter and purer in the ears of angels, because it is sung in a base voice instead of a sulfereno. I never could see why men couldn't do somethin' in the angel line themselves, as well as to put it all on to the wimmen, when they have got everything else under the sun to do. Not but what" says I, "I am willen' to do my part. I never was a shirk, and Josiah Allen will tell you so, I am willin' to do my share of the angel business." And says I, in a generous way, "I would do it all, if I only had time. But I love to see justice and reason. Nature feathers out geese and gander's equally, or if there is any difference the gander's wings are the most foamin' lookin'. Men's shoulders are made jest the same way that wimmen's are; feathers would look jest as well on 'em as on a woman, they can cultivate wings with jest as little trouble. What is the purest and whitest unseen feathers on a livin' angel's hidden wing, Theodore and Victory? They are purity, goodness, and patience, and men can grow these unbeknown feathers jest as easy as a woman can if they only set out."

I had spoke real eloquent, and I knew it, but I felt that I had been carried away slightly by my emotions, from the mission I had come on — to try to convince Miss Woodhull where she was wrong. And so after a minutes silence, I broke out agin mildly, for I felt that if I give way to anger or impatience my mission was lost.

"Another thing you are wrong in, Victory, is to think you can be lawfully married without any minister or justice of the peace. I knew that all you needed was to have it set before you plain by some female that wished you well; you are wrong in it, Victory, and I tell you so plain, and to show you that I am your well wisher, I thought after I had convinced you that you was in the wrong, I would make you this offer. That if you and Col. Blood will go home with Betsey and me, Elder Wesley Minkley shall marry you right in my parlor, and it shan't cost you a cent, for I will pay him myself in dried apples."

Says she, "I don't want any ceremony, I want the only tie to hold me to my husband to be love, the one sacred tie."

"Love is a first rate tie," says I, mildly, holdin' on to my temper first rate, "upwards of 15 years ago, I give one of the most remarkable proofs of it, that has ever been seen in this country;" (and for a minute my mind wandered off onto that old revery, *why* did I love Josiah Allen?) But collectin' my mind together I spoke onwards, with firm and cast iron principle. "Still, although I felt that sacred tie unitin' Josiah and me in a double beau knot that couldn't be untwisted, the first time we met, still, if Elder Wesley Minkley hadn't united us at the alter — or mother's parlor, I should have felt dreadful floatin' round in my mind. It would have seemed too curious and onstiddy kinder, as if Josiah and me was liable to fall all to pieces at any time, and waver off in the air like two kites that had broke loose from thier strings." Says I, firmly, "Thier would be a looseness to it, I couldn't stand."

She said I would get accustomed to it, and that custom made many things seem holy that were unholy, and many things sinful that were pure in the sight of God.

But still I murmured with a sad look, but firm as old Bunker Hill, "I couldn't stand it, Victory, it would seem too much like a circus."

"And then agin, Victory, you are in the wrong of it about divorces. 'What God has joined togather let no man put asunder.'"

Says she, "Josiah Allen's wife, if divorces were free to-morrow, would you get one from Josiah?"

"Never!" says I, and my best dress most bust open at the breast (them biases always was took up a little too snug) at the idee of partin' from Josiah.

"Well, what is it that would hold you so fast to each other that nothin' but death could separate you? was it the few words you said before the minister?"

"It was love, Victory! love, that wouldn't let me eat a mite, nor sleep a wink, if I couldn't put my hand onto Josiah Allen any time day or night."

"Then," says she, "why not give other good men and women credit for bein' actuated by the same sentiments? Those that God has joined togather, no man *can* put asunder. Those who are really married heart and sole, would never separate, it would only correct abuses, and separate those that man, and not God, had joined togather."

Says I, "Victory, is there any particular need of folks lettin' man join 'em togather, when God hasn't?" says I; "if folks was obleeged to marry, there would be some sense in such talk," says I, "they haint no business to marry if they don't love each other. All sin brings its punishment, and them that commit the crime aginst thier own sole, of marryin' without love, ought to be punished by unhappiness in thier domestic relations, what else can they expect?" says I. "Marriage is like baptism, now some folks say it is a savin' audence, I say nobody haint any right to be baptised unless they are saved already. Nobody haint any business to put on the outward form of marriage, if they haint got the inward marriage of the spirit."

"Some folks marry for a home," says she.

"Wall, they haint no business to," says I warmly. "I had ruther live out doors under a umberell, all my days."

"Those are my sentiments exactly, Josiah Allen's wife. But you can't deny that people are liable to be decieved."

"If they are such poor judges the first time, what would hender 'em from bein' decieved the next time, and so on, ad infinitum, to the twentieth and thirtieth time?" says I firmly. "Instead of folks bein' tied together looser, they ought to be tied as tight agin. If folks knew they couldn't marry agin, how many divorces do you suppose there would be? No doubt there are individual cases, where there is great wrong, and great sufferin'. But we ought to look out for the greatest good to the greatest number. And do you realize, Victory, what a condition society would be in, if divorces was absolutely free? The recklessness with which new ties would be formed, the lovin' wimmen's hearts that would be broken by desertion, the children that would be homeless and uncared for. When a fickle man or woman gets thier eyes onto somebody they like better than they do thier own lawful pardners, it is awful easy to think that man, and not God, has jined 'em. But let folks once get the idee into thier heads, that marriage is a solemn thing, and lasts as long as thier lives do, and they can't get away from each other, they will be ten times as careful to live peacible and happy with thier companions." Says I, "When a man realizes that he can if he wants to, start up and marry a woman before breakfast, and get divorced before dinner, and have a new one before supper time, it has a tendency to make him onstiddy and worrysome."

Says I, "Victory, men are dreadful tryin' by spells, do you suppose I have lived with one for upwards of 15 years, and hain't found it out? But suppose a mother deserts a child because he is wormy, and tears his breeches. She brought him into the world, and it is her duty to take care of him. Do you suppose a store keeper ought to take back a pink calico dress, after you have made it up, and washed it because the color washes out of it, you ought to have tried it before it was cut off. I married Josiah Allen with both eyes open, I didn't wear spectacles then, I wasn't starved to it nor thumbscrewed into it, and it is my duty to make the best of him."

Says she, "When a woman finds that her soul is clogged and hampered, it is a duty she owes to her higher nature to find relief."

Says I, "When a woman has such feelin's, instead of leavin' her lawful husband and goin' round huntin' up a affintee, let her take a good thoroughwert puke. Says I, in 9 and ½ cases out of 10, it is folkes'es stomachs that are clogged up insted of their souls. Says I, there is nothin' like keepin' the stomach in good order to make the moral sentiments run good. Now our Tirzah Ann, Josiah's girl by his first wife, I kinder mistrusted that she was fallin' in love with—" I almost said it right out Shakespeare Bobbet, but I thought of Betsey, and turned it "with a little feller that hadn't hardly got out of his roundabouts, she bein' at the same time in pantalettes. Well I give her a good thoroughwert puke, and it cured her, and if his mother," says I with a keen look onto Betsey, as I thought of my night of troubles, "If his mother had served him in the same way, it would have saved some folks a good deal of sufferin'."

I see that agin I was wanderin' off'en the subject, and I says in a deep solemn tone,

"I don't believe in this divorcin'."

Mr. Tilton spoke up for most the first time, and says he, "I think you are wrong in your views of divorce, Josiah Allen's wife."

I looked into his handsome face and my feelin's rose up strong I couldn't throw 'em, they broke loose and says I, in almost tremblin' tones,

"It is you that are in the wrong on it, Theodore," says I, "Theodore, I have read your poetry when it seemed as if I could ride right up to heaven on it, though I weigh 200 and 10 pounds by the steelyards. There is one piece by the name of 'Life's Victory.' I haint much of a hand for poetry, but I read it for the first time when I was sick, and it seemed as if it carried me so near to heaven, that I almost begun to feather out. And when I found out who the author was, he seemed as near to me as Thomas Jefferson, Josiah's boy by his first wife. Theodore, I have kept sight of you ever sense, jest as proud of you, as if you was my own son-in-law, and when you went off into this free love belief I felt bad." I took out my white 25 cent handkerchif, for a tear came within I should say half or three quarters of a inch from my eye-winkers. I held my handkerchif in my hand, the tear come nearer and nearer — he looked agitated — when up spoke Miss Woodhull.

"It is perfectly right; I believe in free divorce, free love, freedom in everything."

I jest jammed my handkerchif back into my pocket, for that tear jest turned round and traveled back to where it come from. I thought I had used mildness long enough, and I says to her in stern tones,

"Victory, can you look me straight in the spectacles, and say that you think this abominable doctrine of free love is right?"

"Yes mom, I can, I believe in perfect freedom."

Says I, "That is what burglers and incendiarys say," says I, "that is the word murderers and Mormans utter," says I "that is the language of pirates, Victory Woodhull."

She pretty near quailed, and I proceeded on, "Victory, there haint but one true liberty, and that is the liberty of the Gospel, and it haint Gospel liberty to be surrounded by a dozen husbands'es and ex-husbands'es," says I, "this marryin' and partin' every day or to, haint accordin' to Skripter."

Says she in a scornful tone, "What is skripter?" If I had been her mother I would have spanked her then and there. But I wasn't, and I jest turned my back to her, and says I, "Mr. Tilton you believe the bible don't you?"

"Yes mom, I do, but the bible justifies divorce."

"Yes," says I, "for one cause, and no other, and the Saviour says that whosoever marries a woman put away for any but the bible cause, commits adultery, and I don't believe in adulteration, nor Josiah don't either. But," says I, convulsivly, "You know a man will part with a woman nowadays if the butter don't come quick, and she will part with him if he don't hang up the bootjack. Is that bible Theodore?" Says I, "don't the bible say that except for that one reason, man and wife are married till death parts 'em. Says I, "is a lawyer in a frock coat, with a lot of papers stickin' out of his breast pocket, death?" Says I, "tell me Theodore is he death?"

He looked convinced, and says he, "No mom, he haint."

"Well then, what business has that little snip of a livin' lawyer to go round tryin' to make out he is death? tell me?" says I almost wildly.

I see my emotions was almost carryin' me off, and I ketched holt of my dignity, and continued in deep solemn tones,

"True marriage is a sacred thing, and it is a solemn thing, it is as solemn as bein' baptized. And if you are baptized once in the way you ought to be, it is enough. But the best way you can fix it, it is a solemn thing Victory. To give your whole life and soul into the keepin' of somebody else. To place all your hopes, and all your happiness in another human bein' as a woman will. A true woman if she loves truly, never gives half of her heart or three quarters, she gives it all. She never asks how much shall I get back in money and housen and finery? or whether she could do better in another direction. No; True Love is a river that runs onward askin' no questions of anybody, sweepin' right on with a full heart. And where does that river empty Theodore and Victory?"

They both looked as solemn as a protracted meetin', almost, as I looked at 'em, first one, then the other, through my specs; but they didn't reply. Says I, in a deep solemn tone, the name of the place where that river emptys is Eternity." Says I, "That river of True Love as it flows through the world gets riley sometimes, by the earthly mud on its banks. Sometimes it gets mad and precipitates itself over precipices, and sometimes it seemin'ly turns backward a spell. But in its heart it knows where it is bound for, it keeps on growin' broader, and deeper, and quieter like, and as it jines the ocian it leaves all its mud on the banks, for God cleanses it, and makes it pure as the pure waters it flows into."

I felt real eloquent as I said this, and it seemed to impress 'em as I wanted it to. They both of 'em have got good faces. Though I didn't like their belief, I liked their looks. They looked sincere and honest.

Agin I repeated, "Marriage is a solemn thing."

I heard a deep sithe behind me, and a sorrowful voice exclaimed,

"It is solemn then both ways, you say it is solemn to marry, and I know"—here was another deep sithe "I *know* it is solemn not to." It was Betsey, she was a thinkin' of the Editer of the Augur, and of Ebineezer, and of all the other dear gazelles, that lay cold and lifeless in her buryin' ground. I felt that I could not comfort her, and I was silent.

Miss Woodhull is a well bread woman, and so to kinder notice Betsey, and make talk with her, says she,

"I believe you are the author of these lines

'If wimmen had a mice's will,
They would arise and get a *bill?*' "

"Yes" says Betsey, tryin' to put on the true modesty of jenieus look. Miss Woodhull said "she had heard it sung to several free love conventions."

"How true it is" says Betsey glancin' towards Mr. Tilton, "that deathless fame sometimes comes by reason of what you feel in your heart haint the best part of you. Now in this poem I speak hard of man, but I didn't feel it Miss Woodhull, I didn't feel it at the time, I wrote it jest for fame and to please Prof. Gusheh. I love men," says she, glancin' at Mr. Tilton's handsome face, and hitchin' her chair up closer to his'en.

"I almost worship 'em."

Theodore began to look uneasy, for Betsey had sot down close by the side of him and says she,

"Did you ever read the soul stirrin' lines that Miss Woodhull refers to, I will rehearse them to you, and also three others of 25 verses apeice which I have wrote since on the same subject."

I see a cold sweat begin to break on his white and almost marble forward, and with a agitated move he ketched out his watch and says he,

"I have a engagement."

Says Betsey, beseechin'ly layin' her hand on his coat sleeve, "I can rehearse them in 26 or 27 minutes, and oh how sweet your sympathy would be to me, let me repeat them to you deah man."

A haggard look crept into his handsome eyes, and says he, wildly turnin' 'em away, "It is a case of life and death," and he hurried to the door.

But Betsey started up and got ahead of him, she got between him and the door, and says she, "I will let you off about hearin' the poetry — but oh! listen to my otheh prayer."

"I *wont* listen to your prayer," says he, firmly.

"In the name of the female wimmen of America who worship you so, pause, and heah my prayer."

He paused deeply agitated, and says he. "In their name I will hear you, what is your request Betsey Bobbet?"

She clasped her hands in a devotional way, and with as beseechin' and almost heart meltin' a look as a dog will give to a bone held above its head, she murmured,

"A lock of youh haih deah man, that I may look at it when the world looks hollow to me, a lock of youh haih to make my life path easier to me."

I turned my spectacles on which principle sot enthroned, towards 'em, and listened in awful deep interest to see how it would end. Would he yield or not? He almost trembled. But finally he spoke.

"Never! Betsey Bobbet! never!" and he continued in low, agitated tones, "I have got jest enough to look well now."

My heart throbbed proudly, to see him comin' so nobly through the hot furnace of temptation, without bein' scorched. To see him bein' lifted up in the moral steelyards, and found full weight to a notch. But alas! Jest as small foxes will gnaw into a grape vine, jest so will dangerous and almost loose principles gnaw into a noble and upright nature unbeknown to them.

Agin Betsey says in harrowin' tones, at the same time ketchin' holt of his coat skirts wildly,

"If you can't part with any more, give me one haih, to make my life path smootheh."

Alas! that my spectacles was ever bought to witness the sad sight. For with a despairin', agonized countenance such as Lucifer, son of Mr. Mornin' might have wore as he fell doun, Theodore plucked a hair out of his foretop, threw it at Betsey's feet, and rushed out doors. Betsey with a proud, haughty look, picked it up, kissed it a few times, and put it into her portmoney.

But I sithed.

I hadn't no heart to say anything more to Victory. I bid her farewell. But after we got out in the street, I kept a sithin'.

NOTES

1. Victoria Woodhull, "a woman of beauty and wit, championed woman's rights, as well as free love, spiritualism and quack healing. . . ." (Flexner, *Century of Struggle*, pp. 153–54). With her sister, Tennessee Claflin, she published a weekly in which she publicized the affair between Rev. Henry Ward Beecher and Mrs. Elizabeth Tilton. Mrs. Woodhull was also a protégeé of Commodore Cornelius Vanderbilt and ran for President in 1872. Says Kraditor in *Ideas of the Woman*

Suffrage Movement 1890–1920: "Suffragists never advocated lowering women's moral standards to the level of men's. Victoria Woodhull and her sister Tennessee Claflin, never for a moment represented suffragist thinking" (p. 93).

Henry Ward Beecher, one of the most popular preachers in America and the first President of the American Women Suffrage Association, was accused of seducing Elizabeth Tilton, one of his parishioners and wife of reform editor Theodore Tilton. Tilton brought Beecher to trial for misconduct; then Tilton himself was accused of misconduct with Victoria Woodhull, who published news of the prolonged Beecher-Tilton love affair in her paper in November 1871. (This "vindication" is reprinted in Cott, *Roots of Bitterness*, pp. 256–60). The sensational trial dragged on for weeks and eventually ended in a hung jury. Meanwhile the American public had taken sides for or against the principles in the case, and the linkage between free love and suffrage as symbolized in the Beecher-Tilton affair was detrimental to the movement. See Andrew Sinclair, *The Emancipation of the American Woman*, p. 192; Kraditor, *Ideas of the Woman Suffrage Movement 1890–1920*, p. 93; Flexner, *Century of Struggle*, p. 154; Clifford Clark, *Henry Ward Beecher: Spokesman for a Middle-Class America* (Urbana, Ill., 1978).

2. Elizabeth Cady Stanton (1815–1902) was a founding mother of the American women's rights movement. An abolitionist, she (and Susan B. Anthony) led the National Woman Suffrage Association formed in 1869 while Lucy Stone and Henry Ward Beecher led the American Woman Suffrage Association formed the same year. Anthony and Stanton thought the Fourteenth Amendment, which gave Negroes the right to vote but inserted the word "male" into the Constitution for the first time, should be defeated. Stone and others disagreed, saying that it was good that Negro men at least had won their political freedom. In 1890 the groups merged into the National American Woman Suffrage Association, with Stanton the first and Anthony the second president of this coalition.

Stanton was instrumental in including the demand for the ballot in the "Declaration of Sentiments" (modeled on the Declaration of Independence) which came out of the 1848 Seneca Falls (New York) meeting which now commonly serves as the originating date for the women's rights movement. In the 1890s she and others wrote *The Woman's Bible*, commentaries in which they demonstrated that the subjection of women was not divinely ordained. This work was not endorsed by the mainstream of the suffrage movement. For accounts of Stanton's contributions to the movement, see the six-volume collections of speeches, writings, etc., *History of Woman Suffrage*, the first three of which were edited by Stanton, Anthony, and Matilda Joslyn Gage. Some of those documents, including the "Declaration of Sentiments" and excerpts from *The Woman's Bible* are reprinted in Kraditor, *Up*

From the Pedestal. For her reminiscences from 1815–97, see Stanton's *Eighty Years and More* (New York, 1971).

3. It is ironic that Samantha sees Isabella, sister of the famous H. W. Beecher, in that both of her half-sisters, Catharine Beecher and Harriet Beecher Stowe, were more famous and probably more recognizable to the reader. Isabella was a women's rights activist, Catharine was an educator and writer who founded Hartford Female Seminary and attempted to expand the domestic power of women, and Harriet was the author of *Uncle Tom's Cabin.*

4. Susan B. Anthony (1820–1906) initially worked in the temperance movement and joined her new cause in 1854 when she organized a drive to petition the New York legislature for three reforms: control by women of their own earnings, guardianship of their children in case of divorce, and the vote. See Flexner, *Century of Struggle*, pp. 83–89, for Anthony's beginnings in the movement. Though there are other, recent biographies, the three-volume biography by Ida Husted Harper remains a good source for information both on the movement and the role played by Anthony.

Says Flexner of Anthony's political insight and her role over the years: "Such political acumen was something new in a woman; so was the organizational ability required for the job. If Lucretia Mott typified the moral force of the movement, if Lucy Stone was its most gifted orator and Mrs. Stanton its outstanding philosopher, Susan Anthony was its incomparable organizer, who gave it force and direction for half a century" (*Century of Struggle*, p. 84). Unlike Stanton who married and bore seven children, Anthony remained single.

Holley has provided Samantha with an illustrious group to drop in on.

13 "A Wimmen's Rights' Lecturer"

As we wended our way back to Miss Asters'es to dinner, Betsey said she guessed after all she would go and take dinner to her cousin Ebeneezer's, for her Pa hadn't give her much money. Says she,

"I hate to awfully. It is revoltin' to all the fineh feelings of my nature to take dinneh theah, afteh I have been so—" she stopped suddenly, and then went on agin. "But Pa didn't make much this yeah, and he didn't give me much money, he nor Ma wouldn't have thought they could have paid my faih heah on the cars if they hadn't thought certain, that Ebeneezah's wife would be took from us, and I—should do my duty by coming. So I guess I will go theah and get dinneh."

Thinks'es I to myself, "If your folks had brought you up to emanual labor, if they had brought you up to any other trade only to get married, you might have money enough of your own to buy one dinner independent, without dependin' on some man to earn it for you." But I didn't say nothin', but proceeded onwards to the tavern where I put up. When I got there I met Johnothan Beane'es ex wife, and says she,

"Oh, I forgot, there is a lady here that wanted to see you when you got back."

"Who is it," says I.

"It is a female lecturer on wimmen's rights," says she.

"Well," says I, "Principle before vittles, is my theme, fetch her on."

Says she, "Go into your room and I'll tell her you have come, and bring her there. She is awful anxious to see you."

"Well," says I, "I'm visible to the naked eye, she won't have to take a telescope," and in this calm state of mind I went into my room and waited for her.

Pretty soon she came in.

Jonothan Beans'es ex wife introduced us, and then went out. I rose

From *My Opinions and Betsey Bobbet's* (Hartford, 1891), pp. 336–46.

up and took holt of her hand, but I give sort of a catious shake, for I
didn't like her looks.[1] Of all the painted, and frizzled, and ruffled, and
humped up, and laced down critters I ever see, she was the cap sheaf.
She had a hump on her back bigger than any camel's I ever see to a
managery, and no three wimmen ever grew the hair that critter had
piled on to her head.

I see she was dissapointed in my looks. She looked dreadful kinder
scornful down onto my plain alpaca, which was made of a sensible
length. Her's hung down on the carpet. I'll bet there was more'n a
bushel basket of puckers and ruffles that trailed down on to the floor
behind her, besides all there was on the skirt and waist.

She never said a word about my dress, but I see she looked awful
scornful on to it. But she went on to talk about Wimmen's Rights, and I
see she was one of the wild eyed ones, that don't use no reason. I see
here was another chance for me to do good — to act up to principle.
And as she give another humiliatin' look onto my dress, I become fully
determined in my own mind, that I wouldn't shirk out from doin' my
duty by her, and tell her jest what I thought of her looks. She said she
had just returned from a lecturin' tower out in the Western States, and
that she had addressed a great many audiences, and had come pretty
near gettin' a Wimmen's Right's Governor chosen in one of the States.[2]
She got to kinder preachin' after a while, and stood lookin' up towards
the cealin', and her hands stretched out as if she was a lecturin'. Says
she,

"Tyrant man shan't never rule us." Says I, "I haint no objection to
your makin' tyrant man better, if you can — there is a chance for im-
provement in 'em — but while we are handlin' 'motes,' sister, let us remember that we have got considerable to do in the line of 'beams.'"
Says I, "To see a lot of immortal wimmen together, sometimes, you
would think the Lord had forgot to put any brains into their heads, but
had filled it all up with dress patterns, and gossip, and beaux, and
tattan."

"Tyrant man has encouraged this weakness of intellect. He has for
ages made woman a plaything; a doll; a menial slave. He has encouraged her weakness of comprehension, because it flattered his self love
and vanity, to be looked up to as a superior bein'. He has enjoyed her
foolishness."

"No doubt there is some truth in what you say, sister, but them days
are past. A modest, intelligent woman is respected and admired now,

more than a fool. It is so in London and New York village, and," says I with some modesty, "it is so in Jonesville."

"Tyrant man," begun the woman agin. "Tyrant man thinks that wimmen are weak, slavish idiots, that don't know enough to vote. But them tyrants will find themselves mistaken."

The thought that Josiah was a man, came to me then as it never had before. And as she looked down from the cealin' a minute on to my dress with that scornful mene, principle nerved me up to give her a piece of my mind.

Says I, "No wonder men don't think that we know enough to vote when they see the way some wimmen rig themselves out. Why says I, a bachelder that had always kept house in a cave, that had read about both and hadn't never seen neither, would as soon take you for a dromedary as a woman."

She turned round quicker'n lightnin', and as she did so, I see her hump plainer'n ever.

Says she, "Do you want to insult me?"

"No," says I, "my intentions are honorable, mom."

"But," says I, puttin' the question plain to her, "would you vote for a man, that had his pantaloons made with trails to 'em danglin' on the ground, and his vest drawed in to the bottom tight enough to cut him into, and his coat tails humped out with a bustle, and somebody else's hair pinned on the back of his head? Would you?" says I solemnly fixin' my spectacles keenly onto her face. "Much as I respect and honor Horace Greeley, if that pureminded and noble man should rig himself out with a bustle and trailin' pantaloons, I wouldn't vote for him, and Josiah shouldn't neither."

But she went right on without mindin' me—"Man has always tried to dwarf our intellects; cramp our souls. The sore female heart pants for freedom. It is sore! and it pants."

Her eyes was rolled up in her head, and she had lifted both hands in a eloquent way, as she said this, and I had a fair view of her waist, it wasn't much bigger than a pipe's tail. And I says to her in a low, friendly tone, "Seein' we are only females present, let me ask you in a almost motherly way, when your heart felt sore and pantin' did you ever loosen your cosset strings? Why," says I, "no wonder your heart feels sore, no wonder it pants, the only wonder is, that it don't get discouraged and stop beatin' at all."

She wanted to waive off the subject, I knew, for she rolled up her eyes higher than ever, and agin she began "Tyrant man—"

Agin I thought of Josiah, and agin I interrupted her by sayin', "Men haint the worst critters in the world, they are as generous and charitable agin, as wimmen are, as a general thing."

"Then what do you want wimmen to vote for, if you think so?"

"Because I want justice done to every human bein'. Justice never hurt nobody yet, and rights given through courtesy and kindness, haint so good in the long run, as rights given by law. And besides, there are exceptions to every rule. There are mean men in the world as well as good ones. Justice to wimmen won't prevent charitable men from bein' charitable, generous men from bein' generous, and good men from bein' good, while it will restrain selfishness and tyrany. One class was never at the mercy of another, in any respect, without that power bein' abused in some instances. Wimmen havin' the right to vote haint a goin' to turn the world over to once, and make black, white, in a minute, not by no means. But I sincerely believe it will bring a greater good to the female race and to the world."

Says I, in my most eloquent way, "There is a star of hope a risin' in the East for wimmen. Let us foller on after it through the desert of the present time, not with our dresses trailin' down onto the sandy ground, and our waists lookin' like pismires, and our hair frizzled out like maniacs. Let us go with our own hair on our heads, soberly, decently, and in order; let us behave ourselves in such a sober, christian way, that we can respect ourselves, and then men will respect us."

"I thought" says she, that you was a pure Wimmen's Righter! I thought you took part with us in our warfare with our foeman man! I thought you was a firm friend to wimmen, but I find I am mistaken."

"I *am* a friend to wimmen," says I, "and because I am, I don't want her to make a natural born fool of herself. And I say agin, I don't wonder sometimes, that men don't think that wimmen know enough to vote, when they see 'em go on. If a woman don't know enough to make a dress so she can draw a long breath in it, how is she goin' to take deep and broad views of public affairs? If she puts 30 yards of calico into a dress, besides the trimmin's, how is she goin' to preach acceptably on political economy? If her face is covered with paint, and her curls and frizzles all danglin' down onto her eyes, how can she look straight and keenly into foreign nations and see our relations there? If a woman don't know enough to keep her dress out of the mud, how is she goin' to steer the nation through the mud puddle of politics? If a woman humps herself out, and makes a camel of herself, how is she goin' through the eye of a needle?"

I said these last words in a real solemn camp meetin' tone, but they seemed to mad her, for she started right up and went out, and I didn't care a cent if she did, I had seen enough of her. She ketched her trail in the door and tore off pretty nigh a yard of it, and I didn't cry about that, not a mite. I don't like these bold brazen faced wimmen that go a rantin' round the country, rigged out in that way, jest to make themselves notorious. Thier names hadn't ought to be mentioned in the same day, with true earnest wimmen who take thier reputations in thier hands, and give thier lives to the cause of Right, goin' ahead walkin' afoot through the wilderness, cuttin' down trees, and diggin' out stumps, makin' a path for the car of Freedom, that shall yet roll onward into Liberty . . .

NOTES

1. In this selection and the two following (On Pantaloons, On Miss Flamm's Ideal Goddess)) Samantha gives considerable attention to the extremes of dress and the relationship between mode of dress, ideas and practicality. In confronting the wild-eyed feminist, the dedicated woman physician, and the frivolous lady of fashion, Samantha finds all of their "costooms" wanting in "megumness" and common sense.

The relationship of one's clothing and the social role one is expected to play was not new to nineteenth-century America. In her article, "The Exquisite Slave: The Role of Clothes in the Making of the Victorian Woman," Helene Roberts underscores both Thackeray's and Carlyle's *(Sartor Resartus)* observations that clothing was not mere ornament but "emblems of society's hierarchy and symbols of the spirit." One of the obvious definitions made by dress, says Roberts, is sex role. "Normal or not, Victorian women had been taught that submissiveness and pain were related." Roberts describes the fashions of the 1830s and 1840s with sleeves set so low over the shoulder that the tightly encased arm could hardly be raised to shoulder height and with skirts that twisted about the knees, doubling fatigue and inhibiting movement. From the mid-1850s through most of the 1860s the crinoline, or cage, replaced the numerous floor-long petticoats. This "helpful invention . . . literally transformed women into caged birds surrounded by hoops of steel." Besides arresting convenient movement, these crinolines were flammable. Roberts quotes figures from the *English-Woman's Domestic Magazine* of 1867 reporting 3,000 women burned to death annually and another 20,000 injured because of the crinoline. By the late 1860s this fashion was in turn replaced by the tied-back skirt and train.

But the item of clothing in the nineteenth century that was most restraining was the corset, a "garment" designed to "change the configurations of the body to accord more closely with the feminine ideal of the small waist which haunted the period." It constricted the waist, thus enlarging hips and bust, but it also constricted the diaphragm, leading to various degrees of physical disability. Though historians of costume disagree about the waist size attained by the tightly laced woman, dimensions of seventeen or eighteen inches are often mentioned.

For her discussion of nineteenth-century dress, the practice of "baby stays" to train young waists, physical consequences, etc., see Roberts's article in Signs: Journal of Women in Culture and Society, 2:3 (Spring, 1977), 554–69. See also in the same volume David Kunzle's rebuttal, "Dress Reform as Antifeminism: A Response to Helene E. Roberts's 'The Exquisite Slave: The Role of Clothes in the Making of the Victorian Women,'" 570–79.

The "Bloomer costume," so called because Amelia Bloomer advocated it in The Lily (a temperance sheet converted to a women's rights paper) and wore it herself, consisted "of a tunic loosely belted at the waist, a skirt not much more than knee length, and—the most sensational feature—Turkish pantaloons which reached to the ankle." Though this costume afforded much more physical comfort than the aforementioned ones, the wearers became the butt of incessant ridicule. Eventually, the ridicule was seen by Elizabeth Cady Stanton, one of the first to adopt the bloomers, as a detriment to the cause and she urged Susan B. Anthony, who wanted to continue wearing them, to discard the costume. See Flexner, Century of Struggle, pp. 83–84, and Sinclair, The Emancipation of the American Woman, pp. 106–7. Also see the section "The Relation of Women's Fashions to Woman's Status," in Kraditor, Up From the Pedestal, pp. 122–36.

2. Women in some states did have either limited or full suffrage before the 1920 amendment. Specifically, the territory of Wyoming decreed full political equality in 1869 and in 1890 entered the union as the first state with full suffrage for women. Other western states followed—Colorado in 1893, Utah and Idaho in 1896. After that, women were not enfranchised again until the State of Washington in 1910. In 1911, California followed suit and in 1912 suffrage was adopted in Oregon, Kansas, and Arizona. The first state east of the Mississippi to give women the vote (though it was the vote for presidential electors rather than full suffrage) was Illinois in 1913. Thus over the next few years state after state enfranchised its women, electing representatives with women constituents. In 1917 New York voters approved a consti-

tutional amendment for full suffrage, and the ultimate success of national victory seemed assured.

As early as 1838 limited suffrage was exercised in some states. That year Kentucky gave its women the right to vote in school elections (under certain conditions); the next states to adopt school suffrage were Kansas in 1861, Michigan and Minnesota in 1875, and 13 other states by 1890. See Kraditor, *Ideas of the Woman Suffrage Movement 1890–1920*, pp. 3–4.

In her book *Frontier Women: The Trans-Mississippi West 1840–80*, Julie Roy Jeffrey argues that suffrage and coeducation were neither a liberating influence nor an indication of different attitudes toward women in the west. The motives, she says, were practical ones. The basis for suffrage defense was the domestic conception of women. In Utah, there was no argument that women were men's equals. They were to keep their place and vote as they were told by their men. The Mormon women's votes were seen as a device to neutralize the political power of Gentiles against polygamy. Jeffrey contends that the motives in Wyoming, though differing in detail, were inspired by equally conservative impulses. The territory had only a small permanent population; by granting women's suffrage, more stable and responsible settlers might be attracted to the territory.

14 On Pantaloons

. . . And as I stood there lookin' at the stiddy passin' crowd and philosophizin' on it as my nater is, I wuz accosted by a strange lookin' man, as I took it to be (I say It for reasons named hereafter).

"Josiah Allen's wife, I am happy to meet you; I knew you at once though it is so long since we met." In the meantime it had gripped holt of my hand with fervor.

I drawed back and sez, "sir!" (I thought it favored that gender most) "Sir, I think you are mistook."

"Oh, no, you are Josiah Allen's wife; I am Dr. Mary Walker."[1]

"Oh!" sez I in a relieved axent, as I returned the warm grasp of her hand, "I am glad to meet you, Mary."

She's done some good things in her life, takin' care of poor wounded soldiers, etc., and I honored her for 'em. Though I don't approve of her costoom, as I told her in the conversation that ensued, after we'd talked considerable about the Fair and kindred matters. For I see as we stood there behavin' ourselves, curious eyes wuz bent on her and onbecomin' epithets hurled at her by them who knowed no better. She seemed oblivious to 'em, but I asked her if she wouldn't rather wear less noticeable attire.

And she said she cared not for ribald remarks as long as her motives wuz pure.

And I said we could carry pure motives under a headdress of peacock's feathers standin' up straight over our foreheads, but wouldn't it be better to carry 'em under a bunnet?

"No better!" sez she. "Not a whit."

"Well, easier?" sez I. "Wouldn't it be easier for ourselves and bystanders?"

Sez she, "I care not for Public Opinion!"

From *Samantha at the St. Louis Exposition* (New York, 1904), pp. 145–49.

"But," sez I, "as long as we've got to live clost neighbor to Public Opinion wouldn't it be easier for us to fall in with his ideas a little on comparatively unimportant things than to keep him riled up all the time? It seems to me that if folks want to impress their personality on the world it is better to do it by noble deeds and words than by startlin' costooms."

Sez she, "My dress is fur more comfortable than the ordinary dress of females."

Sez I reasonably, "Short dresses are a boon and a blessin', but in my opinion they can be short enough for comfort and still not infringe on man's chosen raiment. And as for pantaloons, men are welcome to 'em so fur as I'm concerned, and also tall hats, they hain't nothin' I hanker for either on 'em."

Sez she, "We have a right to wear any clothes we see fit."

Sez I, "We have a right to plow green sword, shingle a steep barn ruff, or break a yoke of steers. But the question is, will it pay in comfort or economy to do this? As for me, I'd ruther be in the house in a comfortable dress and clean apron, cookin' a good dinner for Josiah, or settin' down knittin' his socks whilst he duz the harder work he is by nater and education fitted for. But everybody to their own mind. And so fur as I am concerned I'd ruther attract attention by doin' sunthin' worth while, sunthin' really noble and good, than by tyin' a red rag round my fore-top. But as I say, folks are different, and I am fur from sayin' that my way is the only right way."

Mary kinder waived off some of my idees and went on and spoke of her work on the battlefield and how necessary her dress wuz in such a place.

And I sez, "Mary, I've always honored you for your noble work there. But I believe I could lift up the head of a dyin' man easier in a loose gingham dress and straw bunnet tied on, than I could in your tight pantaloons and high hat, but howsumever the main thing is that the man is lifted, and he doubtless wouldn't quarrel about the costoom of his preserver. The main thing in this world, Mary, is the work we do, the liftin', or tryin' to lift; the day's work we do in the harvest field of Endeavor. And I spoze a few trousers more or less hain't goin' to count when we carry in our sheaves. Though I must say to the last, Mary Walker, I could carry 'em easier in my dress than I could in yourn."

In the heat of our good-natered conversation Mary had slipped her hand through my arm and neither of us noticed it, so wropped up wuz we in the topics under discussion, when I hearn Blandina's voice behind me sayin', "Oh, what a noble lookin' man Aunt Samantha is talkin' to and how affectionate actin'; how sweet it will be to meet him." And then I hearn a sharp raspin' voice clost to me sayin':

"Sir, I will thank you to onhand my wife!"

I wouldn't hardly have knowed my pardner's voice, such burnin' anger showed in it and wuz depictered on his liniment as I turned round and faced him. And he went on.

"Samantha, have I lived with you most a century to be deceived in you now?"

His turrible emotions had onhinged his reasonin' faculties, we hain't lived together so long as that, but I didn't dane to argy, I only sez with calm dignity:

"Miss Walker, this is my pardner, Josiah Allen."

"*Miss!*" sez he in a overbearin' axent, "*Miss* Walker!" He looked as if he thought it wuz a conspiracy hatched up between us to deceive him.

"Yes," sez I coolly, "Miss Walker, Dr. Mary Walker."

"Oh!" sez Josiah, in his surprise and relief not offerin' to bow or shake hands or nothin'. "Dear Samantha, I've hearn on her." And he turned and linked his hand in my other arm so for a minute we looked like three twins perambulatin' along. In the meantime I introduced Blandina, who looked bewildered and disappinted.

But Dr. Mary Walker remembered a engagement, and to my relief took leave on us . . .

NOTE

1. A long-time women's rights advocate, Dr. Mary Walker served as nurse then spy then assistant surgeon in the Union army and routinely wore men's clothing. The Medal of Honor was originally awarded to Dr. Walker on November 11, 1865, by President Andrew Johnson, but was later rescinded when the criteria for the award were changed. Walker refused to return the medal and made numerous attempts to have the decision reversed. On June 10, 1977, the assistant secretary of the army signed an order to reinstate the award and correct the official records. A commemorative stamp now honors Dr. Mary Walker for her unique achievement.

15   On Miss Flamm's Ideal Goddess

. . . And Miss Flamm took her dog into her arms seemin'ly glad to get holt of him ag'in, and kissed it several times with a deep love and devotedness. She takes good care of that dog. And what makes it harder for her to handle him is, her dress is so tight, and her sleeves. I s'pose that is why she can't breathe any better, and what makes her face and hands red, and kinder swelled up. She can't get her hands to her head to save her, and if a assassin should strike her, she couldn't raise her arm to ward off the blow if he killed her. I s'pose it worrys her.

And she has to put her bunnet on jest as quick as she gets her petticoats on, for she can't lift her arms to save her life after she gets her corsets on. She owned up to me once that it made her feel queer to be a walkin' round her room with not much on only her bunnet all trimmed off with high feathers and artificial flowers.

But she said she wuz willin' to do anythin' *necessary*, and she felt that she *must* have her waist taper, no matter what stood in the way on't. She loves the looks of a waist that tapers. That wuz all the fault she found with the goddus of Liberty enlightenin' the world in New York Harber. We got to talkin' about it and she said, "If that Goddus only had corsets on, and sleeves that wuz skin tight, and her overskirt looped back over a bustle, it would be perfect!"

But I told her I liked her looks as well ag'in as she wuz. Why, sez I, "How could she lift her torch above her head? And how could she ever enlighten the world, if she wuz so held down by her corsets and sleeves that she couldn't wave her torch?"

She see in a minute that it couldn't be done. She owned up that she couldn't enlighten the world in that condition, but as fur as looks went, it would be perfectly beautiful.

From *Samantha at Saratoga* (Philadelphia, 1887), pp. 295–7.

16 "A Male Magdalene"

I attended a beautiful party yesterday; it wuz a anniversary, and carried on regardless of style and expense. Over seven wuz invited, besides the happy folks who gin the party. And the cookin' wuz, I do almost believe, as good as my own. That's dretful high praise, but Miss Chawgo deserves it. It wuz to celebrate their weddin' day, which occurred the year before at half past two, and dinner wuz on the table at exactly that hour.

There wuz Josiah and me, Miss Bizer Kipp and Lophemia, she that wuz Submit Tewksbury, and her husband, and Widder Bassett and her baby. That made a little over seven; the baby hadn't ort to count so high as a adult. The party wuz all in high sperits, and all dressed well and looked well, though Miss Bassett whispered to me that Miss Kipp had flammed out a little too much.

She wuz very dressy in a pink flowered shally with lots of ribbins kinder floatin', but she felt and said that she wuz celebratin' a very auspicious occasion with very dear friends, which made us lenitent to her. Weddin' anniversaries are now and agin happy and agreeable, and the male party here, Nelt Chawgo, how much! how much that young man had to be thankful for! yes indeed!

And Id'no but I might jest as well tell about it now as any time while in history's pages the gay party is settin' 'round the bountifully spread table.

I'll make the story short as possible. Most three years ago we had a new arrival in Jonesville, a young grocery man by the name of Nelson Chawgo; the young folks all called him Nelt. He bought out old uncle Simon Pettigrew, his good will and bizness, though so fur as the good will went I wouldn't paid a cent fur it, or not more than a cent, anyway. Uncle Sime abused his wife, wuz clost as the bark to a tree, and

From *Samantha vs. Josiah* (New York, 1906), pp. 297–311, 316–19.

some mentioned the word "sand" in connection with his sugar, and "peas" with his coffee, and etcetery, etcetery. But his bizness wuz what might be called first rate; he had laid up money and retired triumphant at seventy-one.

But to resoom. Uncle Sime Pettigrew's place of bizness wuz a handsome one, a new brick block with stun granite trimmin's, some stained glass over the doors and winders, and everything else it needed for comfort and respectability. He had a big stock of goods and whoever bought 'em and set up bizness in that handsome new block would have been looked up to even if he had been an old man with a bald head, rumatiz and a wooden leg.

But when it wuz a young, handsome, unmarried man, you may imagin he made a sensation to once, and he wuz as handsome a chap as you would often see, light complected with sort o' melancholy blue eyes and curly brown hair and mustash.

The Jonesvillians and Loontowners went into ecstacies over him the first day he appeared in meetin', he wuz so beautiful. They acted fairly foolish; they praised him up so and wuz so enthusiastick. But it is my way to keep calmer and more demute. I will try to restrain my emotions if I have to tie a string to 'em and haul 'em back if I find 'em liable to go too fur. I never could bear anybody or anything that slopped over, from a oriter to a kettle of maple syrup, and I kep' holt of my faculties and common sense in this case, and several of the sisters in the meetin'-house got mad as hens at me, and importuned me sharp as to why I didn't go into spazzums of admiration over him.

And I sez, "He is sweet-lookin', I can't deny that, but there is a kinder weak and waverin' expression to his face that would cause me anxiety if I wuz his Ma."

But when I promulgated these idees to the other sistern, sister Bizer Kipp especially, she most took my head off. She said his face wuz "Be-a-u-tiful, just perfection."

But I still repeated what I had said in a megum tone, and with my most megumest mean, but I agreed with her in a handsome way that Nelt wuz what would be called very, very sweet and winsome, and would be apt to attract female attention and be sought after. And so he wuz. As days rolled on he grew to be the rage in Jonesville, a he-belle, as you may say. Groceries lay in piles on wimmen's buttery shelves and sickness wuz rampant, caused by a too free use of raisins and cinnamon and all-spice. They are too dryin'.

And still the wimmen flocked to his counters as if they couldn't buy enough stuff, and they priced peanuts, and got samples of cast-steel soap, and acted. No place of amusement wuz considered agreeable or endurable without Nelt Chawgo; no party wuz gin without his name stood first on the list, and when he got there he wuz surrounded by a host of the fair sect showerin' attention on him, anxious to win a smile from him.

He wuz doin' dretful well in bizness, and doin' well in morals so fur as I knew. He wuz payin' attention in a sort of a languid, half-hearted way, to Lophemia Kipp. She wuz a pretty girl, sister Kipp's only child. It wuz very pleasin' to her Ma. Folks thought she wuz the one that had brought it about; she acted so triumphant and big feelin' about it, and told everybody how active Nelt wuz in the meetin'-house, and how well he wuz doin' in bizness, and how strong and stimulatin' his tea and coffee wuz.

Folks thought, as I say, that she had more to do about his payin' attention to Lophemia than she did, fur it wuz thought that she had gin her heart to young Jim Carter, old lawyer Carter's youngest boy. He had gone west on a ranch, and it wuz spozed he carried her heart with him. It wuz known he carried her picture, took standin', with a smile on the pretty lips and a happy glow in the eyes, rousted up it wuz spozed by young Jim himself. He went with her to the photographer's; that wuz known, too. Miss Kipp had boasted a sight about him, his good looks and his good bizness and his attentions to Lophemia till Nelt come.

Sister Kipp hain't megum, she is one of the too enthusiastick ones whose motto is not "Love me little love me long," but "Love me a immense quantity in a short time." It stands to reason that if the stream is over rapid the pond will run out sooner; if the stream meanders slow and stiddy, it will last longer.

Well, 'tennyrate she wuz all took up with Nelt Chawgo, and praisin' him up as she had to the very skies you may imagin my feelin's when one day she fairly bust into my settin'-room, out of breath and red in the face, and sez: "I've discovered the dretfulest thing! the awfulest, the most harrowin'! Nelt Chawgo, that young he-hussy, shall never enter my doors agin!"

"Whyee!" sez I, "what's the matter?"

Sez she, "He's a lost young man, a ruined feller!"

"Whyee!" sez I agin, and I sunk right down in my tracts in a rockin'-chair, she havin' sunken down in one opposite; and sez I, "I hain't mistrusted it. He has acted modest and moral; I can't believe it!" "But it is so," sez he. "He has been ruined. Angerose Wilds, a dashin' young woman up in the town of Lyme, is responsible."

"I have hearn of her," sez I. "She had quite a lot of money left her, and is cuttin' a great swath."

"Well," sez sister Kipp, "she has deceived and ruined Nelt Chawgo, and then deserted him; it has all been proved out, and he shall never speak to Lophemia agin, the miserable outcaster!"

Well, I wuz dumbfoundered and horrowstruck like all the rest of Jonesville, but I, as my way is, made inquiries and investigations into the matter. And the next time I see Miss Kipp, and she begun to me awful about Nelt, runnin' him down all to nort, I sez to her, "I have found out some things that makes me feel more lenitent towards Nelson Chawgo."

Oh, how she glared at me. "Lenitent!" sez she, "I'd talk about lenity to that villian, that low ruined creeter!"

"Well," sez I, "I have inquired and found out that Angerose Wilds jest follered Nelt up with attentions and flatteries, and it is spozed up in Lyme that he wuz tempted and fell under a promise of marriage." And I spoke with considerable indignation about this woman who wuz beautiful and rich and holdin' her head high.

But Miss Kipp treated it light and sez: "Oh, young wimmen must sow their wild oats, and then they most always settle down and make the best of wives."

But agin I mentioned extenuatin' circumstances. Sez I, "Miss Wilds wuz noble and galliant in her bearin'; she wuz rich and handsome, and she turned his thoughtless head with her flatteries, and won his pure and unsophistocated heart, so it wuz like wax or putty in her designin' hands, and then at the last she turned her back on him and wouldn't have nothin' to say to him." But these mitigatin', extenuatin' circumstances didn't mitigate or extenuate a mite with Miss Kipp.

Sez she bitterly, "Couldn't he have repulsed her attentions? Couldn't he have kep' his manly modesty if he had been a mind to? Wuz there any need of his fallin' to the depths of infamy he sunk to? No, he is lost, he is ruined!" sez she.

Sez I, "Sister Kipp, don't talk so scornfully; don't say ruined," sez I. "Fall is a good word to use in such a case; folks can fall and git up agin — mebby he will. But ruined is a big word and a hard one; it don't carry any hope with it; it breathes of despair, agony and eternal loss."

"Well," sez she, "it ort to in his case. I shall draw my skirts away from him and go by on the other side. Before his ruin he wuz a sweet, lovely young man but now he is lost. I shall have nothin' to do with him, nor Lophemia shan't."

But I still tried to draw her attention to the facts I had promulgated that Miss Wilds, too, wuz not guiltless. But she wuz sot and wouldn't yield.

She said his sect wuz considered stronger-minded than our sect, with heftier brains and mightier wills, and so it stood to reason that if he wuz tempted by one of the weaker and more feather-brained, he could have saved himself and her, too, from ruin.

There wuz some sense in her talk, I had to admit that there wuz. But I kep' on wavin' my mantilly of charity as high as I could, hopin' that some of the folds, even if it wuzn't nothin' but the end of the tabs, might sort o' shadder Nelt a little, for he wuz indeed a object of pity.

And we couldn't none of us look ahead and see the thrillin' eppisode that wuz in front on him. No, a thick veil of despair seemed to hang down in front on him. And I didn't mistrust that it wuz my hands that wuz goin' to push that veil aside and let some rays lighten up the darkness. But more of that anon and bimeby.

When the news got out about Nelt Chawgo, Jonesville society wuz rent to its very twain. The two factions led on by Miss Kipp and Nelt's friends waged a fearful warfare, some jinin' one side and some the other.

Some on 'em, the old conservative ones, wuz for overlookin' the hull matter so fur as Nelt wuz concerned and throwin' the hull blame onto the female woman up to Lyme on the safe old ground, trod so long by the world at large, that he wuz a man and so such sin in him wuzn't a sin. It wuz sin in a woman, a deep and hopeless sin that forever barred the guilty one from the pail of respectable society.

But I held to the firm belief that if she carried the pail he ort to, and visey versey. My idee wuz that they ort to carry the pail between 'em. They said it wuz sin in the woman, a turrible and hopeless sin, but in him it wuzn't. It come under the head of wild oats, which when planted thick in youth and springin' up rank, prepared the ground for a rich after crop of moral graces.

This wuz old well-established doctrine that had been follered for years and years, so they felt it wuz safe.

But one night to a church sociable when Miss Kipp had brung the subject up and one of our foremost deacons, Deacon Henzy, wuz advancin' these idees, she that wuz Nancy Butterick, who had come to Jonesville to deliver a lecture in the interests of the W. C. T. U., she sassed Deacon Henzy right back and sez she:

"The idee of thinkin' that the same sin when committed by a man and a woman ort to be laid entirely onto the party that is in the law classed with lunaticks and idiots." Sez she, "That hain't good logic. If a woman is a fool she hadn't ort to be expected to have her brain tapped and run wisdom and morality, and if she is a lunatick she might be expected to cut up and act."

She wuz educated high, Nancy wuz, and knew a sight in the first place, as folks have to, to amount to much, for all education can do anyway is to sharpen the tools that folks use to hew their way through the wilderness of life.

Sez she, "The male sect is in the eyes of the Law the gardeens of females, and ort to act like gardeens to 'em and try to curb their folly and wickedness and restrain it instead of takin' advantage of it, and fallin' victims to their weakness." Sez she, "When a oak tree falls it falls heavier than a creepin' vine, a creepin' up and hangin' to it, and it would be jest as sensible to lay the hull of the blame on the creeper for the fall of the oak, as to put the hull of the blame on the Lyme woman."

Why, she brung up lots of simelys that fairly bristled with eloquence, and Deacon Henzy sassed her back in his way of thinkin'; it wuz a sight to hear 'em talkin' pro and con. . . .

. . . I thought Jane Ann looked queer, but I went on and sez: "Oh, if that woman could look and see the wreck she has made of that once happy and good young man, it must be she would be struck with remorse. They say she is handsome and well off, and holds her head high, while her victim is dyin' under the contempt and scorn of the world. Nobody will associate with him. Why, my Josiah draws his pantaloons away from him for fear of the contamination of his touch. He's weighed down under the scorn of the world and his own remorse. He is ruined in his bizness, and he's goin' into the gallopin' consumption as fast as he can gallop."

Jane Ann gin me such a queer look here that I involuntary follered her gaze and looked at the handsome stranger. Her work had fell into her lap, her face wuz red as blood, and she busted into tears, sayin:

"I am Angerose Wilds! I am the guilty wretch that wuz the means of that sweet and innocent young creature's fall; I am the one to blame. But," sez she with her streamin' eyes lifted to mine, "I never realized until you brung it before me the extent of my crime, but I will atone for the evil as fur as I can. I will marry him and so do all I can to lift him up and make an honest man of him, and set him right in the eyes of the community. And," sez she, while the tears chased each other down her cheeks, "Poor Nelt! poor boy! how you have suffered; and I alone am the guilty cause!"

But here I interfered agin, held up by Justice and Duty. "Don't say, mom, that you alone are to blame; divide it into two bundles of guilt, take one on your own back and pack the other onto hisen. It hain't fair for one to bear it alone, male or female."

Josiah come that very minute and I had to bid them a hasty adoo. But the last words that galliant appearin' handsome woman whispered to me wuz: "I will make an honest man of him; I will marry him."

And if you'll believe it, she did. It all ended first rate, almost like a real novel story. It seems that woman wuz so smut with remorse when it wuz brought before her in a eloquent and forcible manner; and she realized the almost irreparable wrong she had committed aginst that lovely and innocent young man, she offered him the only reparation in her power; she offered him honorable marriage, which he accepted gladly, and they got married the next week, and he brought her to Jonesville the follerin' Monday, and they sot up housekeepin' in a handsome two-story-and-a-half house, and are doin' well and bid fair to make a respectable couple.

We buy the most of our groceries there; not all, for I am megum in groceries as well as in everything else. I buy some of the other grocer, not bein' willin' to hurt his feelin's, his wife bein' a member of the same meetin'-house. But Miss Kipp can't be megum any more than my own dear pardner can. She come 'round immegiate and unanimous, and said their marriage made 'em both all that could be desired. She buys all her groceries of him; she sez his tea is cheaper and takes a spunful less in a drawin'. But I don't believe it; I believe she steeps it longer. 'Tennyrate she bought of him all her fruit and candy and stuff for Lophemia Carter's weddin', which took place some time ago.

Well, this party I sot out to tell you about wuz to celebrate the first anniversary of the Chawgo and Wilds weddin', and wuz a joyful event.

After we got home Josiah wuz so nerved up (part on't wuz the strong coffee), that I had to read three truthful articles out of the scrap-book; he a settin' leanin back in his chair a listenin' and a makin' comments on each one on 'em as I finished readin' 'em.

His talk bein' some like the little pieces they play between songs, interludes, I believe they call 'em, only his talk wuzn't all the time melogious; no, indeed; fur from it. There wuz minor cords in it, and discords, and flats and sharps, yes indeed!

17 "The Jonesville Singin' Quire"

Thomas Jefferson is a good boy. His teacher to the Jonesville Academy
told me the other day, says he,

"Thomas J. is full of fun, but I don't believe he has a single bad habit;
and I don't believe he knows any more about bad things, than Tirzah
Ann, and she is a girl of a thousand."

This made my heart beat with pure and fervent emotions of joy, for I
knew it was true, but I tell you I have had to work for it. I was determined from the first, that Thomas Jefferson needn't think because he
was a boy he could do anything that would be considered disgraceful if
he was a girl. Now some mothers will worry themselves to death about
thier girls, so afraid they will get into bad company and bring disgrace
onto 'em. I have said to 'em sometimes,

"Why don't you worry about your boys?"

"Oh things are winked at in a man that haint in a woman."

Says I, "There is one woman that no man can get to wink at 'em, and
that is Samantha Allen, whose maiden name was Smith." Says I, "It is
enough to make anybody's blood bile in thier vains to think how different sin is looked upon in a man and woman. I say sin is sin, and you
can't make goodness out of it by parsin' it in the masculine gender, no
more'n you can by parsin' it in the feminine or neutral.

And wimmin are the most to blame in this respect. I believe in givin'
the D — — I won't speak the gentleman's name right out, because I belong to the Methodist Meetin' house,[1] but you know who I mean, and I
believe in givin' him his due, if you owe him anything, and I say men
haint half so bad as wimmen about holdin' up male sinners and stomp-
in' down female ones.

Wimmen are meaner than pusly about some things, and this is one of
'em. Now wimmen will go out and kill the fatted calf with thier own

From *My Opinions and Betsey Bobbet's* (Hartford, 1891), pp. 112–20.

hands to feast the male prodigal that has been livin' on husks. But let
the woman that he has been boardin' with on the same bundle of husks,
ask meekly for a little mite of this veal critter, will she get it? No! She
won't get so much as one of the huffs. She will be told to keep on eatin'
her husks, and after she has got through with 'em to die, for after a
woman has once eat husks, she can't never eat any other vittles. And if
she asks meekly, why is her stomach so different from the male husk
eater, *he* went right off from husks to fatted calves, they'll say to her
'what is sin in a woman haint sin in a man. Men are such noble creatures that they *will* be a little wild, it is expected of 'em, but after they
have sowed all thier wild oats, they always settle down and make the
very best of men."

"'Can't I settle down too?' cries the poor woman. '*I* am sick of wild
oats too, *I* am sick of husks — I want to live a good life, in the sight of
God and man — can't I settle down too?'"

"'Yes you can settle down in the grave,' they say to her — 'When a
woman has sinned once, that is all the place there is for her — a woman
cannot be forgiven.' There is an old sayin' 'Go and sin no more.' But
that is eighteen hundred years old — awful old fashioned.'"

And then after they have feasted the male husk eater, on this gospel
veal, and fell on his neck and embraced him a few times, they will take
him into thier houses and marry him to their purest and prettiest
daughter, while at the same time they won't have the female husker in
thier kitchen to wash for 'em at 4 cents an article.

I say it is a shame and a disgrace, for the woman to bear all the
burden of sufferin' and all the burden of shame too; it is a mean, cowardly piece of business, and I should think the very stuns would go to
yellin' at each other to see such injustice.

But Josiah Allen's children haint been brought up in any such kind of
a way. They have been brought up to think that sin of any kind is jest as
bad in a man as it is in a woman. And any place of amusement that was
bad for a woman to go to, was bad for a man.

Now when Thomas Jefferson was a little feller, he was bewitched to
go to circuses, and Josiah said,

"Better let him go, Samantha, it haint no place for wimmin or girls,
but it won't hurt a boy."

Says I, "Josiah Allen, the Lord made Thomas Jefferson with jest as
pure a heart as Tirzah Ann, and no bigger eyes and ears, and if Thomas
J. Goes to the circus, Tirzah Ann goes too."

That stopped that. And then he was bewitched to get with other boys that smoked and chewed tobacco, and Josiah was jest that easy turn, that he would have let him go with 'em. But says I —

"Josiah Allen, if Thomas Jefferson goes with those boys, and gets to chewin' and smokin' tobacco, I shall buy Tirzah Ann a pipe."

And that stopped that.

"And about drinkin'," says I. "Thomas Jefferson, if it should ever be the will of Providence to change you into a wild bear, I will chain you up, and do the best I can by you. But if you ever do it yourself, turn yourself into a wild beast by drinkin', I will run away, for I never could stand it, never. And," I continued, "if I ever see you hangin' round bar-rooms and tavern doors, Tirzah Ann shall hang too."

Josiah argued with me, says he, "It don't look so bad for a boy as it does for a girl."

Says I, "Custom makes the difference; we are more used to seein' men. But," says I, "when liquor goes to work to make a fool and a brute of anybody it don't stop to ask about sect, it makes a wild beast and a idiot of a man or a woman, and to look down from Heaven, I guess a man looks as bad layin' dead drunk in a gutter as a woman does," says I; "things look different from up there, than what they do to us — it is a more sightly place. And you talk about *looks*, Josiah Allen. I don't go on clear looks, I go onto principle. Will the Lord say to me in the last day, 'Josiah Allen's wife, how is it with the sole of Tirzah Ann — as for Thomas Jefferson's sole, he bein' a boy it haint of no account?' No! I shall have to give an account to Him for my dealin's with both of these soles, male and female. And I should feel guilty if I brought him up to think that what was impure for a woman, was pure for a man. If man has a greater desire to do wrong — which I won't dispute," says I lookin' keenly on to Josiah, "he has greater strength to resist temptation. And so," says I in mild accents, but firm as old Plymouth Rock, "if Thomas Jefferson hangs, Tirzah Ann shall hang too."

I have brought Thomas Jefferson up to think that it was jest as bad for him to listen to a bad story or song, as for a girl, or worse, for he had more strength to run away, and that it was a disgrace for him to talk or listen to any stuff that he would be ashamed to have Tirzah Ann or me hear. I have brought him up to think that manliness didn't con-sist in havin' a cigar in his mouth, and his hat on one side, and swearin' and slang phrases, and a knowledge of questionable amusements, but in layin' holt of every duty that come to him, with a brave heart and a cheerful face; in helpin' to right the wrong, and protect the weak, and makin' the most and the best of the mind and the soul God had given him. In short, I have brought him up to think that purity and virtue are both masculine and femanine gender, and that God's angels are not necessarily all she ones.

Tirzah Ann too has come up well, though I say it, that shouldn't, her head haint all full, runnin' over, and frizzlin' out on top of it, with thoughts of beaux and flirtin'. I have brought her up to think that marriage wasn't the chief end of life, but savin' her soul. Tirzah Ann's own grandmother on her mother's side, used to come visatin' us and stay weeks at a time, kinder spyin' out I spose how I done by the children, — thank fortune, I wasn't afraid to have her spy, all she was a mind too, I wouldn't have been afraid to had Benedict Arnold, and Major Andre come as spys. I did well by 'em, and she owned it, though she did think I made Tirzah Ann's night gowns a little too full round the neck, and Thomas Jefferson's roundabouts a little too long behind. But as I was a sayin', the old lady begun to kinder train Tirzah Ann up to the prevailin' idee of its bein' her only aim in life to catch a husband, and if she would only grow up and be a real good girl she should marry.

I didn't say nothin' to the old lady, for I respect old age, but I took Josiah out one side, and says I,

"Josiah Allen, if Tirzah Ann is to be brought up to think that marriage is the chief aim of her life, Thomas J. shall be brought up to think that marriage is his chief aim." Says I, "it looks just as flat in a woman, as it does in a man."

Josiah didn't make much of any answer to me, he is an easy man. But as that was the old lady's last visit (she was took bed rid the next week, and haint walked a step sense), I haint had no more trouble on them grounds.

When Tirzah Ann gets old enough, if a good true man, a man for instance, such as I think Whitfield Minkley, our minister's oldest boy is a goin' to make, if such a man offers Tirzah Ann his love which is the greatest honor a man can do a woman, why Tirzah will, I presume, if she loves him well enough, marry him. I should give my consent, and so would Josiah. But to have all her mind sot onto that hope and expectatin' till she begins to look wild, I have discouraged it in her.

I have told her that goodness, truth, honor, vertue and nobility come first as aims in life. Says I,

"Tirzah Ann, seek these things first, and then if a husband is added unto you, you may know it is the Lord's will, and accept him like any other dispensation of Providence, and—" I continued as dreamy thoughts of Josiah floated through my mind, "make the best of him."

I feel thankful to think they have both come up as well as they have. Tirzah Ann is more of a quiet turn, but Thomas J., though his morals are sound, is dreadful full of fun, I worry some about him for he haint made no professions, I never could get him forred onto the anxious seat. He told Elder Minkley last winter that "the seats were all made of the same kind of basswood, and he could be jest as anxious out by the door, as he could on one of the front seats.

Says Elder Minkley, "My dear boy, I want you to find the Lord."

"I haint never lost him," says Thomas Jefferson.

It shocked Elder Minkley dreadfully—but it sot me to thinkin'. He was always an odd child, always askin' the curiousest questions, and I brought him up to think that the Lord was with him all the time, and see what he was doin', and mebby he was in the right of it, mebby he felt as if he hadn't never lost Him. He was always the greatest case to be out in the woods and lots, findin' everything—and sometimes I have almost thought the trash he thinks so much of, such as shells and pieces of rock and stun, and flowers and moss, are a kind of means of grace to him, and then agin I don't know. If I really thought they was I don't suppose I should have pitched 'em out of the winder so many times as I have, clutterin' up the house so.

I worry about him awfully sometimes, and then agin I lay holt of the promises . . .

NOTE

1. The code for good Methodists such as Samantha would prohibit such activities as sex outside of marriage, drinking, dancing, cursing, card-playing, and smoking.

18   On Winkin' at Men's Sins

. . . "As I said sister Minkley, I have made the subject of wimmen my theme for quite a number of years — ever sense the black African and the mortgage on our farm was released. I have meditated on what wimmen has done, and what she haint done; what treatment she has received, and what she haint received. Why sometimes, sister Minkley, when I have got onto that theme, my mind has soared to that extent that you wouldn't have any idee of, if you never had seen anything done in the line of soarin'. It has sailed back to the year one, and sailed onwards through the centuries that lie between to that golden year we both believe in sister Minkley. It has soared clear from the east to the west, and seen sad eyed Eastern wimmen with veiled faces, toys, or beasts of burden, not darin' to uncover their faces to the free air and light of heaven, because man willed it so. It has seen Western wimmen, long processions of savages, the wimmen carryin' the babies, the house, and household furniture on their backs, while the men, unburdened and feathered out nobly, walked in front of 'em, smoking calmly, and meditatin' on the inferiority of wimmen.

I never contended that wimmen was perfect, far from it. You have heerd me say in the past, that I thought wimmen was meaner than pusly about some things. I say so still. My mind haint changed about wimmen, nor about pusly. But justice is what I have been a contendin' for; justice, and equal rights, and a fair dividin' of the burdens of life is my theme; and I say they haint been used well.

Now in the year one, when Adam and Eve eat that apple, jest as quick as Adam swallowed it — probable he most choked himself with the core, he was in such a awful hurry to get his mouth clear, so he could lay the blame onto Eve. "The woman did tempt me, and I did eat."

From *Samantha at the Centennial* (Hartford, 1884), pp. 178–84.

"But thank fortin, he didn't make out much, for Eternal Goodness, which is God, is forever on the side of Right. And Adam and Eve — as any two ort to be who sin together — got turned out of Eden, side by side, out of the same gate, into the same wilderness; and the flaming sword that kept Eve back from her old life of beauty and innocence, kept Adam back, too. Sister Minkley, that is my theme. When two human souls turn the Eden of their innocence into a garden of guilt, punish 'em both alike, and don't turn her out into the wilderness alone; don't flash the flamin' sword of your righteous indignation in her eyes and not in hisen.

"And then, there was Hagar'ses case, — when Abraham turned Hagar and his baby out into the desert. If I had lived neighbor to 'em, at the time, I should have give him a talkin' to about it; I should have freed my mind, and felt relieved so fur, anyway. I should have said to the old gentleman, in a pleasant way, so's not to git him mad: — 'I think a sight of you, Abraham, in the patriarch way. You are a good man, in a great many respects; but standin' up for wimmen is my theme (and also promiscous advisin') and do you think you are doin' the fair thing by Hagar, to send her and your baby off into the desert with nothin' but one loaf of bread and a bottle of water between them and death?' Says I, 'It is your child, and if it hadn't been for you, Hagar would probable now be a doin' housework round in Beersheba, a happy woman with no incumbrances. It is your child as well as hern, and you, to say the least of it, are as guilty as she is; and don't you think it is a little ungenerous and unmanly in you, to drive her off into the desert — to let her in her weakness, take all the consequences of the sin you and she committed, when she had paid for it already pretty well, in the line of sufferin'?' Says I, 'I think a sight of you, Abraham, but in the name of principle, I say with the poet, — that what is sass for the goose, ort to be sass for the gander — and if she is drove off into the desert, you ort to lock arms with her and go too.'

"I'll bet a cent I could have convinced Abraham that he was a doin' a cowardly and ungenerous act by Hagar. But then I wasn't there; I didn't live neighbor to 'em. And I presume Sarah kep' at him all the time; kep' a tewin' at him about her; kep' him awake nights a twittin' him about her, and askin' him to start her off. I persume Sarah acted meaner than pusly.

"Human nater, and especially wimmen human nater is considerable the same in the year 18 and 1800, and I'll bet a cent (or I wouldn't be afraid to bet a cent, if I believed in bettin') that if Sarah had had her way, Hagar wouldn't have got even that loaf of bread and bottle of water. It says, Abraham got up early — probable before Sarah was up — and give 'em to her, and started her off. I shouldn't wonder a mite if Sarah twitted Abraham about that loaf of bread every time she did a bakin', for a number of years after. And that bottle. I dare persume to say, if the truth was known, that she throwed that bottle in his face more'n a hundred times, deplorin' it as the toughest-hided, soundest bottle in all Beersheba.

"But as I said, I wasn't there, and Abraham turned her out, and Hagar had a hard time of it out in the desert, toilin' on alone through its dreary wastes, hungry for bread, and hungry for love; dying from starvation of soul and body; deceived; despised; wronged; deserted; lonely; broken-hearted; and carrying with all the rest of her sorrow — as mothers will — the burden of her child's distress. Why, this woman's wrongs and misery opened the very gates of Heaven, and God's own voice comforted and consoled her; again Eternal Justice and Mercy spoke out of Heaven for wimmen. Why is it that his children on earth will continue to be so deaf and dumb — deaf as a stun — for 6000 years.

"But from that time to this, take it between the Abrahams and the Sarahs of this world, the Hagars have fared hard, and the Abrahams have got along first rate; the Hagars have been turned out into the desert to die there, and the Abrahams that ruined 'em, have increased in flocks and herds; are thought a sight of and are high in the esteem of wimmen. Seems as though the more Hagars they fit out for the desert business, the more feathers it is in their cap. Every Hagar they start out is a new feather, till some get completely feathered out; then they send 'em to Congress, and think a sight on 'em.

"I declare for't it is the singularest thing I ever see, or hearn tell on, how folks that are so just in every thing else, are so blinded in this one. And" says I almost wildly — for I grew more and more agitated every minute, and eloquent — "the female sect are to blame for this state of affairs;" says I, "men as a general thing, all good men, have better idees in this matter than we do, enough sight. Wimmen are to blame — meetin' house wimmen and all, — you and I are to blame sister Minkley," says I. "As a rule the female sect wink at men's sins, but not a wink can you ever git out of them about our sins. Not a wink. *We* have got to toe the mark in morals, and we ort to make *them* toe the mark. And if we did, we should rise 25 cents in the estimation of every good man, and every mean one too, for they can't respect us now, to toady and keep a winkin' at 'em when they wont at us; they can't respect us. We ort to require as much purity and virtue in them, as they do in us, and stop winkin'." Says I, "Winkin' at men's sins is what is goin' to ruin us all, the hull caboodle of us; ruin men, ruin wimmen, Jonesville, and the hull nation. Let the hull female race, fur and near, bond and free, in Jonesville and the world, stop winkin'."

I don't believe I had been any more eloquent sense war times; I used to get awful eloquent then, talkin' about the colored niggers. And I declare I don't know where, to what heights and depths my eloquence would have flown me off to, if I hadn't jest that minute heard a low, lady-like snore — sister Minkley was asleep. Yes, she had forgot her troubles; she was leanin' up ag'inst the high pile of rag carpetin', that kinder fenced us in, fast asleep. But truly, she haint to blame. She has bad spells, — a sort of weakness she can't help. But jest at that very minute my Josiah came up and says he:

"Come Samantha! haint you about ready to go?"

"Yes," says I, for truly principle had tuckered me out. Josiah's voice had waked up sister Minkley, and she give a kind of a start, and says she:

"Amen, sister Allen! I can say amen to that with all my heart. You talked well sister Allen, especially towards the last. You argued powerful." . . .

IV

Women's Powerlessness before the Law: The Need for Suffrage

> "But I'll bet that Abagail Flanders beat our old
> Revolutionary 4 mothers in thinkin' out new
> laws, when she lay round under stairs, and
> behind barrells, in her night-dress.
> You see, when a man hides his wive's corset
> and petticoat, it is governin' without the 'consent
> of the governed.' "
>
> — Samantha

The following selections pertain particularly to the question of suffrage. The woeful tales of Burpy family women illustrate the suffering that results from the convergence of two evils: intemperance and the lack of the vote for women. Women helplessly endure financial disaster, personal humiliation, and maternal disenfranchisement because the government licenses the sale of liquor. Without the right to vote, women will remain victims of the whimsies of drunkards and will be unable to protect their own children or administer properties according to their own consciences. Samantha bemoans the "lawful sufferin's of them wimmen. For there wuzn't nothin illegal about one single trouble of theirn."

In "Polly's Eyes Growed Tender," Samantha assures both male and female opponents of suffrage of the positive consequences of women's votes: equal pay for equal work, end to child labor and attention to children's welfare, moral uprightness in government, the opening of schools to teach girls to be capable wives and mothers. In this selection, Samantha tackles Lorinda, who considers voting unwomanly, and praises Polly, who sticks to her women's rights principles even when it may cost her the attentions of her beloved.

Finally, as usual, Josiah offers a tour-de-force of his distinctive logic, which fits his own self-interest whenever the situation dictates. In this case, it is perfectly womanly for Samantha to go to the poll if it is to purchase buttons for his shirts. To go to the poll to vote, of course, would be "revoltin'." One of the suffragist complaints—that intelligent women are denied the vote while ignorant men sell their votes to the highest bidder—is embodied in the tale of Josiah's "corruption."

"Eunice in Jail"

19   On the Sufferings of the Burpy Women

[Dorlesky Burpy] come for a all day's visit; and though she is a vegetable widow, and very humbly, I wuz middlin' glad to see her. But thinks'es I to myself as I carried away her things into the bedroom, "She'll want to send some errent by me;" and I wondered what it wouldn't be.

And so it didn't surprise me any when she asked me the first thing when I got back "if I would lobby a little for her in Washington."

And I looked agreeable to the idee; for I s'posed it wuz some new kind of tattin', mebby, or fancy work. And I told her, "I shouldn't have much time, but I would try to buy her some if I could."

And she said "she wanted me to lobby, myself."

And then I thought mebby it wus some new kind of waltz; and I told her, "I was too old to lobby, I hadn't lobbied a step since I was married."

And then she said "she wanted me to canvass some of the senators."

And I hung back, and asked her in a cautius tone "how many she wanted canvassed, and how much canvass it would take?"

I knew I had a good many things to buy for my tower; and, though I wanted to obleege Dorlesky, I didn't feel like runnin' into any great expense for canvass.

And then she broke off from that subject, and said "she wanted her rights, and wanted the Whiskey Ring broke up."[1]

And then she says, going back to the old subject agin, "I hear that Josiah Allen has political hopes: can I canvass him?"

And I says, "Yes, you can for all me." But I mentioned cautiously, for I believe in bein' straightforward, and not holdin' out no false hopes, —

From *Sweet Cicely* (New York, 1887), pp. 144–60. The tale of Dorlesky Burpy family women is repeated in *Samantha on the Woman Question* (New York, 1913), using Serepta Pester as the character on pp. 22–42.

I said "she must furnish her own canvass, for I hadn't a mite in the house."

But Josiah didn't get home till after her folks come after her. So he wuzn't canvassed.

But she talked a sight about her children, and how bad she felt to be parted from 'em, and how much she used to think of her husband, and how her hull life wus ruined, and how the Whiskey Ring had done it, — that, and wimmen's helpless condition under the law. And she cried, and wept, and cried about her children, and her sufferin's she had suffered; and I did. I cried onto my apron, and couldn't help it. A new apron too. And right while I wus cryin' onto that gingham apron, she made me promise to carry them two errents of hern to the President, and to get 'em done for her if I possibly could.

"She wanted the Whiskey Ring destroyed, and she wanted her rights; and she wanted 'em both in less than 2 weeks."

I wiped my eyes off, and told her I didn't believe she could get 'em done in that length of time, but I would tell the President about it, and "I thought more'n as likely as not he would want to do right by her." And says I, "If he sets out to, he can haul them babys of yourn out of that Ring pretty sudden."

And then, to kinder get her mind off of her sufferin's, I asked her how her sister Susan wus a gettin' along. I hadn't heard from her for years — she married Philemon Clapsaddle; and Dorlesky spoke out as bitter as a bitter walnut — a green one. And says she, —

"She is in the poorhouse."

"Why, Dorlesky Burpy!" says I. "What do you mean?"

"I mean what I say. My sister, Susan Clapsaddle, is in the poorhouse."

"Why, where is their property all gone?" says I. "They was well off — Susan had five thousand dollars of her own when she married him."

"I know it," says she. "And I can tell you, Josiah Allen's wife, where their property is gone. It has gone down Philemon Clapsaddle's throat. Look down that man's throat, and you will see 150 acres of land, a good house and barns, 20 sheep, and 40 head of cattle."

"Why-ee!" says I.

"Yes, you will see 'em all down that man's throat." And says she, in still more bitter axents, "You will see four mules, and a span of horses, two buggies, a double sleigh, and three buffalo-robes. He has drinked 'em all up — and 2 horse-rakes, a cultivator, and a thrashin'-machine."

"Why! Why-ee!" says I agin. "And where are the children?"

"The boys have inherited their father's evil habits, and drink as bad as he duz; and the oldest girl has gone to the bad."

"Oh, dear! oh, dear me!" says I. And we both sot silent for a spell. And then, thinkin' I must say sunthin', and wantin' to strike a safe subject, and a good-lookin' one, I says, —

"Where is your aunt Eunice'es girl? that pretty girl I see to your house once."

"That girl is in the lunatick asylum."

"Dorlesky Burpy!" says I. "Be you a tellin' the truth?"

"Yes, I be, the livin' truth. She went to New York to buy millinary goods for her mother's store. It wus quite cool when she left home, and she hadn't took off her winter clothes: and it come on brilin' hot in the city; and in goin' about from store to store, the heat and the hard work overcome her, and she fell down in the street in a sort of a faintin'-fit, and was called drunk, and dragged off to a police court by a man who wus a animal in human shape. And he misused her in such a way, that she never got over the horror of what befell her — when she come to, to find herself at the mercy of a brute in a man's shape. She went into a melancholy madness, and wus sent to the asylum. Of course they couldn't have wimmen in such places to take care of wimmen," says she bitterly.

I sithed a long and mournful sithe, and sot silent agin for quite a spell. But thinkin' I *must* be sociable, I says, —

"Your aunt Eunice is well, I s'pose?"

"She is a moulderin' in jail," says she.

"In jail? Eunice Keeler in jail?"

"Yes, in jail." And Dorlesky's tone wus now like wormwood, wormwood and gall.

"You know, she owns a big property in tenement-houses, and other buildings, where she lives. Of course her taxes wus awful high; and she didn't expect to have any voice in tellin' how that money, a part of her own property, that she earned herself in a store, should be used.

"But she had jest been taxed high for new sidewalks in front of some of her buildin's.

"And then another man come into power in that ward, and he natrully wanted to make some money out of her; and he had a spite aginst her, too, so he ordered her to build new sidewalks. And she wouldn't tear up a good sidewalk to please him or anybody else, so she was put to jail for refusin' to comply with the law."

Thinks'es I to myself, I don't believe the law would have been so hard on her if she hadn't been so humbly. The Burpys are a humbly lot. But I didn't think it out loud. And I didn't uphold the law for feelin' so, if it did. No: I says in pityin' tones, — for I wus truly sorry for Eunice Keeler, —

"How did it end?"

"It hain't ended," says she. "It only took place a month ago; and she has got her grit up, and won't pay: and no knowin' how it will end. She lays there a moulderin'."

I myself don't believe Eunice wus "mouldy;" but that is Dorlesky's way of talkin', — very flowery.

"Wall," says I, "do you think the weather is goin' to moderate?"

I truly felt that I dassent speak to her about any human bein' under the sun, not knowin' what turn she would give to the conversation, bein' so embittered. But I felt the weather wus safe, and cotton stockin's, and factory-cloth; and I kep' her down onto them subjects for more'n two hours.

But, good land! I can't blame her for bein' embittered aginst men and the laws they have made; for, if ever a woman has been tormented, she has.

It honestly seems to me as if I never see a human creeter so afflicted as Dorlesky Burpy has been, all her life.

Why, her sufferin's date back before she wus born; and that is goin' pretty fur back. You see, her father and mother had had some difficulty: and he wus took down with billious colic voyolent four weeks before Dorlesky wus born; and some think it wus the hardness between 'em, and some think it wus the gripin' of the colic at the time he made his will; anyway, he willed Dorlesky away, boy or girl, whichever it wuz, to his brother up on the Canada line.

So, when Dorlesky wus born (and born a girl, entirely onbeknown to her), she wus took right away from her mother, and gin to this brother. Her mother couldn't help herself: he had the law on his side. But it jest killed her. She drooped right away and died, before the baby wus a year old. She was a affectionate, tender-hearted woman; and her husband wus kinder overbearin', and stern always.

But it wus this last move of hisen that killed her; for I tell you, it is pretty tough on a mother to have her baby, a part of her own life, took right out of her arms, and gin to a stranger.

For this uncle of hern wus a entire stranger to Dorlesky when the will wus made. And almost like a stranger to her father, for he hadn't seen him sence he wus a boy; but he knew he hadn't any children, and s'posed he wus rich and respectable. But the truth wuz, he had been a runnin' down every way, — had lost his property and his character, wus dissipated and mean (onbeknown, it wus s'posed, to Dorlesky's father). But the will was made, and the law stood. Men are ashamed now, to think the law wus ever in voge; but it wuz, and is now in some of the States. The law wus in voge, and the poor young mother couldn't help herself. It has always been the boast of our American law, that it takes care of wimmen. It took care of her. It held her in its strong, protectin' grasp, and held her so tight, that the only way she could slip out of it wus to drop into the grave, which she did in a few months. Then it leggo.

But it kep' holt of Dorlesky: it bound her tight to her uncle, while he run through with what little property she had; while he sunk lower and lower, until at last he needed the very necessaries of life; and then he bound her out to work, to a woman who kep' a drinkin'-den, and the lowest, most degraded hant of vice.

Twice Dorlesky run away, bein' virtuous but humbly; but them strong, protectin' arms of the law that had held her mother so tight, jest reached out, and dragged her back agin. Upheld by them, her uncle could compel her to give her service wherever he wanted her to work; and he wus owin' this woman, and she wanted Dorlesky's work, so she had to submit.

But the 3d time, she made a effort so voyalent that she got away. A good woman, who, bein' nothin' but a woman, couldn't do any thing towards onclinchin' them powerful arms that wuz protectin' her, helped her to slip through 'em. And Dorlesky come to Jonesville to live with a sister of that good woman; changed her name, so's it wouldn't be so easy to find her; grew up to be a nice, industrious girl. And when the woman she was took by, died, she left Dorlesky quite a handsome property.

And finally she married Lank Rumsey, and did considerable well, it was s'posed. Her property, put with what little he had, made 'em a comfortable home; and they had two pretty little children, — a boy and a girl. But when the little girl was a baby, he took to drinkin', neglected his business, got mixed up with a whisky-ring, whipped Dorlesky — not so very hard. He went accordin' to law; and the law of the United States don't approve of a man whippin' his wife enough to endanger her life — it says it don't. He made every move of hisen lawful, and felt that Dorlesky hadn't ort to complain and feel hurt. But a good whippin' will make anybody feel hurt, law or no law. And then he parted with her, and got her property and her two little children. Why, it seemed as if every thing under the sun and moon, that *could* happen to a woman, had happened to Dorlesky, painful things, and gaulin'.

Jest before Lank parted with her, she fell on a broken sidewalk: some think he tripped her up, but it never was proved. But, anyway, Dorlesky fell, and broke her hipbone; and her husband sued the corporation, and got ten thousand dollars for it. Of course, the law give the money to him, and she never got a cent of it. But she wouldn't never have made any fuss over that, knowin' that the law of the United States was such. But what made it gaulin' to her wuz, that, while she was layin' there achin' in splints, he took that very money and used it to court up another woman with. Gin her presents, jewellry, bunnets, head-dresses, artificial flowers, and etcetery, out of Dorlesky's own hip-money.

And I don't know as any thing could be much more gaulin' to a woman than that wuz, — while she lay there, groanin' in splints, to have her husband take the money for her own broken bones, and dress up another woman like a doll with it.

But the law gin it to him; and he was only availin' himself of the glorious liberty of our free republic, and doin' as he was a mind to.

And it was s'posed that that very hip-money was what made the match. For, before she wus fairly out of splints, he got a divorce from her. And by the help of that money, and the Whisky Ring, he got her two little children away from her.

And I wonder if there is a mother in the land, that can blame Dorlesky for gettin' mad, and wantin' her rights, and wantin' the Whisky Ring broke up, when they think it over, — how she has been fooled round with by men, willed away, and whipped and parted with and stole from. Why, they can't blame her for feelin' fairly savage about 'em — and she duz. For as she says to me once when we wus a talkin' it over, how every thing had happened to her that could happen to a woman, and how curious it wuz, —

"Yes," says she, with a axent like boneset and vinegar, — "and what few things there are that hain't happened to me, has happened to my folks."

And, sure enough, I couldn't dispute her. Trouble and wrongs and sufferin's seemed to be epidemic in the race of Burpy wimmen. Why, one of her aunts on her father's side, Patty Burpy, married for her first husband Eliphalet Perkins. He was a minister, rode on a circuit. And he took Patty on it too; and she rode round with him on it, a good deal of the time. But she never loved to: she wus a woman who loved to be still, and be kinder settled down at home.

But she loved Eliphalet so well, she would do anything to please him: so she rode round with him on that circuit, till she was perfectly fagged out.

He was a dretful good man to her; but he wus kinder poor, and they had hard times to get along. But what property they had wuzn't taxed, so that helped some; and Patty would make one doller go a good ways.

No, their property wasn't taxed till Eliphalet died. Then the supervisor taxed it the very minute the breath left his body; run his horse, so it was said, so's to be sure to get it onto the tax-list, and comply with the law.

You see, Eliphalet's salary stopped when his breath did. And I s'pose mebby the law thought, seein' she was a havin' trouble, she might jest as well have a little more; so it taxed all the property it never had taxed a cent for before.

But she had this to console her anyway, — that the law didn't forget her in her widowhood. No: the law is quite thoughtful of wimmen, by spells. It says, the law duz, that it protects wimmen. And I s'pose in some mysterious way, too deep for wimmen to understand, it was protectin' her now.

Wall, she suffered along, and finally married agin. I wondered why she did. But she was such a quiet, homelovin' woman, that it was s'posed she wanted to settle down, and be kinder still and sot. But of all the bad luck she had! She married on short acquaintance, and he proved to be a perfect wanderer. Why, he couldn't keep still. It was s'posed to be a mark.

He moved Patty thirteen times in two years; and at last he took her into a cart, — a sort of a covered wagon, — and travelled right through the Eastern States with her. He wanted to see the country, and loved to live in the wagon: it was his make. And, of course, the law give him the control of her body; and she had to go where he moved it, or else part with him. And I s'pose the law thought it was guardin' and nourishin' her when it was a joltin' her over them praries and mountains and abysses. But it jest kep' her shook up the hull of the time.

It wus the regular Burpy luck.

And then, another one of her aunts, Drusilla Burpy, she married a industrius, hard-workin' man, — one that never drinked a drop, and was sound on the doctrines, and give good measure to his customers: he was a grocer-man. And a master hand for wantin' to foller the laws of his country, as tight as laws could be follered. And so, knowin' that the law approved of "moderate correction" for wimmen, and that "a man might whip his wife, but not enough to endanger her life," he bein' such a master hand for wantin' to do every thing faithful, and do his very best for his customers, it was s'posed that he wanted to do his best for the law; and so, when he got to whippin' Drusilla, he would whip her *too* severe — he would be *too* faithful to it.

You see, the way ont was, what made him whip her at all wuz, she was cross to him. They had nine little children. She always thought that two or three children would be about all one woman could bring up well "by hand," when that one hand wuz so awful full of work, as will be told more ensuin'ly. But he felt that big families wuz a protection to the Government; and "he wanted fourteen boys," he said, so they could all foller their father's footsteps, and be noble, law-making, law-abiding citizens, jest as he was.

But she had to do every mite of the housework, and milk cows, and make butter and cheese, and cook and wash and scour, and take all the care of the children, day and night, in sickness and in health, and spin and weave the cloth for their clothes (as wimmen did in them days), and then make 'em, and keep 'em clean. And when there wuz so many of 'em, and only about a year's difference in their ages, some of 'em — why, I s'pose she sometimes thought more of her own achin' back than she did of the good of the Government; and she would get kinder discouraged sometimes, and be cross to him.

And knowin' his own motives was so high and loyal, he felt that he ought to whip her. So he did.

And what shows that Drusilla wuzn't so bad as he s'posed she wuz, what shows that she did have her good streaks, and a deep reverence for the law, is, that she stood his whippin's first-rate, and never whipped him.

Now, she wuz fur bigger than he wuz, weighed 80 pounds the most, and might have whipped him if the law had been such.

But they was both law-abidin', and wanted to keep every preamble; so she stood it to be whipped, and never once whipped him in all the seventeen years they lived together.

She died when her twelfth child was born: there wus jest 13 months difference in the age of that and the one next older. And they said she often spoke out in her last sickness, and said, —

"Thank fortune, I have always kept the law."

And they said the same thought wus a great comfort to him in his last moments.

He died about a year after she did, leaving his 2nd wife with twins and a good property.

Then, there was Abagail Burpy. She married a sort of a high-headed man, though one that paid his debts, and was truthful, and considerable good-lookin', and played well on the fiddle. Why, it seemed as if he had almost every qualification for makin' a woman happy, only he had jest this one little excentricity, — that man would lock up Abagail Burpy's clothes every time he got mad at her.

Of course the law give her clothes to him; and knowin' it was one of the laws of the United States, she wouldn't have complained only when she had company. But it was mortifyin', and nobody could dispute it, to have company come, and nothin' to put on.

Several times she had to withdraw into the wood-house, and stay most of the day, shiverin', and under the cellar-stairs, and round in clothes-presses.

But he boasted in prayer-meetin's, and on boxes before grocery-stores, that he wus a law-abidin' citizen; and he wuz. Eben Flanders wouldn't lie for anybody.

But I'll bet that Abagail Flanders beat our old Revolutionary 4 mothers in thinkin' out new laws, when she lay round under stairs, and behind barrells, in her nightdress.

You see, when a man hides his wive's corset and petticoat, it is governin' without the "consent of the governed." And if you don't believe it, you ort to have peeked round them barrells, and seen Abagail's eyes. Why, they had hull reams of by-laws in 'em, and preambles, and "declarations of independence." So I have been told.

Why, it beat every thing I ever heard on, the lawful sufferin's of them wimmen. For there wuzn't nothin' illegal about one single trouble of theirn. They suffered accordin' to law, every one of 'em. But it wus tuff for 'em — very tuff.

And their all bein' so dretful humbly wuz and is another drawback to 'em; though that, too, is perfectly lawful, as everybody knows. . . .

NOTE

1. Many suffragists found the popular connection between prohibition and suffrage to be a dangerous one. While several feminist leaders either came to the suffrage movement via the temperance reform movement or subscribed to the idea of prohibition of liquor, the popular notion that a woman's vote was a "dry" vote threatened suffrage because male "wets" were often consequently antisuffrage. Samantha clearly supports both suffrage and temperance, but among various leaders it was at best an uneasy, often unwilling, alliance. The Woman's Christian Temperance Union (WCTU) was founded in 1869 and by the beginning of the twentieth century its membership outnumbered the suffragists more than ten to one (Sinclair, p. 222). As reforms go, temperance was eminently respectable in pitting religion (often evangelical religions, Baptists, Methodists) and purity against drunkenness and vice, and it gained many converts in the small towns and rural areas of America.

Susan B. Anthony, an early worker for temperance, later refused to publicly endorse it. However, she influenced Frances Willard to support passage of a federal suffrage amendment, so Willard was publicly associated with both reforms. In fact, as president of WCTU in the 1880s she was instrumental in securing the organization's endorsement for woman suffrage. Both Anthony and Willard sent writings to Marietta Holley expressing ideas that often took their folksy form in Jonesville or on "tower." Like Willard, Samantha claims that temperance was a necessary reform to protect the home and the children. After Willard's death in 1898, the WCTU — whose suffrage department had been producing more literature even than the suffragists — pulled back to their former concentration on the liquor prohibition issue (Sinclair, pp. 222–29).

Unlike the suffragists who needed statewide and/or federal passage of their reform, the prohibitionists could attack the liquor interests one saloon or one town or one county at a time once local-option bills had passed the legislatures. The first state prohibition law was passed in Maine in 1846. Eventually the prohibition movement claimed a national victory in 1919 with passage of the Eighteenth Amendment to the United States Constitution (commonly known as the Volstead Act), which made illegal the manufacture, sale, or transportation of alcoholic beverages. Interestingly, it didn't prohibit the purchase of such spirits. Prohibition brought its own problems, however, and was repealed in 1933 with passage of the Twenty-first Amendment.

20 On Women Bein' Angels

. . . "Wimmen had ruther be a flyin' round than to do all this, but they can't. If men really believe all they say about wimmen, and I think some of 'em do, in a dreamy way — if wimmen are angels, give 'em the rights of angels. Who ever heard of a angel foldin' up her wings, and goin' to a poorhouse or jail through the fault of somebody else? Who ever heard of a angel bein' dragged off to a police court by a lot of men, for fightin' to defend her children and herself from a drunken husband that had broke her wings, and blacked her eyes, himself, got the angel into the fight, and then she got throwed into the streets and the prison by it? Who ever heard of a angel havin' to take in washin' to support a drunken son or father or husband? Who ever heard of a angel goin' out as wet nurse to get money to pay taxes on her home to a Government that in theory idolizes her, and practically despises her, and uses that same money in ways abominable to that angel?

"If you want to be consistent — if you are bound to make angels of wimmen, you ort to furnish a free, safe place for 'em to soar in. You ort to keep the angels from bein' meddled with, and bruised, and killed, etc."

"Ahem," says he. "As it were, ahem."

But I kep' right on, for I begun to feel noble and by the side of myself.

"This talk about wimmen bein' outside and above all participation in the laws of her country, is jest as pretty as I ever heard any thing, and jest as simple. Why, you might jest as well throw a lot of snowflakes into the street, and say, 'Some of 'em are female flakes, and mustn't be trampled on.' The great march of life tramples on 'em all alike: they

This conversation between Semantha and a government official is found in *Sweet Cicely* (New York, 1887), pp. 214–16. Nearly the same conversation (including the analogy to the dog) takes place in "Serepta's Errants" in *Samantha on the Woman Question* (New York, 1913), pp. 80–99.

fall from one common sky, and are trodden down into one common ground.

"Men and wimmen are made with divine impulses and desires, and human needs and weaknesses, needin' the same heavenly light, and the same human aids and helps. The law should meet out to them the same rewards and punishments.

"Dorlesky says you call wimmens angels, and you don't give 'em the rights of the lowest beasts that crawls upon the earth. And Dorlesky told me to tell you that she didn't ask the rights of a angel: she would be perfectly contented and proud if you would give her the rights of a dog — the assured political rights of a yeller dog. She said 'yeller;' and I am bound on doin' her errent jest as she wanted me to, word for word.

"A dog, Dorlesky says, don't have to be hung if it breaks the laws it is not allowed any hand in making. A dog don't have to pay taxes on its bone to a Government that withholds every right of citizenship from it.

"A dog hain't called undogly if it is industrious, and hunts quietly round for its bone to the best of its ability, and wants to get its share of the crumbs that fall from that table that bills are laid on.

"A dog hain't preached to about its duty to keep home sweet and sacred, and then see that home turned into a place of torment under laws that these very preachers have made legal and respectable.

"A dog don't have to see its property taxed to advance laws that it believes ruinous, and that breaks its own heart and the hearts of other dear dogs.

"A dog don't have to listen to soul-sickening speeches from them that deny it freedom and justice — about its bein' a damosk rose, and a seraphine, when it knows it hain't: it knows, if it knows any thing, that it is a dog.

"You see, Dorlesky has been kinder embittered by her trials that politics, corrupt legislation, has brought right onto her. She didn't want nothin' to do with 'em; but they come right onto her unexpected and unbeknown, and she feels jest so. She feels she must do every thing she can to alter matters. She wants to help make the laws that have such a overpowerin' influence over her, herself. She believes from her soul that they can't be much worse than they be now, and may be a little better."

"Ah! if Dorlesky wishes to influence political affairs, let her influence her children, — her boys, — and they will carry her benign and noble influence forward into the centuries."

"But the law has took her boy, her little boy and girl, away from her. Through the influence of the Whisky Ring, of which her husband was a shinin' member, he got possession of her boy. And so, the law has made it perfectly impossible for her to mould it indirectly through him. What Dorlesky does, she must do herself." . . .

21 "Polly's Eyes Growed Tender"

Lorinda wuz dretful glad to see us and so wuz her husband and Polly. But the Reunion had to be put off on account of a spell her husband wuz havin'. Lorinda said she could not face such a big company as she'd invited while Hiram wuz havin' a spell, and I agreed with her.

Sez I, "Never, never, would I have invited company whilst Josiah wuz sufferin' with one of his cricks."

Men hain't patient under pain, and outsiders hain't no bizness to hear things they say and tell on 'em. So Polly had to write to the relations puttin' off the Reunion for one week. But Lorinda kep' on cookin' fruit cake and such that would keep, she had plenty of help, but loved to do her company cookin' herself. And seein' the Reunion wuz postponed and Lorinda had time on her hands, I proposed she should go with me to the big out-door meetin' of the Suffragists, which wuz held in a nigh-by city.

"Good land!" sez she, "nothin' would tempt me to patronize anything so brazen and onwomanly as a out-door meetin' of wimmen, and so onhealthy and immodest." I see she looked reproachfully at Polly as she said it. Polly wuz arrangin' some posies in a vase, and looked as sweet as the posies did, but considerable firm too, and I see from Lorinda's looks that Polly wuz one who had to leave father and mother for principle's sake.

But I sez, "You're cookin' this minute, Lorinda, for a out-door meetin'" (she wuz makin' angel cake). "And why is this meetin' any more onwomanly or immodest than the camp-meetin' where you wuz converted, and baptized the next Sunday in the creek?"

"Oh, them wuz religious meetin's," sez she.

"Well," sez I, "mebby these wimmen think their meetin' is religious. You know the Bible sez, 'Faith and works should go together,' and some

From *Samantha on the Woman Question* (New York, 1913), pp. 47–67.

of the leaders of this movement have showed by their works as religious a sperit and wielded aginst injustice to young workin' wimmen as powerful a weepon as that axe of the 'Postles the Bible tells about. And you said you went every day to the Hudson-Fulton doin's and hearn every out-door lecture; you writ me that there wuz probable a million wimmen attendin' them out-door meetin's, and that wuz curosity and pleasure huntin' that took them, and this is a meetin' of justice and right."

"Oh, shaw!" sez Lorinda agin, with her eye on Polly. "Wimmen have all the rights they want or need." Lorinda's husband bein' rich and lettin' her have her way she is real foot loose, and don't feel the need of any more rights for herself, but I told her then and there some of the wrongs and sufferin's of Serepta Pester, and bein' good-hearted (but obstinate and bigoted) she gin in that the errents wuz hefty, and that Serepta wuz to be pitied, but she insisted that wimmen's votin' wouldn't help matters.

But Euphrasia Pottle, a poor relation from Troy, spoke up. "After my husband died one of my girls went into a factory and gits about half what the men git for the same work, and my oldest girl who teaches in the public school don't git half as much for the same work as men do, and her school rooms are dark, stuffy, onhealthy, and crowded so the children are half-choked for air, and the light so poor they're havin' their eyesight spilte for life, and new school books not needed at all, are demanded constantly, so some-one can make money."

"Yes," sez I, "do you spoze, Lorinda, if intelligent mothers helped control such things they would let their children be made sick and blind and the money that should be used for food for poor hungry children be squandered on *on*-necessary books they are too faint with hunger to study."

"But wimmen's votin' wouldn't help in such things," sez Lorinda, as she stirred her angel cake vigorously.

But Euphrasia sez, "My niece, Ellen, teaches in a state where wimmen vote and she gits the same wages men git for the same work, and her school rooms are bright and pleasant and sanitary, and the pupils, of course, are well and happy. And if you don't think wimmen can help in such public matters just go to Seattle and see how quick a bad man wuz yanked out of his public office and a good man put in his place, mostly by wimmen's efforts and votes."

"Yes," sez I, "it is a proved fact that wimmen's votes do help in these matters. And do you think, Lorinda, that if educated, motherly, thoughtful wimmen helped make the laws so many little children would be allowed to toil in factories and mines, their tender shoulders bearin' the burden of constant labor that wears out the iron muscles of men?"

Polly's eyes growed tender and wistful, and her little white hands lingered over her posies, and I knowed the hard lot of the poor, the wrongs of wimmen and children, the woes of humanity, wuz pressin' down on her generous young heart. And I could see in her sweet face the brave determination to do and to dare, to try to help ondo the wrongs, and try to lift the burdens from weak and achin' shoulders. But Lorinda kep' on with the same old moth-eaten argument so broke down and feeble it ort to be allowed to die in peace.

"Woman's suffrage would make women neglect their homes and housework and let their children run loose into ruin."

I knowed she said it partly on Polly's account, but I sez in surprise, "Why, Lorinda, it must be you hain't read up on the subject or you would know wherever wimmen has voted they have looked out first of all for the children's welfare. They have raised the age of consent, have closed saloons and other places of licensed evil, and in every way it has been their first care to help 'em to safer and more moral surroundin's, for who has the interest of children more at heart than the mothers who bore them, children who are the light of their eyes and the hope of the future."

Lorinda admitted that the state of the children in the homes of the poor and ignorant wuz pitiful. "But," sez she, "the Bible sez 'ye shall always have the poor with you,' and I spoze we always shall, with all their sufferin's and wants. But," sez she, "in well-to-do homes the children are safe and well off, and don't need any help from woman legislation."

"Why, Lorinda," sez I, "did you ever think on't how such mothers may watch over and be the end of the law to their children with the father's full consent during infancy when they're wrastlin' with teethin', whoopin'-cough, mumps, etc., can be queen of the nursery, dispensor of pure air, sunshine, sanitary, and safe surroundin's in every way, and then in a few years see 'em go from her into dark, overcrowded, unsanitary, carelessly guarded places, to spend the precious hours when they are the most receptive to influence and pass man-made pitfalls on their way to and fro, must stand helpless until in too many cases the innocent healthy child that went from her care returns to her half-blind, a physical and moral wreck. The mother who went down to death's door for 'em, and had most to do in mouldin' their destiny during infancy should have at least equal rights with the father in controllin' their surroundin's during their entire youth, and to do this she must have equal legal power or her best efforts are wasted. That this is just and right is as plain to me as the nose on my face and folks will see it bom-bye and wonder they didn't before.

"And wimmen who suffer most by the lack on't, will be most interested in openin' schools to teach the fine art of domestic service, teachin' young girls how to keep healthy comfortable homes and fit themselves to be capable wives and mothers. I don't say or expect that wimmen's votin' will make black white, or wash all the stains from the legislative body at once, but I say that jest the effort to git wimmen's suffrage has opened hundreds of bolted doors and full suffrage will open hundreds more. And I'm goin' to that woman's suffrage meetin' if I walk afoot."

But here Josiah spoke up, I thought he wuz asleep, he wuz layin' on the lounge with a paper over his face. But truly the word, "Woman's Suffrage," rousts him up as quick as a mouse duz a drowsy cat, so, sez he, "I can't let you go, Samantha, into any such dangerous and onwomanly affair."

"Let?" sez I in a dry voice; "that's a queer word from one old pardner to another."

"I'm responsible for your safety, Samantha, and if anybody goes to that dangerous and onseemly meetin' I will. Mebby Polly would like to go with me." As stated, Polly is as pretty as a pink posy, and no matter how old a man is, nor how interestin' and noble his pardner is, he needs girl blinders, yes, he needs 'em from the cradle to the grave. But few, indeed, are the female pardners who can git him to wear 'em.

He added, "You know I represent you legally, Samantha; what I do is jest the same as though you did it."

Sez I, "Mebby that is law, but whether it is gospel is another question. But if you represent me, Josiah, you will have to carry out my plans; I writ to Diantha Smith Trimble that if I went to the city I'd take care of Aunt Susan a night or two, and rest her a spell; you know Diantha is a widder and too poor to hire a nurse. But seein' you represent me you can set up with her Ma a night or two; she's bed-rid and you'll have to lift her round some, and give her her medicine and take care of Diantha's twins, and let her git a good sleep."

"Well, as it were — Samantha — you know — men hain't expected to represent wimmen in everything, it is mostly votin' and tendin' big meetin's and such."

"Oh, I see," sez I; "men represent wimmen when they want to, and when they don't wimmen have got to represent themselves."

"Well, yes, Samantha, sunthin' like that."

He didn't say anything more about representin' me, and Polly said she wuz goin' to ride in the parade with some other college girls. Lorinda's linement looked dark and forbiddin' as Polly stated in her gentle, but firm way this ultimatum. Lorinda hated the idee of Polly's jinin' in what she called onwomanly and immodest doin's, but I looked beamin'ly at her and gloried in her principles.

After she went out Lorinda said to me in a complainin' way, "I should think that a girl that had every comfort and luxury would be contented and thankful, and be willin' to stay to home and act like a lady."

Sez I, "Nothin' could keep Polly from actin' like a lady, and mebby it is because she is so well off herself that makes her sorry for other young girls that have nothin' but poverty and privation."

"Oh, nonsense!" sez Lorinda. But I knowed jest how it wuz. Polly bein' surrounded by all the good things money could give, and bein' so tender-hearted her heart ached for other young girls, who had to spend the springtime of their lives in the hard work of earnin' bread for themselves and dear ones, and she longed to help 'em to livin' wages, so they could exist without the wages of sin, and too many on 'em had to choose between them black wages and starvation. She wanted to help 'em to better surroundin's and she knowed the best weepon she could put into their hands to fight the wolves of Want and Temptation, wuz the ballot. Polly hain't a mite like her Ma, she favors the Smiths more, her grand-ma on her pa's side wuz a Smith and a woman of brains and principle.

Durin' my conversation with Lorinda, I inquired about Royal Gray, for as stated, he wuz a great favorite of ourn, and I found out (and I could see it gaulded her) that when Polly united with the Suffragists he shied off some, and went to payin' attention to another girl. Whether it wuz to make Polly jealous and bring her round to his way of thinkin', I didn't know, but mistrusted, for I could have took my oath that he loved Polly deeply and truly. To be sure he hadn't confided in me, but there is a language of the eyes, when the soul speaks through 'em, and as I'd seen him look at Polly my own soul had hearn and understood that silent language and translated it, that Polly wuz the light of his eyes, and the one woman in the world for him. And I couldn't think his heart had changed so sudden. But knowin' as I did the elastic nature of manly affection, I felt dubersome.

This other girl, Maud Vincent, always said to her men friends, it wuz onwomanly to try to vote. She wuz one of the girls who always gloried in bein' a runnin' vine when there wuz any masculine trees round to lean on and twine about. One who always jined in with all the idees they promulgated, from neckties to the tariff, who declared cigar smoke wuz so agreeable and welcome; it did really make her deathly sick, but she would choke herself cheerfully and willin'ly if by so chokin' she could gain manly favor and admiration.

She said she didn't believe in helpin' poor girls, they wuz well enough off as it wuz, she wuz sure they didn't feel hunger and cold as rich girls did, their skin wuz thicker and their stomachs different and stronger, and constant labor didn't harm them, and working girls didn't need recreation as rich girls did, and woman's suffrage wouldn't help them any; in her opinion it would harm them, and anyway the poor wuz ongrateful.

She had the usual arguments on the tip of her tongue, for old Miss Vincent, the aunt she lived with, wuz a ardent She Aunty and very prominent in the public meetin's the She Auntys have to try to compel the Suffragists not to have public meetin's. They talk a good deal in public how onwomanly and immodest it is for wimmen to talk in public. And she wuz one of the foremost ones in tryin' to git up a school to teach wimmen civics, to prove that they mustn't ever have anything to do with civics.

Yes, old Miss Vincent wuz a real active, ardent She Aunty, and Maud Genevieve takes after her. Royal Gray, his handsome attractive personality, and his millions, had long been the goal of Maud's ambition. And how ardently did she hail the coolness growing between him and Polly, the little rift in the lute, and how zealously did she labor to make it larger.

Polly and Royal had had many an argument on the subject, that is, he would begin by makin' fun of the Suffragists and their militant doin's, which if he'd thought on't wuz sunthin' like what his old revolutionary forbears went through for the same reasons, bein' taxed without representation, and bein' burdened and punished by the law they had no voice in making, only the Suffragettes are not nearly so severe with their opposers, they haven't drawed any blood yet. Why, them old Patriots we revere so, would consider their efforts for freedom exceedingly gentle and tame compared to their own bloody battles.

And Royal would make light of the efforts of college girls to help workin' girls, and the encouragement and aid they'd gin 'em when they wuz strikin' for less death-dealin' hours of labor, and livin' wages, and so forth. I don't see how such a really noble young man as Royal ever come to argy that way, but spoze it wuz the dead hand of some rough onreasonable old ancestor reachin' up out of the shadows of the past and pushin' him on in the wrong direction.

So when he begun to ridicule what Polly's heart wuz sot on, when she felt that he wuz fightin' agin right and justice, before they knowed it both pairs of bright eyes would git to flashin' out angry sparks, and hash words would be said on both sides. That old long-buried Tory ancestor of hisen eggin' him on, so I spoze, and Polly's generous sperit rebellin' aginst the injustice and selfishness, and mebby some warlike ancestor of hern pushin' her on to say hash things. 'Tennyrate he had grown less attentive to her, and wuz bestowin' his time and attentions elsewhere.

And when she told him she wuz goin' to ride in the automobile parade of the suffragists, but really ridin' she felt towards truth and justice to half the citizens of the U.S., he wuz mad as a wet hen, a male wet hen, and wuz bound she shouldn't go.

Some men, and mebby it is love that makes 'em feel so (they say it is), and mebby it is selfishness (though they won't own up to it), but they want the women they love to belong to them alone, want to rule absolutely over their hearts, their souls, their bodies, and all their thoughts and aims, desires, and fancies. They don't really say they want 'em to wear veils, and be shet in behind lattice-windowed harems, but I believe they would enjoy it.

They want to be foot loose and heart loose themselves, but always after Ulysses is tired of world wandering, he wants to come back and open the barred doors of home with his own private latch-key, and find Penelope knitting stockings for him with her veil on, waitin' for him.[1]

That sperit is I spoze inherited from the days when our ancestor, the Cave man, would knock down the woman he fancied, with a club, and carry her off into his cave and keep her there shet up. But little by little men are forgettin' their ancestral traits, and men and wimmen are gradually comin' out of their dark caverns into the sunshine (for women too have inherited queer traits and disagreeable ones, but that is another story).

Well, as I said, Royal wuz mad and told Polly that he guessed that the day of the Parade he would take Maud Vincent out in the country in his motor, to gather May-flowers. Polly told him she hoped they would have a good time, and then, after he had gone, drivin' his car lickety-split, harem skarum, owin' to his madness I spoze, Polly went upstairs and cried, for I hearn her, her room wuz next to ourn.

And I deeply respected her for her principles, for he had asked her first to go May-flowering with him the day of the Suffrage meeting. But she refused, havin' in her mind, I spoze, the girls that couldn't hunt flowers, but had to handle weeds and thistles with bare hands (metaforically) and wanted to help them and all workin' wimmen to happier and more prosperous lives.

NOTE

1. In Homer's *The Odyssey* Ulysses wanders the world for twenty years before returning home. His wife, Penelope, had waited, remaining faithful to him despite two decades' absence.

22 "How I Went to 'Lection"

. . . Josiah looked up from the *World*, and says he:

"I am goin' to Jonesville to 'lection bime by, Samantha; you'd better ride down, and get the stuff for my shirts." Says he, "The Town Hall, as you know, is bein' fixed, and the pole is sot up right in the store. It will be handy, and you can go jest as well as not."

But I looked my companion in the face with a icy, curious mean, and says I in low, strange tones:

"Wouldn't it be revoltin' to the finer feelin's of your sole, to see a tender woman, your companion, a crowdin' and elboin' her way amongst the rude throng of men surroundin' the pole; to have her hear the immodest and almost dangerous language, the oaths and swearin'; to see her a plungin' down in the vortex of political warfare, and the arena of corruption?" Says I, "How is the shrinkin' modesty and delicacy of my sect a goin' to stand firm a jostlin' its way amongst the rude masses, and you there to see it?" Says I, "Aint it a goin' to be awful revoltin' to you, Josiah Allen?"

"Oh no!" says he in calm gentle axents, "not if you was a goin' for shirt buttons."

"Oh!" says I almost wildly, "a woman can plunge up head first ag'inst the pole, and be unharmed if she is in search of cotton flannel; she can pursue shirt buttons into the very vortex of political life, into the pool of corruption, and the mirey clay, and come out white as snow, and modest as a lilly of the valley. But let her step in them very tracks, a follerin' liberty and freedom, and justice, and right, and truth and temperance, and she comes out black as a coal." And says I in a almost rapped way, liftin' up my eyes to the ceelin': "Why are these things so?"

"Yes," says the Widder Doodle, that is jest what Mr. Doodle used to say. He said it would make a woman's reputation black as a coal,

From *Samantha at the Centennial* (Hartford, 1884), pp. 145–46, 155–61, 185–92.

would spile her modesty entirely to go to the pole, and be too wearin' on her. Says he, "Dolly it would spile you, and I would rather give my best cow than to see you spilte." Poor Mr. Doodle! there was a heavy mortgage on old Lineback then—it was a cow I brought to him when we was married, and Mr. Doodle was obleeged to mortgage her to git his tobacco through the winter; it was foreclosed in the spring, and had to go, but his speakin' as he did, and bein' so willin' to give up my cow, showed jest how much he thought of me. Oh! he almost worshipped me, Mr. Doodle did."

Jest at that very minute, Josiah laid down the *World*, and says he: "I am a goin to hitch up the old mare, Samantha. I guess you had better go, for I am a sufferin for them shirts; my old ones are a gettin' so thin; I am cold as a frog." . . .

But all the while I was on my tower towards 'lection—and the old mare went slow, all the time—though my face was calm, my mind was worked up and agitated and felt strange, and I kep' s'posen things. I said to myself, here I be started for 'lection, my companion settin' by my side, affection on his face, sweetness and peace throned onto his eyebrow, and at home is a Widder Doodle a helpin' me off to 'lection. Everything is peace and harmony and gay, because I am a goin' to 'lection after buttons and gussets for men's shirts. . . .

. . . I picked out my buttons, five cents a dozen, and bought my cotton flannel, and no Josiah. I felt worried in my mind. I thought of that mysterious bundle, and my companion's strange and curious looks as he brought it out from the barn, seemin'ly unbeknown to me, and his dretful curious actions about it as he meached out of the buggy with it. And I felt worried, and almost by the side of myself. But I kep' a cool demeanor on the outside of me—it is my way in the time of trouble to be calm, and put my best foot forred.

Jest then a man come up to me that I never laid eyes on before. He was a poor lookin' shack; his eyes was white mostly, and stood out of his head as if in search for some of the sense he never could git holt of, and his mouth was about half open. A dretful shiftless lookin' critter, and ragged as a Jew—all but his coat, and I'll be hanged if that didn't look worse than if his clothes was all of a piece. It was a blue broadcloth coat, swaller tailed, and had been a dretful genteel coat in the day of it—which I should judge was some fifty or sixty years previous to date. It was awful long waisted, and small round, and what they call single breasted; it turned back at the breast in a low, genteel way, over his old ragged vest; and ragged, red woolen shirt, and pinched him in at the bottom of his waist like a pismire, and the tails floated down behind, so polite over his pantaloons, which was fairly rags and tatters. As I said, I never laid eyes on him before, and still as he come up, and stood before me, I felt a curious, and strange feelin' go most through me; sunthin' in the arrer way. A curiouser more familiar-like, strange feelin', I never felt. But I didn't know then what it meant, I was in the dark. But more of this, anon, and hereafter.

Says the man, says he; "I beg your parding mom, for speaking to you, but you have got such a dretful good look to your face, somehow —," (Truly as I have said prior, and before this, my trials with the Widder Doodle, my martyrdom on the stake of Doodle and particulars, borne like a martyr, have purified my mean and make me look first-rate.) Says the man, says he: "You look so good, somehow, that I want to ask your advice."

Says I kindly, "I am a Promiscous Advisor by trade; advisin' is my mission and my theme. Ask me any advice my honest man, that you feel called to ask, and I will proceed to preform about my mission."

He handed me a ticket, with a awful dirty hand, every finger nail of which was seemin'ly in the deepest of mournin' for the pen-knife and nail-brushes they never had seen; and says he, "Will you tell me mom, whether that ticket is a democrat ticket, or the t'other one?"

I put on my specks, and says I, "It is the t'other one."

"Good Gracious!" says he; "Christopher Columbus! Pocahontas! Jim Crow and Jehosiphat!" says he. But I interrupted of him coldly, and says I:

"Stop swearin', instantly and this minute; and if you want my advice, proceed, and go on."

Says he, "There I have voted that ticket seventeen times, and I was paid to vote the democrat." Says he, "I am a man of my word, I am a poor man but a honest one. And here I have," — says he in a mournful tone — "here I have voted the wrong ticket seventeen times." Says he in a bitter tone, "I had ruther have give half a cent than to had this happen." Says he, "I am a poor man, I haint no capital to live on, and have got to depend on my honesty and principles for a livin'. And if this gets out, I am a ruined man;" says he in awful bitter tones, "what would the man that hired me say, if he should hear of it?"

"What did he give you?" says I, and as I said this, that strange, curious feelin' came over me again, as strange a feelin' as I ever felt.

Says he, "He give me this coat."

Then I knew it all. Then the cast-iron entered my sole, the arrer that
had been a diggin' into me, unbeknown to me as it was, went clear
through me, and come out on the other side (the side furtherest from
sister Minkley). Then I knew the meanin' of the strange feelin' I had
felt. It was Father Allen's coat — one that had fell to Josiah. Then I
knew the meanin' of my companion's mysterious demeanor, as he bore
the bundle from the barn. His plottin's the week before, and his drawin's onto my sympathy, to keep me from puttin' it into the carpet rags,
when I was fairly sufferin for blue in the fancy stripe, and refrained
from takin' it, because he said it would hurt his feelin's so. Oh the fearful agony of that half a moment. What a storm was a ragin' on the inside of my mind. But with a almost terrible effort, I controlled myself,
and kep' considerable calm on the outside. Truly, everybody has their
own private collection of skeletons; but that haint no sign they should
go abroad in public a rattlin' their bones; it don't help the skeletons any
nor their owners, and it haint nothin' highlarious and happyfyin' to the
public. I hadn't no idee of lettin' sister Minkley into the clothes-press
where my skeletons hung, knowin' that she probable had a private
assortment of her own skeletons, that she could look at unbeknown to
me.

"What made you vote the wrong ticket?" Says I, "can't you read?"

"No," says he, "we can't none of us read, my father, nor my brothers;
there is nine of us in all. My father and mother was first cousins," says
he in a confidential tone; "and the rest of my brothers don't know only
jest enough to keep out of the fire. I am the only smart one in the family. But," says he, "my brothers will all do jest as father and I tell 'em to,
and they will all vote a good many times a day, every 'lection; and we
are all willin' to do the fair thing and vote for the one that will pay us
the most. But not knowin' how to read, we git cheated," says he with
that bitter look, "there is so much corruption in politics now-a-days."

"I should think as much," says I. And almost overcome by my emotions, I spoke my mind out loud.

"There couldn't be much worse goin's on, anyway, if wimmen
voted."

"Wimmen vote!" says he in a awful scornful tone. "*Wimmen!*"

"Then you don't believe in their votin'," says I mekanically (as it were) for I was agitated, very.

"No I don't," says he, in a bold, hauty tone. "Wimmen don't *know* enough to vote."

I wouldn't contend with him, and to tell the truth, though I haint hauty, and never was called so, I was fairly ashamed to be catched talkin' with him, he looked so low and worthless. And I was glad enough that that very minute brother Wesley Minkley came up a holdin' out his hand, and says he:

"How do you do sister Allen, seems to me you look some cast down. How do you feel in your mind today, sister Allen?"

Bein' very truthful, I was jest a goin' to tell him that I felt considerable strange. But I was glad indeed that he forgot to wait for my answer, but went on, and says he:

"I heard the words the poor man uttered as I drew near, and I must say that although he had the outward appearance of bein' a shack — an idiotic shiftless shack, as you may say, — still he uttered my sentiments. We will wave the subject, however, of wimmen's incapacity to vote."

Elder Minkley is a perfect gentleman at heart, and he wouldn't for anything, tell me right out to my face that I didn't know enough to vote. I too am very ladylike when I set out, and I wasn't goin' to be out-done by him, so I told him in a genteel tone, that I should think he would want to wave off the subject, after perusin' such a specimen of male sufferage as had jest disappeared from our vision.

"Yes," says Elder Minkley mildly, and in a gentlemanly way, "we will wave it off. But Senator Vyse was a sayin' to me jest now — he has come in to vote, and we got to talkin', the Senator and I did, about wimmen's votin'; and he is bitter ag'inst it. And I believe jest as the Senator does, that woman's sufferage would introduce an element into politics, that would tottle it down from the foundation of justice and purity, on which it now firmly rests.

. . . I don't know as I ever see Josiah Allen in any better spirits, than he was, as we started off on our tower homewards. He had been to the clothin' store and bought him a new Sentinal necktie, red, white and blue. It was too young for him by forty years, and I told him so; but he said he liked it the minute he sot his eyes on it, it was so dressy. That man is vain. And then 'lection bid fair to go the way he wanted it to. He was awful animated, his face was almost wreathed in a smile, and before the old mare had gone several rods, he begun what a neat thing it was, and what a lucky hit for the nation, that wimmen couldn't vote. And he kep' on a talkin', that man did, as he was a carryin' me home from 'lection, about how it would break a woman's modesty down to go to the pole, and how it would devour her time and so 4th, and so 4th. And I was that tired out and fatigued a talkin' to sister Minkley that I let him go on for more'n a mile, and never put in my note at all. Good land! I'd heerd it all over from him, word for word, more'n a hundred times, and so I sot still. I s'pose he never thought how it was my lungs that ailed me, that I had used 'em almost completely up in principle, how I was almost entirely out of wind. And though a woman's will may be good, and her principles lofty, still she can't talk without wind. For truly in the words of a poem, I once perused:

"What's Paul, or Pollus, when a sinner's dead? dead for want of breath."

I don't s'pose he thought of my bein' tuckered out, but honestly s'pose he thought he was convincin' of me; for his mean grew gradually sort of overbearin' like, and contemptible, till he got to be more big feelin' and hauty in his mean than I had ever known him to be, and independenter. And he ended up as follers:

"Now, we have purity, and honesty, and unswervin' virtue, and incorruptible patriotism at the pole. Now, if corruption tries to stalk, honest, firm, lofty minded men stand ready to grip it by the throat. How can it stalk, when it is a chokin'? Wimmen haint got the knowledge, the deep wisdom and insight into things that we men have. They haint got the lofty idees of national honor, and purity, that we men have. Wimmen may mean well — "

He was feelin' so neat that he felt kinder clever towards the hull world, hemale, and female. "Wimmen *may* mean well, and for arguments sake, we'll say they *do* mean well. But that haint the pint, the pint is here — "

And he pinted his forefinger right towards the old mare. Josiah can't gesture worth a cent. He wouldn't make a oriter, if he should learn the trade for years. But ever sense he has been to the Debatin' school, he has seemed to have a hankerin' that way. "The pint is here. Not knowin' so much as we men know, not bein' so firm and lofty minded as we be, if wimmen should vote corruption would stalk; they not havin' a firm enough grip to choke it off. They would in the language of the 'postle be 'blowed about by every windy doctor.' They would be tempted by filthy lucre to 'sell their birth-right for a mess of pottery,' or crockery, I s'pose the text means. They haint got firmness; they are whifflin', their minds haint stabled. And if that black hour should ever come to the nation, that wimmen should ever go to the pole — where would be the lofty virtue, the firm high-minded honesty, the uncorruptible patriotism that now shines forth from politics? Where would be the purity of the pole? Where? oh! where?"

I'll be hanged if I could stand it another minute, and my lungs havin' got considerable rested, I spoke up, and says I:

"You seem to be havin' a kind of a enquiry meetin' in politics, Josiah Allen, and I'll get up in my mind, and speak in meetin'." And then I jest let loose that eloquent tone I keep by me expressly for the cause of principle; I used the very loftiest and awfulest one I had by me, as I fastened my specks immovably on hisen. "Where is that swaller tailed coat of Father Allen's?"

And in slower, sterner, colder tones, I added:

"With the brass buttons. Where is it Josiah Allen? Where? oh! where?"

Oh! What a change came over my companion's mean. Oh, how his feathers drooped and draggled on the ground speakin' in a rooster and allegory way. Oh, what a meachin' look covered him like a garment from head to foot. I declare for't if his boots didn't look meachin', and his hat and his vest. I never seen a meachener lookin' vest than hisen, as I went on:

"I'd talk Josiah Allen about men bein' so pureminded, and honest. I'd talk about wimmens bein' whifflin' and their minds not stabled. I'd talk about the purity of the pole. I'd love to see Josiah Allen's wife buyin' votes; bribin' Miss Gowdey or sister Minkley away from the paths of honesty and virtue, with a petticoat or a bib apron. I'd love to see George Washington offerin' his jack knife to Patrick Henry to get him to vote his ticket; or Benjamin Franklin, or Thomas Jefferson sellin' their votes for store clothes. I should be ashamed to go to the Sentinal Josiah Allen, if I was in your place. I should be perfectly ashamed to set my eyes on that little hatchet that George Washington couldn't tell a lie with. I should think that hatchet would cut your conscience clear to the bone — if you have got a conscience, Josiah Allen.

"Oh! Did I ever expect to see the companion of my youth and middle age, betrayin' his country's honor; trafficin' in bribery and sin; dickerin' with dishonesty; tradin' in treason; buyin' corruption; and payin' for it

with a swaller tailed coat, with his old father's blue swaller tailed coat
that his lawful pardner wanted for carpet rags. Oh, the agony of this
half an hour, Josiah Allen! Oh, the feelin's that I feel."

But Josiah had begun to pick up his crumbs again. Truly it is hard
work to keep men down in the valley of humiliation. You can't keep
'em worked up and mortified for any great length of time, do the best
you can. But I continued on in almost dretful axents.

"You ort to repent in sackcloth and ashes, Josiah Allen."

"We haint got no sackcloth Samantha," says he, "and we have sold
our ashes. Probable the man wouldn't want me to be a repentin' in 'em.
It would be apt to leach 'em, too much lie for 'em."

"I'd try to turn it off into a joke, Josiah Allen, I'd laugh if I was in
your place about lyin'. Your tears ort to flow like a leach barrell. Oh if
you could realize as I do the wickedness of your act. Destroyin' your
country's honor. Sellin' your father's coat when I wanted it for carpet
rags." Says I, "I am as good a mind as I ever was to eat, to color the hull
thing black, warp and all, makin' a mournin' carpet of it, to set down
and bewail my pardner's wickedness from year to year."

"It would look pretty solemn Samantha." I see the idee worried him.

"It wouldn't look no solemner than I feel, Josiah Allen."

And then I kep' perfectly still for a number of minutes, for silence is
the solemn temple with its roof as high as the heavens, convenient for
the human soul to retire into, at any time, unbeknown to anybody; to
offer up thanksgivin's, or repent of iniquities. And I thought my Josiah
was repentin' of hisen.

But truly as I said men's consciences are like ingy rubber, dretful
easy and stretchy, and almost impossible to break like a bruised reed.
For while I was a hopin' that my companion was a repentin', and
thought mebby he would burst out a cryin', overcome by a realizin'
sense of his depravities; and I was a thinkin' that if he did, I should take
up a corner of his bandanna handkerchief and cry on it too—that man
for all his back slidin's is so oncommon dear to me—he spoke out in jest
as chirp a way as I ever seen him, and for all the world, jest as if he
hadn't done nothin':

"I wonder if sister Doodle will have supper ready, Samantha. I
meant to have told her to fried a little o' that beef."

V
Rights Denied by the Church

"I lay out in petickuler to tackle the Meetin'
House. She is in the wrong on't [The Cause of
Eternal Justice], and I want to set her right."
— Samantha

The following selections are taken from Holley's book on the Meetin'
House, *Samantha Among the Brethren*, but they manage to interlace
several of Samantha's "themes to lay holt of" — denial of equal participation in administering church law while being bound to its punishments, the evil of liquor and women's inability to save their sons from
its "poisen," the good that would result from voting power by moral
women who are not blinded as men are by monied interests, the double
standard of morality applied to men and women, women's total economic dependence on men, and the illogic of male arguments inter-
preting the female's proper sphere.

In a publisher's appendix to *Brethren*, arguments actually cited during the 1888 General Conference of the Methodist Episcopal Church
regarding the seating of women delegates are presented. Those who
spoke against admission of women relied either upon strict adherence
to the intention of the rules — which they maintained obviously did not
include women delegates — or upon ludicrous distinctions in definition.

Rev. James Buckley is perhaps most hairsplitting when he contends
that the word "layman" was created to indicate a separate class from
clergyman. Since there was not a separate class called clergywoman,
there was no need for a separate class called laywoman. Therefore,
layman means men who are not clergymen. He continues by referring
to the Gettysburg Address's famous government of, for, and by the people. Although the dictionary would say that "people" means men,
women and children, Lincoln clearly did not intend that women and
children can take any part in the government of the nation. Our fathers
did not intend to put women in. "The fact is, that they only proposed to

allow them to put us in." Every time you put a woman in, you put a man out.

Rev. Theodore Flood had argued for admission of women delegates on the grounds that the right of suffrage, which women had possessed in the church for sixteen years, carried with it the right to hold office. Rev. A. B. Leonard likewise favored seating women on the grounds that women have always been regarded as laymen in the practical work of church and administration; they pay quarterage, contribute to benevolent collections, pray, and testify. They are tried by the same process as men and are subject to the same penalties of suspension and expulsion. There are only two orders of the church — clergy and laity.

Women delegates were denied admission to the conference. Holley puts the Buckley logic in Josiah's mouth as he tries to explain to Samantha the intricacies of interpretation. Samantha, of course, assumes the Flood-Leonard rationale.

"The Methodist Conference had decided that wimmen wuz too weak to set"

23 On Women and the Meetin' House

Again it come to pass, in the fulness of time, that my companion, Josiah Allen, see me walk up and take my ink stand off of the manteltry piece, and carry it with a calm and majestick gait to the corner of the settin' room table devoted by me to literary pursuits. And he sez to me:

"What are you goin' to tackle now, Samantha?"

And sez I, with quite a good deal of dignity, "The Cause of Eternal Justice, Josiah Allen."

"Anythin' else?" sez he, lookin' sort o' oneasy at me. (That man realizes his shortcomin's, I believe, a good deal of the time, he duz.)

"Yes," sez I, "I lay out in petickuler to tackle the Meetin' House. She is in the wrong on't, and I want to set her right."

Josiah looked sort o' relieved like, but he sez out, in a kind of a pert way, es he set there a-shellin corn for the hens:

"A Meetin' House hadn't ort to be called she—it is a he."

And sez I, "How do you know?"

And he sez, "Because it stands to reason it is. And I'd like to know what you have got to say about him any way?"

Sez I, "That 'him' don't sound right, Josiah Allen. It sounds more right and nateral to call it 'she.' Why," sez I, "hain't we always hearn about the Mother Church, and don't the Bible tell about the Church bein' arrayed like a bride for her husband? I never in my life hearn it called a 'he' before."

"Oh, wall, there has always got to be a first time. And I say it sounds better. But what have you got to say about the Meetin' House, anyway?"

"I have got this to say, Josiah Allen. The Meetin' House hain't a-actin' right about wimmen.[1] The Founder of the Church wuz born of woman. It wuz on a woman's heart that His head wuz pillowed first

The selections in this section are found in *Samantha Among the Brethren* (New York, 1890) and appear in sequence pp. vii–xi, 162–5, 241–70, 347–62, 380–87.

and last. While others slept she watched over His baby slumbers and His last sleep. A woman wuz His last thought and care. Before dawn she wuz at the door of the tomb, lookin' for His comin'. So she has stood ever sense — waitin', watchin', hopin', workin' for the comin' of Christ. Workin', waitin' for His comin' into the hearts of tempted wimmen and tempted men — fallen men and fallen wimmen — workin', waitin', toilin', nursin' the baby good in the hearts of a sinful world — weepin' pale-faced over its crucefixion — lookin' for its reserection. Oh how she has worked all through the ages!"

"Oh shaw!" sez Josiah, "some wimmen don't care about anythin' but crazy work and back combs."

I felt took down, for I had been riz up, quite considerble, but I sez, reasonable:

"Yes, there are such wimmen, Josiah, but think of the sweet and saintly souls that have given all their lives, and hopes, and thoughts to the Meetin' House — think of the throngs to-day that crowd the aisles of the Sanctuary — there are five wimmen to one man, I believe, in all the meetin' houses to-day a-workin' in His name. True Daughters of the King, no matter what their creed may be — Catholic or Protestant.

"And while wimmen have done all this work for the Meetin' House, the Meetin' House ort to be honorable and do well by her."

"Wall, hain't *he?*" sez Josiah.

"No, *she* hain't," sez I.

"Wall, what petickuler fault do you find? What has *he* done lately to rile you up?"

Sez I, "*She* wuz in the wrong on't in not lettin' wimmen set on the Conference."

"Wall, I say *he* wuz right," sez Josiah. "*He* knew, and I knew, that wimmen wuzn't strong enough to set."

"Why," sez I, "it don't take so much strength to set as it duz to stand up. And after workin' as hard as wimmen have for the Meetin' House, she ort to have the priveledge of settin'. And I am goin' to write out jest what I think about it."

"Wall," sez Josiah, as he started for the barn with the hen feed, "don't be too severe with the Meetin' House."

And then, after he went out, he opened the door agin and stuck his head in and sez:

"Don't be too hard on *him.*"

And then he shet the door quick, before I could say a word.

But good land! I didn't care. I knew I could say what I wanted to with my faithful pen — and I am bound to say it.

> JOSIAH ALLEN'S WIFE,
> Bonny View,
> near Adams, New York.

Oct. 14th, 1890.

NOTE

1. A debate among Rev. Henry Grew, Lucretia Mott, Hannah Tracy Cutler, William Lloyd Garrison, and Emma R. Coe at the Woman's Rights Convention in 1854 addressed the relation of religion to women's status. Excerpts from this debate as well as those from Elizabeth Cady Stanton's *The Woman's Bible* (1895) and Catherine Waugh McCulloch's comments on the Bible are reprinted in Kraditor, *Up From the Pedestal*, pp. 108–21. A series of commentaries on those parts of the Bible referring to women, *The Woman's Bible* reflected Stanton's belief that women could not achieve equality unless the pernicious influence of organized religion were destroyed. Stanton did not see the Bible as a message from Heaven but rather from man. In reply to her critics, she claims: "The first step in the elevation of women under all systems of religion is to convince them that the great Spirit of the Universe is in no way responsible for these absurdities [women's position as described in the Pentatuch] . . . 'The Woman's Bible' comes to the ordinary reader like a real benediction. It tells her the good Lord did not write the Book; that the garden scene is a fable; that she is in no way responsible for the laws of the Universe."

Catherine Waugh McCulloch, a lawyer and suffragist, took the more typical tact of arguing that if the Bible were properly interpreted, woman's claim to equality would be supported and male-supremacist portions could be accounted for in historical or metaphorical ways. For Holley (and Samantha) it is the male-dominated hierarchy and not God or Christianity as it should be practiced that keeps women active in the "doin's" but invisible in the power of the institutional church.

24   On the Methodist Conference

Submit wuz very skairt to heern him [Josiah] go on (she felt more nervous on account of an extra hard day's work), and I myself wuz beat
out, but I wuzn't afraid at all of him, though he did go on elegant, and
dretful empressive and even skairful.

He stood up on the same old ground that men have always stood up
on, the ground of man's great strength and capability, and wimmen's
utter weakness, helplessness, and incapacity. Josiah enlarged almost
wildly on the subject of how high, how inaccessibley lofty the Conference wuz, and the utter impossibility of a weak, helpless, fragaile bein'
like a women ever gettin' up on it, much less settin' on it.

And then, oh how vividly he depictered it, how he and every other
male Methodist in the land loved wimmen too well, worshipped 'em
too deeply to put such a wearin' job onto 'em. Oh how Josiah Allen
soared up in eloquence. Submit shed tears, or, that is, I thought she did
— I see her wipe her eyes any way. Some think that about the time the
Samuel Danker anniversary comes round, she is more nervous and deprested.[1] It wuz very near now, and take that with her hard work that
day, it accounts some for her extra depression — though, without any
doubt, it wuz Josiah's talk that started the tears.

I couldn't bear to see Submit look so mournful and deprested, and
so, though I wuz that tired myself that I could hardly hold my head up,
yet I did take my bits in my teeth, as you may say, and asked him —

What the awful hard job wuz that he and other men wuz so anxus to
ward offen wimmen.

And he sez, "Why, a settin' on the Conference."

And I sez, "I don't believe that is such a awful hard job to tackle."

"Yes, indeed, it is," sez Josiah in his most skairful axent, "yes, it is."

And he shook his head meenin'ly and impressively, and looked at me
and Submit in as mysterius and strange a way, es I have ever been looked

at in my life, and I have had dretful curius looks cast onto me, from first to last. And he sez in them deep impressive axents of hisen,

"You jest try it once, and see — I have sot on it, and I know."

Josiah wuz sent once as a delegate to the Methodist Conference, so I spozed he did know.

But I sez, "Why you come home the second day when you sot as happy as a king, and you told me how you had rested off durin' the two days, and how you had visited round at Uncle Jenkins'es, and Cousin Henn's, and you said that you never had had such a good time in your hull life, as you did when you wuz a settin'. You looked as happy as a king, and acted so."

Josiah looked dumbfounded for most a quarter of a minute. For he knew my words wuz as true es anything ever sot down in Matthew, Mark, or Luke, or any of the other old patriarks. He knew it wuz Gospel truth, that he had boasted of his good times a settin', and as I say for nearly a quarter of a minute he showed plain signs of mortification.

But almost imegietly he recovered himself, and went on with the doggy obstinacy of his sect:

"Oh, wall! Men can tackle hard jobs, and get some enjoyment out of it too, when it is in the line of duty. One thing that boys em' up, and makes em' happy, is the thought that they are a keepin' trouble and care offen wimmen. That is a sweet thought to men, and always wuz. And there wuz great strains put onto our minds, us men that sot, that wimmen couldn't be expected to grapple with, and hadn't ort to try to. It wuz a great strain onto us."

"What was the nater of the strain?" sez I. "I didn't know as you did a thing only sot still there and go to sleep. You wuz fast asleep there most the hull of the time, for it come straight to me from them that know. And all that Deacon Bobbett did who went with you wuz to hold up his hand two or three times a votin'. I shouldn't think that wuz so awful wearin'."

And agin I sez, "What wuz the strain?"

But Josiah didn't answer, for that very minute he remembered a pressin' engagement he had about borrowin' a plow. He said he had got to go up to Joe Charnick's to get his plow. (*I* don't believe he wanted a plow that time of night.) . . .

. . . Though Josiah Allen made a excuse of borrowin' a plow (a *plow*, that time of night) to get away from my arguments on the Conference, and Submit's kinder skairt face, and so forth, and so on —

He resumed the conversation the next mornin' with more energy than ever. (He never said nuthin' about the plow, and I never see no sign on it, and don't believe he got it, or wanted it.)

He resumed the subject, and kep on a-resumin' of it from day to day and from hour to hour.

He would nearly exhaust the subject at home, and then he would tackle the wimmen on it at the Methodist Meetin' House, while we Methodist wimmen wuz to work.

After leavin' me to the meetin' house, Josiah would go on to the post-office for his daily *World*, and then he would stop on his way back to give us female wimmen the latest news from the Conference, and give us his idees on't.

And sometimes he would fairly harrow us to the very bone, with his dretful imaginins and fears that wimmen would be allowed to overdo herself, and ruin her health, and strain her mind, by bein' permitted to set!

Why Submit Tewksbury, and some of the other weaker sisters, would look fairly wild-eyed for some time after he would go.

He never could stay long. Sometimes we would beset him to stay and do some little job for us, to help us along with our work, such as liftin' somethin' or movin' some bench, or the pulpit, or somethin'.

But he never had the time; he always had to hasten home to get to work. He wuz in a great hurry with his spring's work, and full of care about that buzz saw mill.

And that wuz how it wuz with every man in the meetin' house that wuz able to work any. They wuz all in a hurry with their spring's work, and their buzz saws, and their inventions, and their agency's, etc., etc., etc.

And that wuz the reason why we wimmen wuz havin' such a hard job on the meetin' house.

NOTE

1. The last day she saw her beloved.

25 On Fixin' Over the Meetin' House

. . . Things looked dretful dark. And Sister Bobbet, who is very tender hearted, shed tears several times a-talkin' about the hard times that had come onto our meetin' house, and how Zion wuz a-languishin', etc., etc.

And I told Sister Bobbet in confidence, and also in public, that it wuz time to talk about Zion's languishin' when we had done all we could to help her up. And I didn't believe Zion would languish so much if she had a little help gin her when she needed it.

And Miss Bobbet said "she felt jest so about it, but she couldn't help bein' cast down."

And so most all of the sisters said. Submit Tewksbury wept, and shed tears time and agin, a-talkin' about it, and so several of 'em did. But I sez to 'em —

"Good land!" sez I. "We have seen jest as hard times in the Methodist meetin' house before, time and agin, and we wimmen have always laid holt and worked, and laid plans, and worked, and worked, and with the Lord's help have sailed the old ship Zion through the dark waters into safety, and we can do it agin."

Though what we wuz to do we knew not, and the few male men who didn't jine in the hardness, said they couldn't see no way out of it, but what the minister would have to go, and the meetin' house be shet up for a spell.

But we female wimmen felt that we could not have it so any way. And we jined together, and met in each other's housen (not publickly, oh no! we knew our places too well as Methodist Sisters).

We didn't make no move in public, but we kinder met round to each other's housen, sort o' private like, and talked, and talked, and prayed — we all knew that wuzn't aginst the church rules, so we jest rastled in prayer, for help to pay our honest debts, and keep the Methodist meetin' house from disgrace, for the men wuz that worked up and madded, that they didn't seem to care whether the meetin' house come to nothin' or not.

Wall, after settin' day after day (not public settin', oh, no! we knew our places too well, and wouldn't be ketched a-settin' public till we had a right to).

After settin' and talkin' it over back and forth, we concluded the very best thing we could do wuz to give a big fair and try to sell things enough to raise some money.

It wuz a fearful tuff job we had took onto ourselves, for we had got to make all the things to sell out of what we could get holt of, for, of course, our husbands all kep the money purses in their own hands, as the way of male pardners is. But we laid out to beset 'em when they wuz cleverer than common (owin' to extra good vittles) and get enough money out of 'em to buy the materials to work with, bedquilts (crazy, and otherwise), embroidered towels, shawl straps, knit socks and suspenders, rugs, chair covers, lap robes, etc., etc., etc.

It wuz a tremendus hard undertakin' we had took onto ourselves, with all our spring's work on hand, and not one of us Sisters kep a hired girl at the time, and we had to do our own house cleanin', paintin' floors, makin' soap, spring sewin', etc., besides our common housework.

But the very worst on't wuz the meetin' house wuz in such a shape that we couldn't do a thing till that wuz fixed.

The men had undertook to fix over the meetin' house jest before the hardness commenced. The men and wimmen both had labored side by side to fix up the old house a little.

The men had said that in such church work as that wimmen had a perfect right to help, to stand side by side with the male brothers, and do half, or more than half or even *all* the work. They said it wuzn't aginst the Discipline, and all the Bishops wuz in favor of it, and always had been. They said it wuz right accordin' to the Articles. But when it come to the hard and arjuous duties of drawin' salleries with 'em, or settin' up on Conferences with 'em, why there a line had to be drawed, wimmen must not be permitted to strain herself in no such ways — nor resk the tender delicacy of her nature, by settin' in a meetin' house as a delegate by the side of a man once a year. It wuz too resky. But we could lay holt and work with 'em in public, or in private, which we felt wuz indeed a privelege, for the interests of the Methodist meetin' house wuz dear to our hearts, and so wuz our pardners' approvals — and they wuz all on 'em unanimus on this pint — we could *work* all we wanted to.

So we had laid holt and worked right along with the men from day to day, with their full and free consents, and a little help from 'em, till we had got the work partly done. We had got the little Sabbath-school room painted and papered, and the cushions of the main room new covered, and we had engaged to have it frescoed, but the frescoer had turned out to be a perfect fraud, and, of all the lookin' things, that meetin' house wuz about the worst. The plaster, or whatever it wuz he had put on, had to be all scraped off before it could be papered, the paper wuz bought, and the scrapin' had begun.

The young male and female church members had give a public concert together, and raised enough money to get the paper — it wuz very nice, and fifty cents a roll (double roll).

These young females appearin' in public for this purpose wuz very agreeable to the hull meetin' house, and wuz right accordin' to the rules of the Methodist Meetin' House, for I remember I asked about it when the question first come up about sendin' female delegates to the Conference, and all the male members of our meetin' house wuz so horrified at the idee.

I sez, "I'll bet there wouldn't one of the delegates yell half so loud es she that wuz Mahala Gowdey at the concert. Her voice is a sulferino of the very keenest edge and highest tone, and she puts in sights and sights of quavers."

But they all said that wuz a *very* different thing.

And sez I, "How different? She wuz a yellin' in public for the good of the Methodist Meetin' House (it wuz her voice that drawed the big congregatin, we all know). And them wimmen delegates would only have to 'yea' and 'nay' in a still small voice for the good of the same. I can't see why it would be so much more indelicate and unbecomin' in them" — and sez I, "they would have bonnets and shawls on, and she that wuz Mahala had on a low neck and short sleeves."

But they wouldn't yield, and I wouldn't nuther.

But I am a eppisodin fearful, and to resoom. Wall, as I said, the scrapin' had begun. One side of the room wuz partly cleaned so the paper could go on, and then the fuss come up, and there it wuz, as you may say, neither hay nor grass, neither frescoed nor papered nor nuthin'. And of all the lookin' sights it wuz.

Wall, of course, if we had a fair in that meetin' house, we couldn't have it in such a lookin' place to disgrace us in the eyes of Baptists and 'Piscopals.

No, that meetin' house had got to be scraped, and we wimmen had got to do the scrapin' with case knives.

It wuz a hard job. I couldn't help thinkin' quite a number of thoughts as I stood on a barell with a board acrost it, afraid as death of fallin' and a workin' for dear life, and the other female sisters a standin' round on similar barells, all a-workin' fur beyond their strengths, and all afraid of fallin', and we all a-knowin' what we had got ahead on us a paperin' and a gettin' up the fair.

Couldn't help a-me-thinkin' to myself several times. It duz seem to me that there hain't a question a-comin' up before that Conference that is harder to tackle than this plasterin' and the conundrum that is up before us Jonesville wimmen how to raise 300 dollars out of nuthin', and to make peace in a meetin' house where anarky is now rainin' down.

But I only thought these thoughts to myself, fur I knew every women there wuz peacible and law abidin' and there wuzn't one of 'em but what would ruther fall offen her barell then go agin the rules of the Methodist Meetin' House.

Yes, I tried to curb down my rebellous thoughts, and did, pretty much all the time.

And good land! we worked so hard that we hadn't time to tackle very curius and peculier thoughts, them that wuz dretful strainin' and wearin' on the mind. Not of our own accord we didn't, fur we had to jest nip in and work the hull durin' time.

And then we all knew how deathly opposed our pardners wuz to our takin' any public part in meetin' house matters or mountin' rostrums, and that thought quelled us down a sight.

Of course when these subjects wuz brung up before us, and turned round and round in front of our eyes, why we had to look at 'em and be rousted up by 'em more or less. It was Nater.

And Josiah not havin' anything to do evenin's only to set and look at the ceilin'. Every single night when I would go home from the meetin' house, Josiah would tackle me on it, on the danger of allowin' wimmen to ventur out of her spear in Meetin' House matters, and specially the Conference.

It begin to set in New York the very day we tackled the meetin' in Jonesville with a extra grip.

So's I can truly say, the Meetin' House wuz on me day and night. For workin' on it es I did, all day long, and Josiah a-talkin' abut it till bed time, and I a-dreamin' abut it a sight, that, and the Conference.

Truly, if I couldn't set on the Conference, the Conference sot on me, from mornin' till night, and from night till mornin'.

I spoze it wuz Josiah's skairful talk that brung it onto me, it wuz brung on nite mairs mostly, in the nite time.

He would talk *very* skairful, and what he called deep, and repeat pages of Casper Keeler's arguments, and they would appear to me (drawed also by nite mairs) every page on 'em lookin' fairly lurid.

I suffered.

Josiah would set with the *World* and other papers in his hand, a-perusin' of 'em, while I would be a-washin' up my dishes, and the very minute I would get 'em done and my sleeves rolled down, he would tackle me, and often he wouldn't wait for me to get my work done up, or even supper got, but would begin on me as I filled up my tea kettle, and keep up a stiddy drizzle of argument till bed time, and as I say, when he left off, the nite mairs would begin.

I suffered beyond tellin' almost.

The second night of my arjuous labors on the meetin' house, he began wild and eloquent about wimmen bein' on Conferences, and mountin' rostrums. And sez he, "That is suthin' that we Methodist men can't stand."

And I, havin' stood up on a barell all day a-scrapin' the ceilin', and not bein' recuperated yet from the skairtness and dizziness of my day's work, I sez to him:

"Is rostrums much higher than them barells we have to stand on to the meetin' house?"

And Josiah said, "it wuz suthin' altogether different." And he assured me agin,

"That in any modest, unpretendin' way the Methodist Church wuz willin' to accept wimmen's work. It wuzn't aginst the Discipline. And that is why," sez he, "that wimmen have all through the ages been allowed to do most all the hard work in the church — such as raisin' money for church work — earnin' money in all sorts of ways to carry on the different kinds of charity work connected with it — teachin' the children, nursin' the sick, carryin' on hospital work, etc., etc. But," sez he, "this is fur, fur different from gettin' up on a rostrum, or tryin' to set on a Conference. Why," sez he, in a haughty tone, "I should think they'd know without havin' to be told that laymen don't mean women."

Sez I, "Them very laymen that are tryin' to keep wimmen out of the Conference wouldn't have got in themselves if it hadn't been for wimmen's votes. If they can legally vote for men to get in why can't men vote for them?"

"That is the pint," sez Josiah, "that is the very pint I have been tryin' to explain to you. Wimmen can help men to office, but men can't help wimmen; that is law, that is statesmanship. I have been a-tryin' to explain it to you that the word laymen *always* means woman when she can help men in any way, but *not* when he can help her, or in any other sense."

Sez I, "It seemed to mean wimmen when Metilda Henn wuz turned out of the meetin' house."

"Oh, yes," sez Josiah in a reasonin' tone, "the word laymen always means wimmen when it is used in a punishin' and condemnatory sense, or in the case of work and so fourth, but when it comes to settin' up in high places, or drawin' sallerys, or anything else difficult, it always means men."

Sez I, in a very dry axent, "Then the word man, when it is used in church matters, always means wimmen, so fur as scrubbin' is concerned, and drowdgin' round?"

"Yes," sez Josiah haughtily. "And it always means men in the higher and more difficult matters of decidin' questions, drawin' sallerys, settin' on Conferences, etc. It has long been settled to be so," sez he.

"Who settled it?" sez I.

"Why the men, of course," sez he. "The men have always made the rules of the churches, and translated the Bibles, and everything else that is difficult," sez he. Sez I, in fearful dry axents, almost husky ones, "It seems to take quite a knack to know jest when the word laymen means men and when it means wimmen."

"That is so," sez Josiah. "It takes a man's mind to grapple with it; wimmen's minds are too weak to tackle it. It is jest as it is with that word 'men' in the Declaration of Independence. Now that word 'men', in that Declaration, means men some of the time, and some of the time men and wimmen both. It means both sexes when it relates to punishment, taxin' property, obeyin' the laws strictly, etc., etc., and then it goes right on the very next minute and means men only, as to wit, namely, votin', takin' charge of public matters, makin' laws, etc.

"I tell you it takes deep minds to foller on and see jest to a hair where the division is made. It takes statesmanship.

"Now take that claws, 'All men are born free and equal.'

"Now half of that means men, and the other half men and wimmen. Now to understand them words perfect you have got to divide the tex. 'Men are born.' That means men and wimmen both — men and wimmen are both born, nobody can dispute that. Then comes the next claws, 'Free and equal.' Now that means men only — anybody with one eye can see that.

"Then the claws, 'True government consists.' That means men and wimmen both — consists — of course the government consists of men and wimmen, 'twould be a fool who would dispute that. 'In the consent of the governed.' That means men alone. Do you see, Samantha?" sez he.

I kep' my eye fixed on the tea kettle, fer I stood with my tea-pot in hand waitin' for it to bile — "I see a great deal, Josiah Allen."

"Wall," sez he, "I am glad on't. Now to sum it up," sez he, with some the mean of a preacher — or, ruther, a exhauster — "to sum the matter all up, the words 'bretheren,' 'laymen,' etc., always means wimmen so fur as this: punishment for all offenses, strict obedience to the rules of the church, work of any kind and all kinds, raisin' money, givin' money all that is possible, teachin' in the Sabbath school, gettin' up missionary and charitable societies, carryin' on the same with no help from the male sect leavin' that sect free to look after their half of the meanin' of the word — sallerys, office, makin' the laws that bind both of the sexes, rulin' things generally, translatin' Bibles to suit their own idees, preachin' at 'em, etc., etc. Do you see, Samantha?" sez he, proudly and loftily.

"Yes," sez I, as I filled up my tea-pot, for the water had at last biled. "Yes, I see."

And I spoze he thought he had convinced me, for he acted high headeder and haughtier for as much as an hour and a half. And I didn't say anything to break it up, for I see he had stated it jest as he and all his sect looked at it, and good land! I couldn't convince the hull male sect if I tried — clergymen, statesmen and all — so I didn't try, and I wuz truly beat out with my day's work, and I didn't drop more than one idee more, I simply dropped this remark es I poured out his tea and put some good cream into it — I merely sez:

"There is three times es many wimmen in the meetin' house es there is men."

"Yes," sez he, "that is one of the pints I have been explainin' to you," and then he went on agin real high headed, and skairt, about the old ground, of the willingness of the meetin' house to shelter wimmen in its folds, and how much they needed gaurdin' and guidin', and about their delicacy of frame, and how unfitted they wuz to tackle anything hard, and what a grief it wuz to the male sect to see 'em a-tryin' to set on Conferences or mount rostrums, etc., etc.

And I didn't try to break up his argument, but simply repeated the question I had put to him — for es I said before, I wuz tired, and skairt, and giddy yet from my hard labor and my great and hazardus elevatin'; I had not, es you may say, recovered yet from my recuperation, and so I sez agin them words —

"Is rostrums much higher than them barells to stand on?"

And Josiah said agin, "it wuz suthin' entirely different;" he said barells and rostrums wuz so fur apart that you couldn't look at both on 'em in one day hardly, let alone a minute. And he went on once more with a long argument full of Bible quotations and everything.

And I wuz too tuckered out to say much more. But I did contend for it to the last, that I didn't believe a rostrum would be any more tottlin' and skairful a place than the barell I had been a-standin' on all day, nor the work I'd do on it any harder than the scrapin' of the ceilin' of that meetin house.

And I don't believe it would, I stand jest as firm on it to-day as I did then.

Wall, we got the scrapin' done after three hard and arjous days' works, and then we preceeded to clean the house. The day we set to clean the meetin' house prior and before paperin', we all met in good season, for we knew the hardships of the job in front of us, and we all felt that we wanted to tackle it with our full strengths.

Sister Henzy, wife of Deacon Henzy, got there jest as I did. She wuz in middlin' good spirits and a old yeller belzerine dress.

Sister Gowdy had the ganders and newraligy and wore a flannel for 'em round her head, but she wuz in workin' spirits, her will wuz up in arms, and nerved up her body.

Sister Meechim wuz a-makin' soap, and so wuz Sister Sypher, and Sister Mead, and me. But we all felt that soap come after religion, not before. "Cleanliness *next* to godliness."

So we wuz all willin' to act accordin', and tackle the old meetin' house with a willin' mind.

Wall, we wuz all engaged in the very heat of the warfare, as you may say, a-scrubbin' the floors, and a-scourin' the benches by the door, and a-blackin' the 2 stoves that stood jest inside of the door. We wuz workin' jest as hard as wimmen ever worked — and all of the wimmen who wuzn't engaged in scourin' and moppin' wuz a-settin' round in the pews a-workin' hard on articles for the fair — when all of a suddin the outside door opened and in come Josiah Allen with 3 of the other men bretheren.

They had jest got the great news of wimmen bein' apinted for Deaconesses, and had come down on the first minute to tell us. She that wuz Celestine Bobbet wuz the only female present that had heard of it.

Josiah had heard it to the post-office, and he couldn't wait till noon to tell me about it, and Deacon Gowdy wuz anxius Miss Gowdy should hear it as soon es possible.

Deacon Sypher wanted his wife to know at once that if she wuzn't married she could have become a deaconess under his derectin'.

And Josiah wanted me to know immegietly that I, too, could have had the privilege if I had been a more single woman, of becomin' a deaconess, and have had the chance of workin' all my hull life for the meetin' house, with a man to direct my movements and take charge on me, and tell me what to do, from day to day and from hour to hour.

And Deacon Henzy was anxious Miss Henzy should get the news as quick as she could. So they all hastened down to the meetin' house to tell us.

And we left off our work for a minute to hear 'em. It wuzn't nowhere near time for us to go home.

Josiah had lots of further business to do in Jonesville and so had the other men. But the news had excited 'em, and exhilerated 'em so, that they had dropped everything, and hastened right down to tell us, and then they wuz a-goin' back agin immegietly.

I, myself, took the news coolly, or as cool as I could, with my temperature up to five or five and a half, owin' to the hard work and the heat.

Miss Gowdy also took it pretty calm. She leaned on her mop handle, partly for rest (for she was tuckered out) and partly out of good manners, and didn't say much.

But Miss Sypher is such a admirin' woman, she looked fairly radiant at the news, and she spoke up to her husband in her enthusiastik warm-hearted way —

"Why, Deacon Sypher, is it possible that I, too, could become a deacon, jest like you?"

"No," sez Deacon Sypher solemnly, "no, Drusilly, not like me. But you wimmen have got the privelege now, if you are single, of workin' all your days at church work under the direction of us men."

"Then I could work at the Deacon trade under you," sez she admirin'ly, "I could work jest like you — pass round the bread and wine and the contribution box Sundays?"

"Oh, no, Drusilly," sez he condesendinly, "these hard and arjuous dutys belong to the male deaconship. That is their own one pertickiler work, that wimmen can't infringe upon. Their hull strength is spent in these duties, wimmen deacons have other fields of labor, such as relievin' the wants of the sick and sufferin', sittin' up nights with small-pox patients, takin' care of the sufferin' poor, etc., etc."

"But," sez Miss Sypher (she is so good-hearted, and so awful fond of the deacon), "wouldn't it be real sweet, Deacon, if you and I could work together as deacons, and tend the sick, relieve the sufferers — work for the good of the church together — go about doin' good?"

"No, Drusilly," sez he, "that is wimmen's work. I would not wish for a moment to curtail the holy rights of wimmen. I wouldn't want to stand in her way, and keep her from doin' all this modest, unpretendin' work, for which her weaker frame and less hefty brain has fitted her.

"We will let it go on in the same old way. Let wimmen have the privelege of workin' hard, jest as she always has. Let her work all the time, day and night, and let men go on in the same sure old way of superentendin' her movements, guardin' her weaker footsteps, and bossin' her round generally."

Deacon Sypher is never happy in his choice of language, and his method of argiment is such that when he is up on the affirmative of a question, the negative is delighted, for they know he will bring victory to their side of the question. Now, he didn't mean to speak right out about men's usual way of bossin' wimmen round. It was only his unfortunate and transparent manner of speakin'.

And Deacon Bobbet hastened to cover up the remark by the statement that "he wuz so highly tickled that wimmen wuzn't goin' to be admitted to the Conference, because it would *weaken* the Conference."

"Yes," sez my Josiah, a-leanin' up aginst the meetin' house door, and talkin' pretty loud, for Sister Peedick and me had gone to liftin' round the big bench by the door, and it wuz fearful heavy, and our minds wuz excersised as to the best place to put it while we wuz a-cleanin' the floor.

"You see," sez he, "we feel, we men do, we feel that it would be weakenin' to the Conference to have wimmen admitted, both on account of her own lack of strength and also from the fact that every woman you would admit would keep out a man. And that," sez he (a-leanin' back in a still easier attitude, almust a luxurious one), "that, you see, would tend naterally to weakenin' the strength of a church."

"Wall," sez I, a-pantin' hard for breath under my burden, "move round a little, won't you, for we want to set the bench here while we scrub under it. And," sez I, a-stoppin' a minute and rubbin' the perspiratin and sweat offen my face,

"Seein' you men are all here, can't you lay holt and help us move out the benches, so we can clean the floor under 'em? Some of 'em are very hefty," sez I, "and all of us Sisters almost are a-makin' soap, and we all want to get done here, so we can go home and bile down; we would dearly love a little help," sez I.

"I would help," sez Josiah in a willin' tone, "I would help in a minute, if I hadn't got so much work to do at home."

And all the other male bretheren said the same thing—they had got to git to get home to get to work. (Some on 'em wanted to play checkers, and I knew it.)

But some on 'em did have lots of work on their hands, I couldn't dispute it.

26   On Economics

[Josiah] wuz jest a-countin' out his money prior to puttin' it away in his tin box, and I laid the subject before him strong and eloquent, jest the wants and needs of the meetin' house, and jest how hard we female sisters wuz a-workin', and jest how much we needed some money to buy our ingregiencies with for the fair.

He set still, a-countin' out his money, but I know he heard me. There wuz four fifty dollar bills, a ten, and a five, and I felt that at the very least calculation he would hand me out the ten or the five, and mebby both on 'em.

But he laid 'em careful in the box, and then pulled out his old pocket-book out of his pocket, and handed me a ten cent piece.

I wuz mad. And I hain't a-goin' to deny that we had some words. Or at least I said some words to him, and gin him a middlin' clear idee of how I felt on the subject.

Why, the colt wuz more mine than his in the first place, and I didn't want a cent of money for myself, but only wanted it for the good of the Methodist meetin' house, which he ort to be full as interested in as I wuz.

Yes, I gin him a pretty lucid idee of what my feelin's wuz on the subject — and spozed mebby I had convinced him. I wuz a-standin' with my back to him, a-ironin' a shirt for him, when I finished up my piece of mind. And thought more'n as likely as not he'd break down and be repentent, and hand me out a ten dollar bill.

But no, he spoke out as pert and cheerful as anything and sez he:

"Samantha, I don't think it is necessary for Christians to give such a awful sight. Jest look at the widder's mit."

I turned right round and looked at him, holdin' my flat-iron in my right hand, and sez I:

"What do you mean, Josiah Allen? What are you talkin' about?"

"Why the widder's mit that is mentioned in Scripter, and is talked about so much by Christians to this day. Most probable it wuz a odd one, I dare persume to say she had lost the mate to it. It specilly mentions that there wuzn't but one on 'em. And jest see how much that is talked over, and praised up clear down the ages, to this day. It couldn't have been worth more'n five cents, if it wuz worth that."

"How do you spell mit, Josiah Allen?" sez I.

"Why m-i-t-e, mit."

"I should think," sez I, "that that spells mite."

"Oh well, when you are a-readin' the Bible, all the best commentaters agree that you must use your own judgment. Mite! What sense is there in that? Widder's mite! There hain't any sense in it, not a mite."

And Josiah kinder snickered here, as if he had made a dretful cute remark, bringin' the "mite" in in that way. But I didn't snicker, no, there wuzn't a shadow, or trace of anything to be heard in my linement, but solemn and bitter earnest. And I set the flat-iron down on the stove, solemn, and took up another, solemn, and went to ironin' on his shirt collar agin with solemnety and deep earnest.

"No," Josiah Allen continued, "there hain't no sense in that—but mit! there you have sense. All wimmen wear mits; they love 'em. She most probable had a good pair, and lost one on 'em, and then give the other to the church. I tell you it takes men to translate the Bible, they have such a realizin' sense of the weaknesses of wimmen, and how necessary it is to translate it in such a way as to show up them weaknesses, and quell her down, and make her know her place, make her know that man is her superior in every way, and it is her duty as well as privilege to look up to him."

And Josiah Allen crossed his left leg over his right one, as haughty and over bearin' a-crossin' as I ever see in my life, and looked up haughtily at the stove-pipe hole in the ceilin', and resoomed,

"But, as I wuz sayin' about her mit, the widder's, you know. That is jest my idee of givin', equinomical, savin', jest as it should be."

"Yes," sez I, in a very dry axent, most as dry as my flat-iron, and that wuz fairly hissin' hot. "She most probable had some man to advise her, and to tell her what use the mit would be to support a big meetin' house."

Oh, how dry my axent wuz. It wuz the very dryest, and most irony one I keep by me—and I keep dretful ironikle ones to use in cases of necessity.

"Most probable," sez Josiah, "most probable she did." He thought I wuz praisin' men up, and he acted tickled most to death.

"Yes, some man without any doubt, advised her, told her that some other widder would lose one of hern, and give hers to the meetin' house, jest the mate to hern. That is the way I look at it," sez he "and I mean to mention that view of mine on this subject the very next time they take up a subscription in the meetin' house and call on me."

But I turned and faced him then with the hot flat-iron in my hand, and burnin' indignation in my eys, and sez I:

"If you mention that, Josiah Allen, in the meetin' house, or to any livin' soul on earth, I'll part with you." And I would, if it wuz the last move I ever made.

But I gin up from that minute the idea of gettin' anything out of Josiah Allen for the fair. But I had some money of my own that I had got by sellin' three pounds of geese feathers and a bushel of dried apples, every feather picked by me, and every quarter of apple pared and peeled and strung and dried by me. It all come to upwerds of seven dollars, and I took every cent of it the next day out of my under bureau draw and carried it to the meetin' house and gin it to the treasurer, and told 'em, at the request of the hull on 'em, jest how I got the money.

And so the hull of the female sisters did, as they handed in their money, told jest how they come by it.

Sister Moss had seated three pairs of children's trouses for young Miss Gowdy, her children are very hard on their trouses (slidin' down the banesters and such). And young Miss Gowdy is onexperienced yet in mendin', so the patches won't show. And Sister Moss had got forty-seven cents for the job, and brung it all, every cent of it, with the exception of three cents she kep out to buy peppermint drops with. She has the colic fearful, and peppermint sometimes quells it.

Young Miss Gowdy wuz kep at home by some new, important business (twins). But she sent thirty-two cents, every cent of money she could rake and scrape, and that she had scrimped out of the money her husband had gin her for a woosted dress. She had sot her heart on havin' a ruffle round the bottom (he didn't give her enough for a over-shirt), but she concluded to make it plain, and sent the ruffle money.

And young Sister Serena Nott had picked geese for her sister, who married a farmer up in Zoar. She had picked ten geese at two cents apiece, and Serena that tender-hearted that it wuz like pickin' the feathers offen her own back.

And then she is very timid, and skairt easy, and she owned up that while the pickin' of the geese almost broke her heart, the pickin' of the ganders almost skairt her to death. They wuz very high headed and warlike, and though she put a stockin' over their heads, they would lift 'em right up, stockin' and all, and hiss, and act, and she said she picked 'em at what seemed to her to be at the resk of her life.

But she loved the meetin' house, so she grin and bore it, as the sayin' is, and she brung the hull of her hard earned money, and handed it over to the treasurer, and everybody that is at all educated knows that twice ten is twenty. She brung twenty cents.

Sister Grimshaw had, and she owned it right out and out, got four dollars and fifty-three cents by sellin' butter on the sly. She had took it out of the butter tub when Brother Grimshaw's back wuz turned, and sold it to the neighbors for money at odd times through the year, and besides gettin' her a dress cap (for which she wuz fairly sufferin'), she gin the hull to the meetin' house.

There wuz quite dubersome looks all round the room when she handed in the money and went right out, for she had a errent to the store.

And Sister Gowdy spoke up and said she didn't exactly like to use money got in that way.

But Sister Lanfear sprunted up, and brung Jacob right into the argument, and the Isrealites who borrowed jewelry of the Egyptians, and then she brung up other old Bible characters, and held 'em up before us.

But still we some on us felt dubersome. And then another sister spoke up and said the hull property belonged to Sister Grimshaw, every mite of it, for he wuzn't worth a cent when he married her — she wuz the widder Bettenger, and had a fine property. And Grimshaw hadn't begun to earn what he had spent sense (he drinks). So, sez she, it all belongs to Sister Grimshaw, by right.

Then the sisters all begin to look less dubersome. But I sez:

"Why don't she come out openly and take the money she wants for her own use, and for church work, and charity?"

"Because he is so hard with her," sez Sister Lanfear, "and tears round so, and cusses, and commits so much wickedness. He is willin' she should dress well — wants her to — and live well. But he don't want her to spend a cent on the meetin' house. He is a atheist, and he hain't willin' she should help on the Cause of religeon. And if he knows of her givin' any to the Cause, he makes the awfulest fuss, scolds, and swears, and threatens her, so's she has been made sick by it, time and agin."

"Wall," sez I, "what business is it to him what she does with her own money and her own property?"

I said this out full and square. But I confess that I did feel a little dubersome in my own mind. I felt that she ort to have took it more openly.

And Sister Grimshaw's sister Amelia, who lives with her (onmarried and older than Sister Grimshaw, though it hain't spozed to be the case, for she has hopes yet, and her age is kep). She had been and contoggled[1] three days and a half for Miss Elder Minkley, and got fifty cents a day for contogglin'.

She had fixed over the waists of two old dresses, and contoggled a old dress skirt so's it looked most as well as new. Amelia is a good contoggler and a good Christian. And I shouldn't be surprised any day to see her snatched away by some widower or bachelder of proper age. She would be willin', so it is spozed.

Wall, Sister Henn kinder relented at the last, and brung two pairs of fowls, all picked, and tied up by their legs. And we thought it wuz kinder funny and providential that one Henn should bring four more of 'em.

But we wuz tickled, for we knew we could sell 'em to the grocer man at Jonesville for upwerds of a dollar bill.

And Submit Tewksbury, what should that good little creeter bring, and we couldn't any of us hardly believe our eyes at first, and think she could part with it, but she did bring *that plate*.[2] That pink edged, chiny plate, with gilt sprigs, that she had used as a memorial of Samuel Danker for so many years. Sot it up on the supper table and wept in front of it.

Wall, she knew old china like that would bring a fancy price, and she hadn't a cent of money she could bring, and she wanted to do her full part towerds helpin' the meetin' house along—so she tore up her memorial, a-weepin' on it for hours, so we spozed, and offered it up, a burnt chiny offerin' to the Lord.

Wall, I am safe to say, that nothin' that had took place that day had begun to affect us like that.

To see that good little creeter lookin' pale and considerble wan, hand in that plate and never groan over it, nor nothin', not out loud she didn't, but we spozed she kep up a silent groanin' inside of her, for we all knew the feelin' she felt for the plate.

It affected all on us fearfully.

But the treasurer took it, and thanked her almost warmly, and Submit merely sez, when she wuz thanked:

"Oh, you are entirely welcome to it, and I hope it will fetch a good price, so's to help the cause along."

And then she tried to smile a little mite. But I declare that smile wuz more pitiful than tears would have been.

Everybody has seen smiles that seemed made up, more than half, of unshed tears, and withered hopes, and disappointed dreams, etc., etc.

Submit's smile wuz of that variety, one of the very curiusest of 'em, too. Wall, she gin, I guess, about two of 'em, and then she went and sot down.

NOTES

1. Contoggled means "made over."
2. This plate is the one she set out each year on the anniversary of the last day she had seen her beloved. Since this is one of her most prized possessions because of its symbolic value, Samantha is showing the extreme sacrifice these women made in order to raise money of their own.

27 On Bein' Too Weak to Set

Sister Sylvester Bobbet and I had been voted on es the ones best qualified to lead off in the arjeous and hazerdous enterprize.

And though we deeply felt the honor they wuz a-heapin' on to us, yet es it hes been, time and agin, in other high places in the land, if it hadn't been fer duty that wuz a-grippin' holt of us, we would gladly have shirked out of it and gin the honor to some humble but worthy constituent.

Fer the lengths of paper wuz extremely long, the ceilin' fearfully high, and oh! how lofty and tottlin' the barells looked to us. And we both on us, Sister Sylvester Bobbet and I, had giddy and dizzy spells right on the ground, let alone bein' perched up on barells, a-liftin' our arms up fur, fur beyond the strength of their sockets.

But duty wuz a-callin' us, and the other wimmen also, and it wuzn't for me, nor Sister Sylvester Bobbet to wave her nor them off, or shirk out of hazerdous and dangerous jobs when the good of the Methodist Meetin' House wuz at the Bay.

No, with as lofty looks as I ever see in my life (I couldn't see my own, but I felt 'em), and with as resolute and martyrous feelin's as ever animated two wimmen's breasts, Sister Sylvester Bobbet and I grasped holt of the length of paper, one on each end on it, Sister Arvilly Lanfear and Miss Henzy a-holdin' it up in the middle like Aaron and Hur a-holdin' up Moses'ses arms. We advanced and boldly mounted up onto our two barells, Miss Gowdy and Sister Sypher a-holdin' two chairs stiddy for us to mount up on.

Every eye in the meetin' house wuz on us. We felt nerved up to do our best, even if we perished in so doin', and I didn't know some of the time but we would fall at our two posts. The job wuz so much more wearin' and awful than we had foreboded, and we had foreboded about it day and night for weeks and weeks, every one on us.

The extreme hite of the ceilin'; the slipperyness and fragility of the lengths of paper; the fearful hite and tottlin'ness of the barells; the dizzeness that swept over us at times, in spite of our marble efforts to be calm. The dretful achin' and strainin' of our armpits, that bid fair to loosen 'em from their four sockets. The tremenjous responsibility that laid onto us to get the paper on smooth and onwrinkled.

It wuz, takin' it altogether, the most fearful and wearisome hour of my hull life.

Every female in the room held her breath in deathless anxiety (about thirty breaths). And every eye in the room wuz on us (about fifty-nine eyes — Miss Shelmadine hain't got but one workin' eye, the other is glass, though it hain't known, and must be kep).

Wall, it wuz a-goin' on smooth and onwrinkled — smiles broke out on every face, about thirty smiles — a half a minute more and it would be done, and done well. When at that tryin' and decisive moment when the fate of our meetin' house wuz, as you may say, at the stake, we heard the sound of hurryin' feet, and the door suddenly opened, and in walked Josiah Allen, Deacon Sypher, and Deacon Henzy followed by what seemed to me at the time to be the hull male part of the meetin' house.

But we found out afterwerds that there wuz a few men in the meetin' house that thought wimmen ort to set; they argued that when wimmen had been standin' so long they out to set down; they wuz good dispositioned. But as I sez at the time, it looked to us as if every male Methodist in the land wuz there and present.

They wuz in great spirits, and their means wuz triumphant and satisfied.

They had jest got the last news from the Conference in New York village, and had come down in a body to disseminate it to us.

They said the Methodist Conference had decided that the seven wimmen that had been stood up there in New York for the last week, couldn't set, that they wuz too weak and fraguile to set on the Conference.

And then the hull crowd of men, with smiles and haughty linements, beset Josiah to read it out to us.

So Josiah Allen, with his face nearly wreathed with a smile, a blissful smile, but as high headed a one as I ever see, read it all out to us. But he should have to hurry, he said, for he had got to carry the great and triumphant news all round, up as fur as Zoar, if he had time.

And so he read it out to us, and as we see that that breadth wuz spilte, we stopped our work for a minute and heard it.

And after he had finished it, they all said it wuz a masterly docku-ment, the decision wuz a noble one, and it wuz jest what they had al-ways said. They said they had always known that wimmen wuz too weak, her frame wuz too tender, she was onfitted by Nater, in mind and in body to contend with such hardship. And they all agreed that it would be puttin' the men in a bad place, and takin' a good deal offen their dignity, if the fair sex had been allowed by them to take such hardships onto 'em. And they sez, some on 'em, "Why! what are men in the Methodist meetin' house for, if it hain't to guard the more weaker sect, and keep cares offen 'em?"

And one or two on 'em mentioned the words, "cooin' doves" and "sweet tender flowerets," as is the way of men at such times. But they wuz in too big a hurry to spread themselves (as you may say) in this direction. They had to hurry off to tell the great news to other places in Jonesville and up as fer as Loontown and Zoar.

But Sister Arvilly Lanfear, who happened to be a-standin' in the door as they went off, she said she heard 'em out as fer as the gate a-congratilatin' themselves and the Methodist Meetin' House and the nation on the decesion, for, sez they,

"Them angels hain't strong enough to set, and I've known it all the time."

And Sister Sylvester Gowdy sez to me, a-rubbin' her achin' armpits—

"If they are as beet out as we be they'd be glad to set down on any-thing—a Conference or anything else."

And I sez, a-wipin' the presperatin of hard labor from my forwerd,

"For the land's sake! Yes! I should think so."

And then with giddy heads and strainin' armpits we tackled the meetin' house agin.

VI

History's Treatment of Women: Written Record and Public Symbols

> "I spoze the account of these things bein' writ
> down by males and translated by 'em makes a
> difference; it's sort o' naterel to stand up for your
> own sect.
>   But folks ort to own up, male or female; and
> them old females ort to have justice done 'em."
>
> — Samantha

The recorded culture has generally omitted the accomplishments of women or relegated them to the "woman behind the man" indirectness considered socially appropriate. Samantha conjectures about the lives of those whom history failed to record — in this case the "likely" wives of the Biblical prophets. Maintaining her "megumness" and distaste for condemning men outright without considering the entire question, Samantha "spozes" that we don't know of the wives of the prophets because history has been written and translated by men.

One of her "towers" provides the chance to correct erroneous assumptions regarding women's lack of accomplishment. Public statues reflect symbolically the relative places of men and women, especially as Samantha observes those erected for the World's Fair. The statue of Liberty "depictered" as a woman fills her with hope that Uncle Sam had finally seen the chains bindin' woman and would therefore turn over a new leaf. The selection from *Sweet Cicely*, however, during which the appropriate gender for the "figger of Liberty" is discussed, suggests that to be symbolically and historically correct, Liberty should indeed be a man. But the impressive figure of Columbia flanked by female "figgers" representing Science, Industry, Literature, etc., convince Samantha that Columbia has at last discovered woman and means to do right by her. And a solid silver statue of a woman named Justice must indicate that downtrodden woman had got on top now.

Surely, Samantha reasons, a nation wouldn't make a woman its symbol of Justice if it meant to continue denying her the rights of "the poorest dog that walks the globe."

"I took it as bein' a compliment to my sect the way that fountain wuz laid out — ten or a dozen wimmen and only one or two men"

28 On the Wives of the Prophets

That very night I went into Genieve's room to kiss Snow and Boy good-night.

But both the darlin's wuz fast asleep, Snow in her little white bed and Boy in his crib. Their faces looked like fresh roses aginst their white pillers, and I did kiss 'em both, but light, so as not to wake 'em up.

Sweet little creeters, I think my eyes on 'em.

Genieve, I see, when I went in wuz a readin' some book, and as I looked closter at it I see it wuz the Bible. I see she wuz a readin' about her favorite topick, the old prophets and their doin's and their sayin's.

And as I sot down a few minutes by the side of my sweet darlin's she begun to talk to me about Daniel, and St. John, and some of the rest of them good, faithful old prophets.

Why, she wuz brung up with 'em, as you may say.

She had sot under them old prophets ever sence she had sot at all.

And why shouldn't she went on about 'em and love 'em when she had fairly drinked in their weird, fascinatin' influence with her mother's milk?

She wuz a readin' about Daniel jest as I went in — about how Daniel stood by the deep waters and heard a voice sayin' to him:

"Understand."

And sez she, with her great, beautiful eyes all aglow, "Don't you think that we who stand by deep waters to-day can hear the voice if we listen?"

"Yes," sez I, "I believe it from the bottom of my heart; if we do as Daniel did, 'set our hearts to understand,' we can be kep' from perils as he wuz, and we can hear that Divine Voice a biddin' us to understand and to be strong."

Sez I, "I believe that Voice almost always comes to us in the supreme

From *Samantha on the Race Problem* (Minneapolis, 1892), pp. 308–19.

moments of our greatest need. When we have been mournin' as Daniel
had, and 'eaten no pleasant bread,' and lay with our faces on the ground
by the deep waters, then comes One to us, onseen by them about us,
and touches our bowed heads and sez:

"'Beloved, fear not. Peace be unto thee. Be strong. Yea, be strong.'"

And then we went on and talked considerable, and she told me how
her mother had read to her, as soon as she wuz able to understand anything, all about the prophets, and how she had always loved to think
about 'em and their divine work.

And I told her I felt jest so; I thought they wuz likely old creeters,
them and their wives too.

And Genieve looked up dretful startled and surprised, and said she
had never thought about their wives, not at all.

And I sez, "Like enough, nobody duz. Nobody ever did think anything about old Miss Daniel, or Miss Zekiel, or any of 'em. Nobody ever
thought of givin' the wimmen any credit, but they deserve it," sez I. "I
believe they wuz likely old females, every one of 'em."

Genieve still looked dretful wonderin', and as if I had put a bran
new idee into her head. As much as she had pondered and studied them
prophets, she never had gin a thought to them good old females — faithful, hard-workin' creeters, I believe they wuz.

And she sez, sez she, "I never thought anything about them, whether
they had any troubles or not."

"No," sez I, "I spoze not, but I believe they had 'em, and I believe
they had a tuckerin' time on't more'n half the time.

"Why," sez I, "it stands to reason they had. While their husbands
wuz a sallyin' out a prophesyin', somebody had to stay to home and
work, split kindlin' wood, etc."

Genieve looked kinder shocked, and I sez warmly:

"Not but what I think a sight of them old prophets, sights of 'em. My
soul burns within me, or almost burns, a thinkin' of them old men of
whom the world wuz not worthy, who *had* to tell the secret things that
the Lord had revealed to 'em to the ears of a blasphemin' and gainsayin'
world. I jest about worship 'em when I think of their trials, their persecutions, their death for duty's sake.

"But while I honor them old men up to the very highest pint honor
can go in a human breast, still I have feelin's for their wives — I can't
help feelin' sorry for them poor old creeters."

"Not a word do we hear about them, and it makes me feel bad to see my sect so overlooked and brought down to nort.

"And I'll bet (or would bet if it wuzn't for principle) that old Miss Daniel, and Miss Zekiel, and Miss Hosey, and Miss Maleky, and all the rest of them old female wimmen had a tough time on't.

"Why, if there wuzn't anything else to trouble 'em, it wuz enough to kill any woman to see the torment and persecutions that follered on after the man she loved. To see 'em wanderin' about in sheepskin and goatskin, and bein' afflicted, and destitute, and tormented.

"That wuz enough to break down any woman's happiness; but they had to buckle to and work head work most likely to take care of themselves and their children.

"'Destitute' means privation and starvation for old Miss Prophet and the children, as well as for the husband and father.

"And I'll bet that old Miss Hosey and Miss Maleky jest put to it and worked and made perfect slaves of themselves.

"And with all this work, and care, and privation on their minds and hearts, they couldn't have got such a dretful sight of sympathy and companionship out of their husbands, to say nuthin' of help and out-door chores.

"For though the old prophets wuz jest as likely as likely could be and did what wuz perfectly necessary and right, still while they wuz out in the streets a hollerin' 'Woe! woe! to this wicked city!' etc., etc., they couldn't at the same time be to home a talkin' affectionate to their pardners or a sawin' wood. I'll bet old Miss Maleky picked up more than half she burned, and split pretty nigh all her own kindlin' wood, and killed her hens, and sot 'em, etc. etc.

"Them days seem a good ways off to us, and things seen through the misty, hazy atmosphere of so many years seem sort o' easy to us.

"But I don't spoze water would bile then without a fire no more than it would now. And I spoze the dishes, or whatever they kep' their vittles in then, had to be washed.

"And I spoze the goatskins and sheepskins that them good old men wandered round in had to be cleaned every now and then — it stands to reason they did. And I don't believe them prophets did it; no, I don't believe they had the time to, even if they thought on't.

"No; I dare presume to say that every time you found a prophet you would find some woman a takin' care on him, so he could have the freedom of mind and the absence of domestic cares necessary to keep his soul the calm medium through which divine truth could pour down upon a sinful world.

"The sieve must be held right end up or you can't sift through it; hold it sideways or bottom end up, and where be you?

"No; old Miss Hosey and Miss Maleky, I dare presume to say, jest wrastled round with household cares and left them old men as free as they could.

"I'll bet the minds of them good old prophets wuzn't opset with pickin' geese and ketchin' gobblers, or makin' hens set, or fastenin' down the tent stakes if the wind come up sudden in the night.

"No; I'll bet Miss Hosey, that good old creeter, got up herself and hung onto them flappin' ends and drove down the stakes herself, so's Mr. Hosey could get a little sleep. Or if little Isaac, or Lemuel, or Rebeckah Hosey wuz took sudden with the croup or infantum, I'll bet it wuzn't old Mr. Hosey that got up and hunted round for the goose oil, or groped his way round and started up a fire, and steeped catnip, and heat cloths, and applied 'em.

"No; it wuz that good old female creeter every time, I wouldn't be afraid to say it wuz.

"And ten to one if her pardner didn't wake up and ask her 'what she wuz makin' such a noise for in the middle of the night, and tell her she wuz jest spilin' them children a indulgin' 'em so, and if she had kep' their sandals on, they wouldn't have took cold,' etc., etc., etc.

"And then if she got into bed agin with cold feet he complained bitterly of that.

"And so, I dare presume to say Miss Hosey or Miss Maleky, as the case might be, sot up with them children, pulled one way by her devoted affection for 'em, and the other way by her wifely love, and tried to keep 'em as still as she could, and shet up them babies if they went to cry, for her husband's sake, and tried to doctor 'em up for their own sake, and felt meachin' through it all, borne down by the weight of her husband's onmerited blame and faultfindin'.

"And the next mornin', I dare presume to say, she went round with a headache, and got as good a breakfast as she could with what she had to do with; and if her husband waked up feelin' kind o' chirk and said a kind word to her, or kissed her, I dare say she forgot all her troubles and thought she had the best husband in the world, and she wouldn't change places with anybody on earth.

"For female human nater is about the same from Eve down to she that wuz Samantha Smith.

"And then I dare presume to say that as bad as she felt, and as much as she needed a nap, she jest helped him off on his prophesying trip, did everything she could for his comfort before he went, brushed his goatskin, and mebby cleaned it, and took care of the children till he come back, fed the camels, and watered the goats, and I dare presume to say got kicked by 'em, as bad as she felt.

"Made her butter — like as not she had a big churnin' — or a baggin' I don't know but it ort to be called — I spoze they used a bag instead of a churn.

"And then mebby she had lots of little young goats and camels to bring up by hand. I shouldn't wonder if she had a camel corset that took lots of care.

"And then mebby she had a lot of onexpected company come onto her — old Miss Aminidab and her daughter-in-law, and old Miss Jethro, and Miss Lemuel and her children, a perfect tent full, and she had to buckle to and get dinner for 'em, and mebby dinner and supper; and it would be jest like 'em to stay all night, the hull caboodle of 'em, and mebby she had to pound every mite of corn herself before she cooked for 'em.

"And she all the while with a splittin' headache, and her back a achin' as if it would break in two.

"And then jest as they got onto their camels and sot out home agin, then like as not old Mr. Hosey would come home all wore out and onstrung from the persecutions he had had to contend with, and that good old female, as beat out as she wuz, would have to go to work to string him up agin, and soothe him, and encourage him to go on with his prophesyin' agin.

"But who thinks anything of these old female wimmen's labors and sufferin's? Nobody.

"Who thinks of their martyrdom, their efforts in the good cause, and the help they gin the old male prophets? Nobody, not one.

"I spoze the account of these things bein' writ down by males and translated by 'em makes a difference; it's sort o' naterel to stand up for your own sect.

"But folks ort to own up, male or female; and them old females ort to have justice done 'em.

"And though it is pretty late in the day — thousands of years have flown by, and the dust of the desert lays deep over their modest, un-assumin' graves, where they have lain unnoticed and overlooked by everybody —

"But here is one in Jonesville that is goin' to brush away the thick dust that has drifted down over their memory, and tell my opinion of 'em.

"It is too late now to tell them old Miss Prophets what I think of 'em, thousands of years too late to chirk 'em up, and lighten their achin' hearts, and brighten their sad eyes by lettin' 'em know the deep sympathy and affection I feel for 'em.

"I can't make 'em hear my words, the dust lays too thick over their ears.

"But yet I am a goin' to say them words jest out of a love for justice.

"Justice has stood for ages with the bandage on tight over her eyes on one side, on the side of wimmen, and her scales held out, blind as a bat to what them old females done and suffered.

"But she has got a little corner lifted now on the side of wimmen; Justice is a beginnin' to peek out and notice that 'male and female created He them.'

"Bein' so blind, and believin' jest what wuz told her, Justice had got it into her head that it read:

" 'Male created He them.'

"Justice never so much as hearn the name of wimmen mentioned, so we spoze.

"But she is a liftin' up her bandage and lookin' out; and it stands to reason she can weigh as well agin when she can see how the notches stand.

"Jest even, so I figger it out, jest even, men and wimmen, one weighin' jest as much as the other.

"If there are some ingregiencies in one of 'em that are a little better, that weigh a few ounces more, lo and behold! in the other one's nater and soul are a few ounces of different goodness that even it up, that weigh enough more to make it even.

"If Justice takes my advice — and I spoze mebby she will, knowin' I am a female that always wished her well, even in her blind days — if Justice takes my advice she won't put on her bandages agin, she will look out calm and keen and try to weigh things right by the notch, try to hold her steelyards stiddy.

"And no matter what is put into 'em — men, wimmen, colored folks or white ones — get the right weight to 'em, the hull caboodle of 'em, black or white, rich or poor, bond or free.

"She will get along as well agin, and take more comfort herself.

"It must have been a tejus job for her to be a standin' up there a weighin' things as blind as a bat."

But sez I, as I kinder come to myself, and glanced up at the little clock over the bureau:

"I am a eppisodin', a eppisodin' out loud, and to a greater extent than I ort to, and it is bedtime," sez I.

Genieve looked sort o' bewildered and strange, and said "she had enjoyed my talk," and I dare presume to say she had, for she hain't one to lie.

But it wuz bedtime, and I went to my own peaceful room. My beloved pardner wuz fast asleep and a dreamin' most likely about the farm and Ury; and if he dreamed some about Philury, I didn't care, I hain't one of the jealous kind. And I knew his dreams would be perfectly moral and well-behaved ones anyway.

29 On Public Statues

. . . Here is a bank, post-office, and the department of general information about the Fair.[1]

And never, never sence the creation of the world has old General Information had a better-lookin' place to stay in.

Why, some folks call this high, magnificent buildin', with its great shinin' dome, the handsomest buildin' amongst that city of matchless palaces. It covers four acres, every acre bein' more magnificent than the other acres. Why, the Widder Albert herself gin Mr. Hunt, the architect, a ticket, she was so tickled with his work.

The dome on top of it is the biggest dome in the world, with the exception of St. Peter's in Rome. And it seemed to me, as I looked up at the dome, that Peter might have got along with one no bigger than this.

Howsumever, it hain't for me to scrimp anybody in domes. But this wuz truly enormious.

But none too big, mebby, for the nub on top of the gate of the World's Fair. That needs to be mighty in size, and of pure gold, to correspond with what is on the inside of the gate.

But never wuz there such a gorgeous gate-way before, unless it wuz the gate-way of Paradise.

Why, as you stood inside of that dome and looked way up, up, up towards the top, your feelin's soared to that extent that it almost took you offen your feet.

Noble pictures and statutes you see here, too. Some on 'em struck tremendious hard blows onto my appreciation, and onto my head also.

And a-lookin' on 'em made me feel well, dretful well, to see how much my sect wuz thought on in stun, and canvas, and such.

There wuz Diligence, a good-lookin' woman, workin' jest as she

From *Samantha at the World's Fair* (New York, 1893), pp. 228–34.

always has, and is willin' to; there she sot a-spinnin' and a-bringin' up her children as good as she knew how.

Mebby she wuz a-teachin' a Sunday-school lesson to the boy that stood by her.

He had his arms full of ripe fruit and grapes. I am most afraid for his future, but she wuz a-teachin' him the best she could; you could see that by her looks.

Then there wuz Truth, another beautiful woman, a-holdin' a lookin'-glass in her hand, and a-teachin' another little boy. Mebby it wuz the young Future she wuz a-learnin' to tell the truth, anyway, no matter how much it hurt him, how hard it hit aginst old custom and prejudices. He wuz a-leanin' affectionate on her, but his eyes wuz a-lookin' away — fur off. Mebby he'll hear to her, mebby he will — he's young; but I feel kinder dubersome about it.

She held her glass dretful high. Mebby she laid out that Uncle Sam should see his old features in it, and mebby she wuz a-remindin' him that he ortn't to carve woman as a statute of Truth, and then not be willin' to hear her complaints when she tries to tell him about 'em, in his own place, where he makes his laws, year in and year out.

If he believes she is truthful — and he must, or he wouldn't name her Truth and set her up so high for the nations to look at — what makes him, year after year, act towards wimmen as if he believed she wuz a-lyin'? It is onreasonable in him.

And then there wuz Abundance, a woman and a man. I guess they had an abundance of everything for their comfort, and it looked real good to see they wuz both a-sharin' it.

She wuz a-settin' in a chair, and he wuz on the floor. That might do for a Monument, or Statute, but I don't believe they would foller it up so for day after day in real life, and they hadn't ort to. Men and wimmen ort to have the same settin' accommodations, and standin' too, and ort to be treated one of 'em jest as well as the other. They are both likely creeters, a good deal of the time.

Then there wuz Tradition. Them wuz two old men, as wuz nateral — wimmen wuzn't in that — woman is in the future and the present. Them two men, a-lookin' considerable war-like, wuz a-talkin' over the past — the deeds of Might.

They didn't need wimmen so much there, and I didn't feel as if I cared a cent to have her there.

When they git to talkin' over the deeds of *Right*, I'd want wimmen to be present. *And she will be there.*

And then there wuz Liberty, agin a woman, beautiful and serene, a-depicterin' Liberty, and agin a-holdin' her arms round a young male child, and a-teachin' him.

That, too, filled me with high hope, that Uncle Sam had at last discovered the mean actions that wuz a-goin' on about wimmen; that he had seen the chains that wuz a-bindin' her, and a-gaulin' her.

He wouldn't be likely to depicter her as Liberty, and set her up so high in the gate-way to the World's Fair, if he calculated to keep her on in the slavery she is now, a-bindin' her with her own heartstrings — takin' away her power to help her own heart's dearest, in their fights aginst the evils and temptations of the World.

No, I believe Uncle Sam is a-goin' to turn over a new leaf — anyway, Liberty sot up there, a-lookin' off with a calm mean, and there wuz a smile on her face, as if she see a light in the future that begened to her.

And then, there wuz Charity; of course she wuz a woman — she always is.

She had two little boys by her; one had his hand on her heart, and that faithful heart wuz filled with love and pity for him, jest as it always has been, and always will be. Another wuz a-kneelin' at her feet, with her fosterin' hand on his head. A good-lookin' creeter Charity wuz, and well behaved.

Joy seemed to be enjoyin' herself first rate. Her pretty face seemed to answer back the music that the youth at her feet wuz a-rousin' from his magic flute.

Theology wuz a wise, reverend-lookin' old man, a-thinkin' up a sermon, or a-thinkin' out some new system of religion, I dare presoom to say, for his book seemed to be half closed, and he wuz lost in deep thought.

He looked first rate — a good and well-behaved old man. I hain't a doubt on't.

Then, there wuz Patriotism — a man and a woman. He, a-standin' up ready to face danger, or die for his country; she, with her arms round him, a-lookin' up into his face, as if to say —

"If you must go, I will stay to home with a breakin' heart, and take care of the children, and do the barn chores."

They both looked real good and noble. Mr. Bitters done first rate — Josiah couldn't have begun to done so well, nor I nuther.

Then there wuz a dretful impressive statute there, a grand-lookin' old man, with his hand uplifted, a-tellin' sunthin' to a young child, who wuz a-listenin' eagerly.

I d'no who the old man wuz; there wuz broad white wings a-risin' up all round him, and it might be he wuz meant to depicter the Recordin' Angel; if he wuz, he could have got quills enough out of them wings to do all his writin' with.

And it might be that it wuz Wisdom instructin' youth.

And it might be some enterprisin' old goose-raiser a-tellin' his oldest boy the best way to save the white wings of ganders.

But I don't believe this wuz so. There wuz a riz up, noble look on the old man's face that wuz never ketched, I don't believe, with wrestlin' with geese on a farm, and neighbors all round him.

No, I guess it wuz the gray and wise old World a-instructin' the young Republic what to do and what not to do.

The child looked dretful impetuous and eager, and ready to start off any minute, a good deal as our country does, and I presoom wherever the child wuz a-startin' for it will git there.

A noble statute. Mr. Bitters did first rate.

But when I git started on pictures and statutes—I don't know where or when to stop.[2]

But time hastens, and to resoom . . .

NOTES

1. She is describing the Administration Building, designed by a man.

2. Samantha and Josiah later tour the Woman's Building, where Samantha was "fearfully riz up and by the side of [herself]" to see the "simple, noble perfection of the building." She describes the building and its exhibits at considerable length, taking pride in how it ably represents her "sect." "A woman designed the hull buildin'; a woman modelled the figgers that support the ruff; a woman won fairly in competition the right to decorate the cornice. The interior decoration, much of it carved work, is done by wimmen . . ." (p. 257). Some of the women artists who contributed to the Woman's Building included painters Mary Cassatt and Cecilia Beaux, sculptors Alice Rideout, Vinnie Ream Hoxie, Harriet Hosmer, and architect Sophia Hayden. For a comprehensive account with illustrations of the 1893 World's Fair Woman's Building, see Jeanne M. Weimann, *The Fair Women* (Chicago, 1981).

30 On Columbia Discoverin' Woman

. . . the figger on the throne wuz so impressive, and the female in front so determined.

Wisdom, and courage, and joyful hope and ardor.

Helped by 'em, borne along by 'em in the face of envy, and detraction, and bigotry, and old custom, the boat sails grandly.

"Ho! up there on the high mast! What news?"

"Light! light ahead!"

But to resoom: a-standin' up on each side of that impressive figger wuz another row of females—mebby they had oars in their hands, showin' that they wuz calculatin' to take hold and row the boat for a spell if it got stuck; and mebby they wuz poles, or sunthin'.

But I don't believe they meant to use 'em on that solitary man that stood in back end of the boat, a-propellin' it—it would have been a shame if they had.

No; I believe that they meant to help at sunthin' or ruther with them long sticks.

They wuz all a-lookin' some distance ahead, all a-seemin' bound to get where they started for.

Besides bein' gorgeous in the extreme, I took it as bein' a compliment to my sect, the way that fountain wuz laid out—ten or a dozen wimmen, and only one or two men. But after I got it all fixed out in my mind what that lofty and impressive figger meant, a bystander a-standin' by explained it all out to me.

He said that the female figger way up above the rest wuz Columbia, beautiful, strong, fearless.

And that it wuz Fame that stood at the prow with the bugle, and

From *Samantha at the World's Fair* (New York, 1893), pp. 300–11.

that it wuz Father Time at the hellum, a-guidin' it through the dangers of the centuries.

And the female figgers around Columbia's throne wuz meant for Science, Industry, Commerce, Agriculture, Music, Drama, Paintin', and Literature, all on 'em a-helpin' Columbia along in her grand pathway.

And then I see that what I had hearn wuz true, that Columbia had jest discovered Woman. Yes, the boat wuz headed directly towards Woman, who stood up one hundred feet high in front.

And I see plain that Columbia couldn't help dicoverin' her if she wanted to, when she's lifted herself up so, and is showin' plain in 1893 jest how lofty and level-headed, how many-sided and yet how symmetrical she is.

There she stands (Columbia didn't have to take my word for it), there she wuz a-towerin' up one hundred feet, lofty, serene, and sweet-faced, her calm, tender eyes a-lookin' off into the new order of centuries.

And Columbia wuz a-sailin' right towards her, steered by Time, the invincible.

I see there wuz a great commotion down in the water, a-snortin', and a-plungin', and a-actin' amongst the lower order of intelligences.

But Columbia's eyes wuz clear, and calm, and determined, and Old Time couldn't be turned round by any prancin' from the powers below.

Woman is discovered.

But to resoom. This immense boat wuz in the centre, jest as it should be; and all before it and around wuz the horses of Neptune, and mermaids, and fishes, and all the mystery of the sea.

Some of the snortin' and prancin' of the horses of the Ocean, and pullin' at the bits, so's the men couldn't hardly hold 'em, wuz meant, I spoze, to represent how awful tuckerin' it is for humanity to control the forces of Nater.

Wall, of all the sights I ever see, that fountain wuz the upshot and cap sheaf; and how I would have loved to have told Mr. MacMonnies so! It would have been so encouragin' to him, and it would have seemed to have relieved that big debt of gratitude that Jonesville and America owed to him; and how I wish I could make a good cup of tea for him, and brile a hen or a hen tuckey! I'd do it with a willin' mind.

I wish he'd come to Jonesville and make a all-day's visit — stay to dinner and supper, and all night if he will, and travel round through Jonesville the next day. I would enjoy it, and so would Josiah. Of course, we couldn't show off in fireworks anything to what he does, havin' nothin' but a lantern and a torchlight left over from Cleveland's campain. No; we shouldn't try to have no such doin's. I know when I am outdone.

Bime-by we stood in front of that noble statute of the Republic.

And as I gazed clost at it, and took in all its noble and serene beauty, I had emotions of a bigger size, and more on 'em, than I had had in some time.

Havin' such feelin's as I have for our own native land — discovered by Christopher Columbus, founded by George Washington, rescued, defended, and saved by Lincoln and Grant (and I could preach hours and hours on each one of these noble male texts, if I had time) —

Bein' so proud of the Republic as I have always been, and so sot on wantin' her to do jest right and soar up above all the other nations of the earth in nobility and goodness — havin' such feelin's for her, and such deep and heartfelt love and pride for my own sect — what wuz my emotions, as I see that statute riz up to the Republic in the form of a woman, when I went up clost and paid particular attention to her!

A female, most sixty-five feet tall! Why, as I looked on her, my emotions riz me up so, and seemed to expand my own size so, that I felt as if I, too, towered up so high that I could lock arms with her, and walk off with her arm in arm, and look around and enjoy what wuz bein' done there in the great To-Day for her sect, and mine; and what that sect wuz a-branchin' out and doin' for herself.

But, good land! it wuz only my emotions that riz me up; my common sense told me that I couldn't walk locked arms with her, for she wuz built out in the water, on a stagin' that lifted her up thirty or forty feet higher.

And her hands wuz stretched out as if to welcome Columbia, who wuz a-sailin' right towards her. On the right hand a globe was held; the left arm extended above her head, holdin' a pole.

I didn't know what that pole wuz for, and I didn't ask; but she held it some as if she wuz liable to bring it down onto the globe and gin it a whack. And I didn't wonder.

It is enough to make a stun woman, or a wooden female, mad, to see how the nation always depicters wimmen in statutes, and pictures, and things, as if they wuz a-holdin' the hull world in the palm of their hand, when they hain't, in reality, willin' to gin 'em the right that a banty hen has to take care of their own young ones, and protect 'em from the hoverin' hawks of intemperance and every evil.

But mebby she didn't have no idee of givin' a whack at the globe; she wuz a-holdin' it stiddy when I seen her, and she looked calm, and middlin' serene, and as beautiful, and lofty, and inspirin' as they make.

She wuz dressed well, and a eagle had come to rest on her bosom, symbolical, mebby, of how wimmen's heart has, all through the ages, been the broodin' place and the rest of eagle man, and her heart warmed by its soft, flutterin' feathers, and pierced by its cruel beak.

The crown wore on top of her noble forehead wuz dretful appropriate to show what wuz inside of a woman's head; for it wuz made of electric lights — flashin' lights, and strange, wrought of that mysterious substance that we don't understand yet.

But we know that it is luminous, fur-reachin' in its rays, and possesses almost divine intelligence.

It sheds its pure white light a good ways now, and no knowin' how much further it is a-goin' to flash 'em out — no knowin' what sublime and divine power of intelligence it will yet grow to be, when it is fully understood, and when it has the full, free power to branch out, and do all that is in it to do.

Jest like wimmen's love, and divine ardor, and holy desires for a world's good — jest exactly.

It wuz a good-lookin' head-dress.

Her figger wuz noble, jest as majestic and perfect as the human form can be. And it stood up there jest as the Lord meant wimmen to stand, not lookin' like a hour-glass or a pismire, but a good sensible waist on her, jest as human creeters ort to have.

I don't know what dressmakers would think of her. I dare presoom to say they would look down on her because she didn't taper. And they would probable be disgusted because she didn't wear cossets.

But to me one of the greatest and grandest uses of that noble figger wuz to stand up there a-preachin' to more than a million wimmen daily of the beauty and symmetry of a perfect form, jest as the Lord made it, before it wuz tortured down into deformity and disease by whalebones and cosset strings.

Imagine that stately, noble presence a-scrunchin' herself in to make

a taper on herself — or to have her long, graceful, stately draperies cut
off into a coat-tail bask — the idee!

Here wuz the beauty and dignity of the human form, onbroken by
vanity and folly. And I did hope my misguided sect would take it to
heart.

And of all the crowds of wimmen I see a-standin' in front of it admirin' it, I never see any of 'em, even if their own waists did look like
pismires, but what liked its looks.

Till one day I did see two tall, spindlin', fashionable-lookin' wimmen
a-lookin' at it, and one sez to the other:

"Oh, how sweet she would look in elbow-sleeves and a tight-fittin'
polenay!"

"Yes," sez the other; "and a bell skirt ruffled almost to the waist, and
a Gainsboro hat, and a parasol."

"And high-heel shoes and seven-button gloves," sez the other.

And I turned my back on them then and there, and don't know what
other improvements they did want to add to her — most likely a box of
French candy, a card-case, some eyeglasses, a yeller-covered novel,
and a pug dog. The idee!

And as I wended on at a pretty good jog after hearin' 'em, I sez to
myself —

"Some wimmen are born fools, some achieve foolishness, and some
have foolishness thrust on 'em, and I guess them two had all three of
'em."

I said it to myself loud enough so's Josiah heard me, and he sez in
joyful axents —

"I am glad, Samantha, that you have come to your senses at last, and
have a realizin' sense of your sect's weaknesses and folly."

And I wuz that wrought up with different emotions that I wuz almost perfectly by the side of myself, and I jest said to him —

"Shet up!"

I wouldn't argy with him. I wuz fearful excited a-contemplatin' the
heights of true womanhood and the depths of fashionable folly that a
few — a very few — of my sect yet waded round in.

But after I got quite a considerable distance off, I instinctively turned
and looked up to the face of that noble creeter, the Republic.

And I see that she didn't care what wuz said about her.

Her face wuz sot towards the free, fresh air of the future — the past
wuz behind her. The winds of Heaven wuz fannin' her noble foretop,

her eyes wuz lookin' off into the fur depths of space, her lips wuz wreathed with smiles caught from the sun and the dew, and the fire of the golden dawn.

She wuz riz up above the blame or praise—the belittlin', foolish, personal babblin' of contemporary criticism.

Her head wuz lifted towards the stars.

But to resoom, and continue on.

31 On One-armed Justice

In front of the French section I see another statute of the Republic.

She wuz a-settin' down. Poor creeter, she wuz tired; and then agin she had seen trouble — lots of it.

Her left arm was a-restin' firm on a kind of a square block, with "The Rights of Man" carved on it, and half hidin' them words wuz a sword, which she also held in her left hand.

The rights of Man and a sword wuz held in one hand, jest as they always have been.

But, poor creeter! her right arm wuz gone — her good right hand wuz nowhere to be seen.

I don't like to talk too glib about the judgments of Providence. The bad boys don't always git drownded when they go fishin' Sundays — they often git home with long strings of trout, and lick the good boys on their way home from Sunday-school. Such is real life, too oft.

But I couldn't help sayin' to Josiah —

"Mebby if they had put onto that little monument she holds, 'The Rights of Man and Woman' — mebby she wouldn't had her arm took off."

But anyway, judgment or not, anybody could see with one eye how one-sided, and onhandy, and cramped, and maimed, and everything a Republic is who has the use of only one of her arms. Them that run could read the great lesson —

"Male and female created He them."

Both arms are needed to clasp round the old world, and hold it firm — Justice on one side, Love on the other.

I felt sorry for the Republic — sorry as a dog.

But that wuz the first time I see her. The next time she had had her arm put on.

From *Samantha at the World's Fair* (New York, 1893), pp. 325–27.

I guess Uncle Sam done it. That old man is a-gittin' waked up, and Eternal Right is a-hunchin' him in the sides.

She wuz a-holdin' that right arm up towards the Heavens; the fingers wuz curved a little — they seemed to be begenin' to sunthin' up in the sky to come down and bless the world.

Mebby it wuz Justice she wuz a-callin' on to come down and watch over the rights of wimmen. Anyway, she looked as well agin with both arms on her . . .

32   On Justice Without Blindfolds

But the thing that impressed me the most in the hull buildin', and I thought on't all the time I wuz there, and thought on't goin' home, and waked up and thought on't—

It wuz a statute of woman named Justice—a female big as life, made of solid silver from her head to her heels, and a-standin' on a gold world—

Jest as they do in the streets of the New Jerusalem. Oh, my heart, think on't!

Yes, it tickled me to a extraordinary degree, for sech a thing must mean sunthin'! The world borne on the outspread wings of an eagle is under her feet, and under that is a foundation of solid gold.

First, the riches of the earth to the bottom; then the eagle Ambition, and wavin' wings of power and conquest, carryin' the hull round world, and then, above 'em all, Woman.

Yes, Justice in the form of woman stood jest where she ort to stand— right on top of the world.

Justice and Woman has too long been crumpled down, and trod on. But she has got on top now, and I believe will stay there for some time.

She holds a septer in her right hand, and in her left a pair of scales.

She holds her scales evenly balanced—that is jest as it ort to be; they have always tipped up on the side of man (which has been the side of Might).

But now they are held even, and *Right* will determine how the notches stand, not Might.

I don't believe that the Nation would make a statute of woman out of solid silver, and stand it on top of the world, if it didn't lay out to give her sect a little mite of what she symbolizes.

From *Samantha at the World's Fair* (New York, 1893), pp. 570–73.

They hain't a-goin' to make a silver woman and call it Justice, if they lay out to keep their idee of wimmen in the future, as they have in the past, the holler pewter image stuffed full of all sorts of injustices, and meannesses, and downtroddenness.

They hain't a-goin' to stand the figger of woman and Justice on top of the world, and then let woman herself grope along in the deepest and darkest swamps and morasses of injustice and oppression, taxed without representation, condemned and hung by laws they have no voice in makin'.

Goin' on in the future as in the past — bringin' children into the world, dearer to 'em than their heart's blood, and then have their hearts torn out of 'em to see these children go to ruin before 'em through the foolishness and wickedness of laws they have no power to prevent — nay, if they are rich, to see their loved ones helped to their doom by their own wealth; taxed to extend and perpetuate these means of death and Hell, and they with their hands bound by the chains of Slavery and old Custom.

But things are a-goin' to be different. I see it plain. And I looked on that figger with big emotions in my heart, and my umbrell in my hand.

I knew the Nation wuzn't a-goin' to depicter woman with the hull earth at her feet, and then deny her the rights of the poorest dog that walks that globe. No; that would be makin' too light of her, and makin' perfect fools of themselves.

They wouldn't of their own accord put a septer in her hand, if they laid out to keep her where she is now — under the rule of the lowest criminal landed on our shores, and beneath niggers, and Injuns, and a-settin' on the same bench in a even row with idiots, lunaticks, and criminals.

No; I think better of 'em; they are a-goin' to carry out the idee of that silver image in the gold of practical justice, I believe.

If I hadn't thought so, I would a-histed up my umbrell and hit that septer of hern, and knocked that globe out from under her feet.

And them four mountaineers, a-guardin' her with rifles in their hands, might have led me off to prison for it if they had wanted too — I would a done it anyway.

But, as I sez, I hope for better things, and what give me the most courage of anything about it wuz that Justice had got her bandages off.

That is jest what I have wanted her to do for a long time. I had advised Justice jest as if she had been my own Mother-in-law. I had argued with her time and agin to take that bandage offen her eyes.

And when I see that she had took my advice, and meditated on what happiness and freedom wuz ahead for my sect, and realized plain that it wuz probable all my doin's—why, the proud and happy emotions that swelled my breast most broke off four buttons offen my bask waist. And onbeknown to me I carried myself in that proud and stately way that Josiah asked me anxiously—

"If I had got a crick in my back?"

I told him, "No, I hadn't got any crick, but I had proud and lofty emotions on the inside of my soul that no man could give or take away."

"Wall," sez he, "you walked considerable like our old peacock when she wants to show off." . . .

33 On Sculpting the "Figger" of Liberty

. . . They are buildin' a new court-house at Jonesville. It is most done, and it seemed they got into a dispute that day about the cupelow. They wanted to have the figger of Liberty sculped out on it; and they had got the man there all ready, and he had begun to sculp her as a woman, — the goddess of Liberty, he called her. But at the last minute a dispute had rosen: some of the leadin' minds of Jonesville, uncle Nate Gowdey amongst 'em, insisted on it that Liberty wuzn't a woman, he wuz a man. And they wanted him depictered as a man, with whiskers and pantaloons and a standin' collar, and boots and spurs — Josiah Allen wus the one that wanted the spurs.

He said the dispute waxed furious; and he says to 'em, —

"Leave it to Samantha: she'll know all about it."

And so it was agreed on that they'd leave it to me. And he drove the old mare home, almost beyond her strength, he wus so anxious to have it settled.

I wus jest makin' some cream biscuit for supper as he come in, and asked me about it; and a minute is a minute in makin' warm biscuit. You want to make 'em quick, and bake 'em quick. My mind wus fairly held onto that dough — and needed on it; but instinctively I told him he wus in the right ont. Liberty here in the United States wuz a man, and, in order to be consistent, ort to be depictered with whiskers and over-coat and a standin' collar.

"And spurs!" says Josiah.

"Wall," I told him, "I wouldn't be particular about the spurs." I said, "Instead of the spurs on his boots, he might be depictered as settin' his boot-heel onto the respectful petition of fifty thousand wimmen, who had ventured to ask him for a little mite of what he wus s'posed to have quantities of — Freedom.

From *Sweet Cicely* (New York, 1887), pp. 132–33.

"Or," says I, "he might be depictered as settin' on a judgment-seat, and wavin' off into prison an intelligent Christian woman,[1] who had spent her whole noble, useful life in studyin' the laws of our nation, for darin' to think she had as much right under our Constitution, as a low, totally ignorant coot who would most likely think the franchise wus some sort of a meat-stew."

Says I, "That will give Liberty jest as imperious and showy a look as spurs would, and be fur more historick and symbolical."

Wall, he said he would mention it to 'em; and says he, with a contented look, —

"I told uncle Nate I knew I wus right. I knew Liberty wus a man."

Wall, I didn't say no more . . .

NOTE

1. Refers to Susan B. Anthony, who in 1872 led a group of Rochester, New York, women to the polls, was arrested, found guilty, and fined one dollar. On principle, she refused to pay the fine but was prevented (by a technicality) from appealing her case to a higher court.

The End

Bibliography

Marietta Holley's Works

Around the World With Josiah Allen's Wife. New York: G. W. Dilling-
ham, 1905. Originally published 1899.
"How I Wrote My First Book," *Harper's Bazaar,* (Sept., 1911).
Josiah's Alarm and Abel Perry's Funeral. Philadelphia: J. B. Lippin-
cott, 1895.
Josiah Allen on the Woman Question. New York: Fleming H. Revell,
1914.
Josiah Allen's Wife as a P.A. and P.I. or Samantha at the Centennial.
Hartford: American Publishing, 1884. Also cited from 1887 edition.
The Lament of the Mormon Wife. Hartford: American Publishing Co.,
1880.
Miss Jones' Quilting. New York: J. S. Ogilvie, 1887.
Miss Richards' Boy. Hartford: American Publishing, 1883.
My Opinions and Betsey Bobbet's. Hartford: American Publishing,
1873. Selected readings cited from 1891 edition.
My Wayward Pardner or Trials with Josiah Allen. Hartford: American
Publishing, 1881.
Poems. New York: Funk & Wagnalls, 1887.
Samantha Among the Brethren. New York: Funk & Wagnalls, 1890.
Samantha at Coney Island and A Thousand Other Islands. New York:
Christian Herald, 1911.
Samantha at the St. Louis Exposition. New York: G. W. Dillingham,
1904.
Samantha at Saratoga. Philadelphia: Hubbard Brothers, 1887.
Samantha at the World's Fair. New York: Funk & Wagnalls, 1893.
Samantha in Europe. New York: Funk & Wagnalls, 1896.
Samantha on the Race Problem. Minneapolis: J. C. McClure, 1892.
Also published as *Samantha Among the Colored Folks,* New York:
Dodd, Mead, 1894.
Samantha on Children's Rights. New York: G. W. Dillingham, 1909.

Samantha on the Woman Question. New York: Fleming H. Revell, 1913.
Samantha Vs. Josiah. New York: Funk & Wagnalls, 1906.
The Story of My Life. Watertown, N.Y.: Times Publishing, 1931.
Sweet Cicely. New York: Funk & Wagnalls, 1887. Also cited from 1885 edition.
Tirzah Ann's Summer Trip, and Other Sketches. New York: F. M. Lupton, 1892.
The Widder Doodle's Love Affair. New York: F. M. Lupton, 1893.

About Marietta Holley

Armitage, Shelley. "Marietta Holley: The Humorist as Propagandist," *Rocky Mountain Review,* 34:4 (Fall, 1980), 193–201.
Blair, Walter. *Horse Sense in American Humor.* Chicago: University of Chicago Press, 1942.
Blyley, Katherine Gillette. "Marietta Holley." Ph.D. Dissertation, University of Pittsburgh, 1936.
Butler, Ellis Parker. "The Uniqueness of Marietta Holley." *Mark Twain Journal,* (Spring–Summer, 1958), 11.
Critic, 46:1 (1905), 6.
Curry, Jane. "Samantha 'Rastles' the Woman Question," *Journal of Popular Culture,* VIII:4 (Spring, 1975).
James, Edward T., Janet Wilson James, and Paul S. Boyer, eds. *Notable American Women 1607–1950.* Cambridge: Belknap Press of Harvard University Press, 1971. Vol. II, pp. 202–4. Article by M. Langworthy.
Morris, Linda A. "Women Vernacular Humorists in Nineteenth-Century America: Ann Stephens, Frances Whitcher, and Marietta Holley." Ph.D. Dissertation, University of California, Berkeley, 1978.
Wagnalls, Mabel. "A Glimpse of Marietta Holley." *Ladies Home Journal,* 20 (Nov., 1903), 61.
Walker, Nancy. "Wit, Sentimentality, and the Image of Women in the Nineteenth Century." *American Studies,* XXII:2, 5–22.
Wyman, Margaret. "Women in the American Realistic Novel 1860–1893." Ph.D. Dissertation, Radcliffe College, 1950, 298–317.
Short entries appear in *American Women Writers, Dictionary of American Biography, National Cyclopedia of American Biography,* and *Dictionary of Literary Biography: American Humorists, 1800–1950.*

Index

A Note on the Editor

JANE CURRY has introduced Marietta Holley's characters to audiences of women's studies scholars and laypersons through her stage performances as Samantha Smith Allen. Curry received her B.A. from Hanover College in Indiana in 1967 and her M.A. and Ph.D. degrees from the University of Michigan in 1970 and 1975. She has published articles in the *Journal of Popular Culture* and *Frontiers* and a book on riverboat pilots, *The River's in My Blood* (University of Nebraska Press, 1983).

A thirty-minute recording of Jane Curry performing selections from *Samantha Rastles the Woman Question* is also available on a tape cassette (ISBN 0-252-01062-0) from the University of Illinois Press.